THE UGLY WIFE IS A TREASURE AT HOME

THE UGLY WIFE IS A TREASURE AT HOME

True Stories of Love and Marriage in Communist China

在家醜妻是個寶

MELISSA MARGARET SCHNEIDER

Potomac Books

An imprint of the University of Nebraska Press

Library of Congress Cataloging-in-Publication Data

Schneider, Melissa Margaret.
The ugly wife is a treasure at home: true stories of love and marriage in communist China /
Melissa Margaret Schneider.
pages   cm

Includes bibliographical references.
ISBN 978-1-61234-694-6 (pbk.: alk. paper) — ISBN 978-1-61234-704-2 (pdf) 1. Marriage—
China—History—20th century. 2. Mate selection—China—History—20th century.
3. Sex—China—History—20th century. 4. China—Social life and customs—1949–1976.
5. China—Social life and customs—1976–2002. I. Title.
HQ684.S36 2014
306.810951090′04—DC23
2014014897

Set in Quadraat by Renni Johnson.

For my husband—my best friend,
accomplice, and pundit—for
taking me to China and encouraging
me to follow my dreams.

Many people would not have fallen in love
had they not heard of it.

—La Rochefoucauld, seventeenth-century
French nobleman

People have always loved a love story. But for most of
the past, our ancestors did not try to live in one.

—Stephanie Coontz, marital historian

If you want to be happy and live a king's life /
Never make a pretty woman your wife.

—"Ugly Woman," American calypso song

CONTENTS

ACKNOWLEDGMENTS

I dove into this project armed with little more than my familiarity with Western relationships and a willingness to listen, read, and learn. As such, I owe a debt of cultural and intellectual gratitude to ever so many people, and I want to give special thanks to those who generously shared their time and knowledge.

First and foremost, I thank my storytellers, for openly and vulnerably sharing your hopes, disappointments, and life experiences with me. Listening to you was an unforgettable process that has truly changed my life. I also owe a debt to Dr. Haiyan Lee, associate professor of Chinese and comparative literature at Stanford University, for her fabulous book on the history of sentiment in China and for meeting with me in person to discuss my myriad questions. Dr. Lee is probably a genius, and her work is stunning. Read it if you can. I also thank Professor Stephanie Coontz, whose wonderful book gave me a new perspective on Western marriage traditions, and Dr. Zhenchao Qian, professor of sociology at Ohio State University, for meeting with me and explaining the spousal atmosphere of the early Mao years.

I also want to acknowledge several friends in China whose knowledge and assistance helped make this book possible. The lion's share of gratitude is due to Ms. Lin Ling, or "Linda Lin," as I knew her. Linda took a great personal interest in the subject of this book and faithfully accompanied me to nearly every interview, helping to translate and explain things along the way. Also vital was my friend Emilie Xingli Guo, who believed in this book from the start, demystified my storytellers' customs and traditions, and critiqued the entire manuscript, in English. My neighbor and friend Elly Zhen kindly checked the book's idiom translations and talked openly with me about political situations and cultural realities. Marsha Ma, another friend, proved an invaluable resource as she had spent more than a decade living in the United States and could anticipate what I would not understand about the stories I was collecting. I am also grateful to the dozens of friends, colleagues, and acquaintances in Shenzhen who spent time introducing me to storytellers and sharing their opinions about love and marriage. Finally, thanks are due to Mrs. Rachael Liang, who grew up in China and worked for more than forty years as a librarian at the University of Hawai'i. Thank you for reading my early manuscript, taking me to dim sum, and hating my first conclusion so much that I wised up and wrote a new one.

I offer particular gratitude to Lorraine Hatatia, my friend and faithful writing group partner, who spent hours reading and critiquing the stories in this book. You have single-handedly sharpened my writing and changed this book for the better. Thanks are also due to Virlane Torbit, who gave helpful edits and insight and was always up for a foot massage when I wanted to relax.

I also want to mention the many friends back home and around the world who read early stories via email and gave their comments: Irene Roberson; Rosemary Hinkle; Savina KimJohnson; Joann Phelan; Mary Luithy; and Grace Chiou. Special thanks are due to Ms. Ellen Szeto Lee for reading an early draft of the introduction and helpfully asking what an "ugly wife" was.

This book would never have been published without the practical assistance of many wonderful people. First and foremost among them is my mother-in-law, Mrs. Shirley Schneider, Stateside post office woman extraordinaire. Thank you for printing and mailing dozens of query letters and for being sad about each rejection letter. I also want to covertly acknowledge Paul Silva for his "research assistance." You know what you did. And a big thank you to my brother Philip Haines, for his cheerful legal review of all book-related contracts.

I am extremely thankful to the wonderful staff at Potomac Books and the University of Nebraska Press for taking on this project with so much enthusiasm and professionalism. Ms. Hilary Clagget, I'll never forget the day you wrote back and said, "I'd love to see your book." To Alicia, Tish, Rosemary, Ann, and everyone else who had a hand in this project, thank you so much for your faithful work.

I also want to say thank you to my parents, Mark and Linda Haines. You had four kids when you were even younger than I am now, and yet you always found the time to take me to the library and to creative writing classes, and you never failed to look up the words I didn't know. Thank you for shaping and believing in me.

To my wonderful husband, Matthew Schneider, I just want to say thank you for believing in me and for encouraging me to spend my time on this project. I am grateful for your love and for every day that we share together.

And finally, a shout-out to my adopted cat George, for faithfully sitting on critical manuscripts, hitting the number keys whenever possible, and generally keeping vigil while I typed.

Throughout this book, Chinese words are spelled according to the pinyin system. Most are pronounced as English speakers would expect, with the following exceptions:

c   pronounced like *ts* at the beginning of a syllable (*Licai* is pronounced *Lee-tsi*)

q   pronounced like *ch* (*qīnqíng* is pronounced *chin-ching*)

x   pronounced like *sh* (*Xu* is pronounced *shoe*; *Xing* is pronounced *shing*)

zh pronounced like *j* (*Zhang* is pronounced *Jahng*)

Introduction
Who Wants an Ugly Wife?

"Before marriage, every boy wants a beautiful girlfriend.
If she is beautiful, then when the couple walks outside
together, the man will feel very confident, because everyone
will notice his high status. If the girlfriend is not very
beautiful, well then, maybe he won't take her outside! When
it comes time to marry, however, a common man's thinking
will be totally different. He will hope his wife will be good at
housework and cooking. I think this opinion is the same
for men across all of China: a girlfriend should be a
beautiful girl. But if you want to marry, the woman doesn't
need to be beautiful, just good at housework. A beautiful
wife might bring you bad luck. Or someone else might steal
her away. We have a saying about a good-choice
wife in China: *Chǒu qī jiā zhōng bǎo*, or
'The ugly wife is a treasure at home.'"

Mr. Wang paused, pondering the matter. "Well, maybe a rich man
would want a beautiful wife," he mused, "because she would not really
need to do any housework."

At thirty-one, Mr. Wang was not a rich man. But he was married.

We were talking over tea and snacks in a Starbucks, huddled back
from the bustle of the Chegongmiao metro station in Shenzhen, China.
I was starting work on a collection of true stories about love and marriage in China, and Mr. Wang had generously agreed to share his experiences with me and Ms. Lin Ling, my friend and translator.

While some aspects of his story were romantic and sweet, Mr.
Wang's expectations of a spouse were primarily practical and family
oriented. When I asked him to recall his motivations for marriage,
he named four: wanting a lifelong companion, wanting love, wanting
to satisfy his parents' expectation that he marry, and wanting children. I proposed other possible motivations, which included find-

ing an attractive spouse or enjoying a regular sexual relationship. These suggestions struck Mr. Wang as strange and irrelevant, and he said that he had never thought about marrying for those reasons. His reply surprised me and stoked my curiosity. Clearly he wanted to share love with a lifelong companion, but attraction and a satisfying intimate relationship were not part of his vision. As he said before, he wanted a "good-choice" wife, defined as an ugly wife who would be a treasure at home.

Intrigued, I looked into this ugly wife concept and was rather touched by what I found. Mr. Wang's saying, "The ugly wife is a treasure at home," comes from a folktale about Zhuge Liang (181–234 AD), a well-known historical figure from the Han dynasty. Zhuge was a gifted strategist who rose to become chancellor to the emperor. He also managed to ripen to the advanced age of twenty-five without taking a wife, a worrisome state of bachelorhood for the time. As legend has it, Zhuge Liang ultimately agreed to marry an ugly girl, stricken with yellow hair and sun-blotted skin, because he was so taken with her intelligence and artistic talents. His wise choice rewarded him with a long and happy marriage to a woman whose inner beauty and engaging domesticity far outweighed her outward comeliness. Mr. Wang's utilitarian portrayal of the benefits of having an ugly wife lacked some of the sweeter nuance of this Han-period folktale, but as I was soon to learn, his dream of a quiet wife who would do housework was hardly uncommon.

Why was I prying into this private quarter of Chinese social life? After working for several years as a social worker and relationship counselor in New York City, I moved with my husband to Shenzhen just two days after our own wedding. As I made friends and settled in, curious stories skittered through my unfolding social life. During a get-to-know-you lunch with my husband's Chinese colleagues, one of them, a master's-level engineer, told me he had married a woman after meeting her just three times over a three-month period.

Later on, during a business trip to Hangzhou, some visiting American associates told my husband and I another curious story. They had barely finished dinner with their Chinese business partner, a willowy, thirty-one-year-old guy in blocky black glasses, when he had unabashedly announced that he was "MBA" that weekend: married but available. Laughing nervously, they did their best to explain that they were married, too, but should probably be *unavailable* that weekend.

A few months later a twenty-five-year-old friend of mine, a university graduate who rents her own apartment, announced that she was going on a blind date. She had never been on a date before and confessed that thinking about liking a boy had made her feel ashamed until recently. This date was to include her mother, the intended gentleman, and his aunt. The entire party was expected to share the same table and converse together at a local tea shop. On the appointed day, her date did thoughtfully attempt to remedy their socially cramped situation. Leaning over to their chaperones, he said, "Please feel free to talk with each other, or even to choose a more comfortable table. I'm sure what we have to say is not very interesting for you."

The aunt-mother team waved him off with big smiles. "Oh, no, it's very interesting. We can just listen to you two talk!"

Afterward my friend was expected to report back to his aunt about whether she thought he was "suitable." She didn't think so, since he lived far away, didn't appeal to her, and was too skinny. The aunt informed the man of his unsuitability, and nothing more was said about the matter.

Given my line of work as a counselor, I was naturally curious about the dynamics of Chinese relationships. But I was staggeringly unprepared for just *how* different local attitudes and actions really were. As the first few months rolled by, my curiosity deepened, and eventually I decided I had to know more. By sheer serendipity I was introduced to Ms. Lin Ling, a woman who had long wanted to investigate this very subject. Ms. Lin, who went by "Linda" with her English-speaking friends, met me for a mango smoothie one day. We had such a great time talking about love and marriage in China that we agreed to set up joint interviews and uncover its truth together. Over the next year, Linda accompanied me on more than forty interviews, and proved an invaluable partner, translator and cultural interpreter. I am grateful also to count her among my friends.

I embarked on this journey because I wanted to understand the love and marriage experiences of ordinary people. Along the way I spoke with cabdrivers and factory workers, scholars and businessmen, former "class enemies" and "leftover women"—the government's official label for single ladies over age twenty-seven. I asked Chinese people of all ages and backgrounds to tell me what they learned about love and marriage in their youth, how they met their spouse or significant other, and what other romantic encounters or losses they had experienced. Mostly I just soaked in their fascinating stories and bubbled with questions. Peopled with matchmakers, *tóngyǎngxí* (child brides), mistresses, and Communist "cadres," their memories drew me into a world both fascinating and strange.

All of these conversations took place in Shenzhen, China, which may be the largest city you've never heard of. A southeastern metropolis with ten million "official" residents and many more unofficial ones, Shenzhen is endowed with an unusual and brief history. In the late 1970s, when it was just a tiny fishing village, the future city won something akin to a national lottery. It was christened a "special economic zone" as part of a pilot financial reform program launched in a handful of locations by Deng Xiaoping, China's influential 1980s leader. In these special economic zones, foreign enterprises and private domestic businesses were invited to flourish in ways unseen in China since the 1940s. Over the next thirty years, Shenzhen's backwater tangle of piscatorial huts exploded into a prosperous metropolis, swollen with a flood of ambitious entrepreneurs and poorly educated factory and service workers.

Shenzhen is only now reaching the point where young people have been born and raised within its borders. It is a city without a past, and in many ways, without a strong cultural identity. As one friend said to me, "Shenzhen is rich with the smell of cash." Nothing could better describe this place. People come here to seek their fortune or to make ends meet, and they are willing to work long hours and sleep in cramped apartments to do it. It has none of Shanghai's swanky cosmopolitan vibe or Beijing's stalwart swagger. Shenzhen is raw, urgent, and ruggedly entrepreneurial. Transplants are normal, and many folk think more like villagers or townspeople than jaded urbanites, making Shenzhen's residents a wonderfully unique cross section of broader China.

The twenty-seven stories in this book capture the life and love experiences of people born in each decade since the establishment of Communist China in 1949. Political turmoil and societal change have shifted daily life so often since that pivotal moment in history that Chinese people speak of a new generation with the turn of each decade. Today's older folks, the 1950s and 1960s generations, are infamously bewildered by and disapproving of the bālínghòu and the jiǔlínghòu—the 1980s and 1990s generations. While young people still care a great deal about their traditional responsibility to care for their parents, and many do try to respect their "old ways," they must connect with their parents across a divide of options, values, and ideas that were unimaginable just a few decades ago. Members of the 1970s generation, often raised with conservative opinions but exposed to a flood of new ideas in young adulthood, are awkwardly sandwiched in between.

Again and again my storytellers surprised and perplexed me with their attitudes about love, dating, sex, marriage, and their parents. Tom Liu, born in 1958 to high-ranking soldiers in the People's Liberation Army (PLA), gave a short laugh as he explained that his parents had believed romantic love was capitalist and wrong. Consequently, they did not teach him anything about it and neither did anybody else. The Chinese had not always been so tight-lipped on love, he said, but under Mao's regime, people wanted to be "red, very pure." Talking about romantic love was a "black," or morally rotten, thing to do in those days. Lucy Lai, another woman born in the 1950s, also told me that nobody talked about love when she was young. "Not at school, not in university, not in society . . . it was as though love didn't exist."

While I found it hard to imagine a society that never talked about love, I assumed such reticence was a thing of the past. This assumption, however, was not entirely accurate. Plenty has changed over the past sixty years, but many old ideas and habits linger still, like pickled fragments of a mind-set that China can't quite shake. Carrie, a charming girl born in 1990 to Buddhist parents, described an upbringing very similar to that of Tom Liu, the son of PLA soldiers. Despite being born more than thirty years later than Tom, she too never witnessed an exchange of physical affection between men and women in her hometown, not even between married spouses. Nobody said "I love you" out loud either. As Carrie explained, "If a couple in my hometown kissed in public today, everyone would gossip and say they were bad people."

Bad people? I was only starting to understand that some of my storytellers weren't just chiding the behavior of hormone-charged teens. Instead, they had actually been taught to view expressions of romantic love as morally corrupt, like cheating on an exam or stealing money from a neighbor. For many, romantic love itself was tinged with crookedness, or at best impermanence, rather than heralded as a valuable blessing to those who found it.

Another woman, a villager born in the early 1960s, told me she had never consciously yearned for romance or marital happiness in the first place. "I don't have any special feeling about marriage," she shrugged. To her, marriage was simply a practical arrangement for the making and raising of children. She had grown up in a world where such love was entirely absent from conversation, books, and films. Back then, she recalled, books were only about war or history, topics that would "encourage us to build our country and make the future better."

This village woman had not married for love—this much I was prepared to digest. But she hadn't even thought about whether her marriage would be happy? That admission shocked me. I had assumed that *every* unmarried person thought about such things. Over the course of many interviews, I learned to ask lots of questions about how people felt and what motivated them to do certain things. My American assumptions were simply not a useful guide to the Chinese heart and mind.

Other interesting themes emerged over the course of my interviews. For starters, I learned that Chinese people commonly distinguish between three kinds of love when they speak of marriage: qīnqíng, which is the love between family members; yǒuqíng, the love between friends; and àiqíng, or romantic love. Àiqíng is associated with dating, engagement, and early marriage, but most Chinese prize it far less than yǒuqíng or qīnqíng. Over the life cycle of a healthy marriage, most assume that romance will fade, to be replaced with the quieter and more enduring forms of love that bond a family together.

I had expected to hear about sexually conservative, monogamous marriages, but instead, my storytellers reported a surprising number of affairs. I had also presumed that teenage dating would be ubiquitous and parentally acceptable by now, while in fact it is still prohibited by all but the most liberal parents. In fact, many people of all ages genuinely believed that dating before one reaches one's twenties is an emotionally harmful practice that will inevitably distract young students from their studies.

Mistakenly, I also presumed that the bulk of people born after the mid-1970s would have married for love. While some of them had managed to do so, the practice is not widespread, even in current-day China. Instead, storytellers from every generation bowed to parental and societal pressure to marry at the "right time"—before their late twenties—whether or not they loved their intended spouse. This hardwired sense of timing is rooted in the traditional Confucian belief that everyone must marry and have a child (traditionally, a son) to carry on the family lineage. A nationwide belief, this Confucian philosophy resulted in hundreds of years of near-universal marriage in China. Up until the mid-1980s, 99 percent of women tied the knot before age thirty-five.

Certain elements of family life surprised me as well. To begin with, a number of my storytellers born after 1980 had siblings, despite the enactment of the One Child Policy. Also, while China's adult children have always supported their parents financially, the equation is rapidly changing. Unlike couples from decades past, today's husbands and wives may both be the only child of healthy parents who plan to retire in their fifties and live for thirty to fifty more years. If they are not already living with parents, many couples expect at least one set to move in during their first pregnancy. As newlyweds are supposed to get pregnant right away, this means the cascade of life changes triggered by marriage is sudden and financially taxing. I could see why many people approached their marriage decisions more practically than romantically. How can you focus on love knowing that a baby and your parents will move in ten months later and might stay forever?

One last theme that emerged among my older storytellers was the idea that the Communist Party had actively suppressed romantic love under Mao Zedong, an accusation that mystified me. I imagined that the Chinese people pre-1949 had been arranging marriages, taking concubines, and visiting courtesans rather than going for dates at the local soda fountain. Had romantic love even made its debut in pre-Communist China? If so, what possible political motive could Mao Zedong's political regime have had for stifling it?

To better understand these stories, and to appreciate just how far customs have somersaulted since 1949, it helps to understand something about the history of love and marriage in China. For a thousand years before the establishment of Communism, Chinese family life adhered to Confucian philosophy. Confucius, who was no lover of women or marriage, taught that a son should revere his parents above his wife, always treating them with "filial piety," or deep loyalty. Sons were expected to live with their parents and to provide for them until their death. Wives were expected to join their husbands in the mission of caring for his parents, leaving the care of their own parents to brothers. As such, a man's wife was selected by his parents for the betterment of the family unit, and marriage was the joining of two families, not the creation of a romantic or sexually compatible union. Parents considered things like family reputation, social status, political alliance, and auspicious astrological signs when selecting a daughter-in-law. The newly created couple was meant to blossom with sons, not to fall in love.

Wives, and women in general, were not the proper companions for men anyway, because of their inferior social status. Confucian society taught *nánzūnnǚbēi*, the idea that men were nobles while women were slaves. Various men ruled over a woman throughout her lifetime, according to the Confucian teaching of "three obediences": a woman should obey her father before marriage, obey her husband after marriage, and obey her sons in widowhood.

Simply put, the husband-wife relationship was not the central player in the Chinese family drama. As the son-parent relationship was paramount, the son's expressions of commitment, love, and passion must be to his parents, not to his wife. Any man who did fall in love with his wife needed to conceal that fact, and he certainly could not express his affection publicly. It would have been unthinkable to give

8

her a kiss upon entering a room or call "I love you!" as she left for an errand. Doing so would deeply offend his parents, and they had the power to force him to divorce her. They could send his wife back to her birth family if she didn't work hard enough, failed to bear a son, or upset them in some way. The "jealous mother" of Western archetype, who clutches intrusively after her married sons, had the upper hand in China. She could clutch away for her son's entire lifetime, and no one would criticize her. This Confucian family template may have helped to stabilize lineages and empires, but it was not a recipe for happily married couples.

Romantic and sexually passionate relationships certainly existed in Chinese society, but they almost always occurred outside of the husband-wife relationship. In the kind of maddening moral dichotomy favored by prudish Victorians in the Western world, "good" Chinese wives were supposed to *have* sex but not relish it or long for it. Husbands, on the other hand, were allowed to pursue carnal bliss, but not with their wives. They could take a second wife, known as a concubine. These women were often more like playthings, and while they enjoyed their husband's passion, they did not enjoy a high status in the community. Husbands could also get steamy with courtesans or prostitutes, and wives were expected to look the other way.

I could understand that romantic love between spouses might be less common in a culture of arranged marriages, but traditional attitudes in China clearly took things much further. Displays of affection and expressions of love between spouses were practically taboo, and this attitude confused me. Why couldn't a couple both honor their parents and love one another?

To sort out this mystery, I contacted Haiyan Lee, a Stanford University professor and the author of *Revolution of the Heart: A Genealogy of Love in China*. In a fascinating coffee shop chat, Lee explained that devotion to a spouse was considered almost immoral in Old China because it conflicted directly with the bond between a son and his parents. Marital devotion was considered a slippery slope, one that would ultimately cause a son to side with his wife against his parents. Since denying the wishes of one's parents was one of the worst sins a son could commit, a man really couldn't have it both ways. If he did something to show that he loved his wife, like holding her hand or complimenting her cooking, that was a slap in the face to his parents. To use a more modern analogy, a good husband simply cannot both love his wife and kiss an attractive secretary good night in front of her. His wife would feel deeply offended by this evidence of his care for another woman. Traditional Chinese parents felt the same way. They wanted their son's undivided loyalty and love—they did not expect to share him with his wife.

By the early twentieth century, urban intellectuals started to question this thousand-year-old template for family life. Perhaps it was missing something, some suggested. An influx of foreign books and ideas, facilitated by the arrival of merchants and missionaries and the overseas educations of upper-class Chinese, rapidly fanned the flames of these emerging local ideas about family relationships.

In the space of a few decades, fueled by the explosion of the popular press, the subject of romantic love rocketed from conceptual obscurity into a central spot in the lively discourse of China's educated classes. "Free Love," an essay published in 1903, argued that young people should have the right to marry a person of their own choosing. Romantic fiction, like the 1906 novel *Sea of Regret*, began to appear. Literary societies sprang up, and translated foreign works, including Freud's theories on sexuality and love stories from the European Romantics, poured into the hands of literate Chinese urbanites.

This whirlpool of new ideas catalyzed the call for social revolution. In 1911 the Qing dynasty fell and the Nationalist Party, headed by Sun Yat-sen, rose up. Radical reformers ramped up their attack on oppressive Confucian family values, calling for people to embrace individual happiness and freedom of choice in marriage instead. By the close of a second revolution in 1919, China's literati concocted their wildest idea yet. What if a person could not only choose his or her spouse but also marry for love? The concept of married love was so unprecedented that nobody even knew what to call it. No such word existed in the Chinese language.

The 1920s was the real heyday of àiqíng (romantic love) in pre-Communist China, but the topic was broadly popular from the 1910s to the 1940s. During that time, the unprecedented public clamor over love and sex crammed the columns of fiction and entertainment magazines, newspaper supplements, and even political journals. By 1940 the popular press reached about 4 percent of the Chinese population, or upwards of seventeen million people. From there, kernels of new thought spread quickly through verbal networks.

Not to be outdone, the budding Chinese film industry took up the question of love as well. In fact, the very first Chinese-produced short film, *A Couple in Difficulty* (1913, Shanghai), was a satire criticizing arranged marriages. By 1937 over three hundred movie theaters operated in China, and many indigenous films explored the merits of love and romance. Moreover, three-quarters of the films screened during that period were Hollywood imports, in which love was a perennial theme.

This hubbub demonstrates one important fact: many young people had heard something about romance and marrying for love before 1949. Many could make use of a new vocabulary to describe their natural feelings. Others made a critical philosophical decision, deciding that sexual attraction and romantic love could be socially acceptable, even morally good, between spouses. Spurred on by new ideas and thrilling media depictions, young men and women in the most progressive cities began to meet openly in dance halls, movie theaters, and parks. Dating was born.

In those days, both the Nationalist Party and the newly established Communist Party encouraged young people to marry for love. In fact, both groups forwarded legislation toward that end. A 1931 code offered by the Nationalists abolished the practices of having multiple wives and concubines while demanding equality, easier access to divorce, and more equitable properly rights for women. The Communist Party penned a law as well, calling for the end of "feudal" marriages and banning concubinage, bigamy, the exchange of money and gifts in engagement deals, and the practice of taking in a "child bride" who would later marry a son. A later version of this Communist legislation even specified a no-fault divorce, in which a marriage could be ended if spouses could "find no way to continue living together owing to the absence of affection or love." While issues of influence and clout and the urgency of civil war and the Japanese invasion prevented either party's mandate from having much impact, these attempts to regulate and equalize marriage were truly groundbreaking.

Just as the fledgling project of love unfurled its wings, another ideal swooped into the Chinese heart: patriotism. Rather than living for àiqíng (romantic love), a newly minted crop of social revolutionaries cared more for àiguó, literally "love of country." Young heroes were supposed to feel the higher, purer call of the nation in their gut and bravely relinquish sweethearts, and their mothers, to embrace it. This new ideal was also more useful for recruiting badly needed soldiers to fight the Japanese and man the civil war between the Communists and Nationalists. As such, patriotic zeal was elevated over private romantic love, a moral decision that would affect Chinese society for decades to come.

Throughout the first half of the twentieth century, most of China's far-flung and multitudinous peasantry had heard nothing of this buzz in the cities. They had gone on arranging marriages and caring for aging parents as they always had. But a time was coming in the not-too-distant future when the new idea of marrying for love would be spread far and wide by Mao and his Communist cadres.

By the mid-1940s Japan had surrendered and left China, enabling the Nationalists and the Communists to resume their protracted civil war for control of the country. In 1949 Mao Zedong's troops routed the last of the Nationalist army, sending its tattered remnants scurrying into Taiwan by boat and plane. The People's Republic of China was duly established under the control of the Communist Party.

The newly empowered Communist cadres launched a wave of ideological campaigns intended to win over the hearts and minds of China's people. They wanted to mold their people into modern citizens whose lifestyle and choices would express the spirit of the revolution. Interestingly, one of the very first priorities of the new government was to reshape China's approach to marriage.

In the early 1950s the Communists diligently campaigned across the country, bringing the good news of marriage reform to the remote corners of their freshly liberated nation. They cast a vision of a new breed of "revolutionary couples" who would not marry at their parents' command but instead would freely choose their life partners on the basis of love and shared aspirations for building New China. Young people were encouraged to reject arranged marriages and choose *zhǎo duìxiàng*, or "the search for one's beloved." This vocabulary contrasted sharply with the traditional terms, such words as *chǒu xífù*, "the search for a wife/daughter-in-law," and *zhǎo pójiā*, "the search for the home of one's mother-in-law." Prior to the 1950s, China's marriage vocabulary had focused on the parents, not the couple.

For millions of people, this campaign marked the first time such ideas reached their ears. And the campaign was not just a suggestion, it was now also the law. In 1950 the Communists enacted the New Marriage Law, which outlawed bigamy, concubinage, prostitution, and arranged marriages across the nation. The laudable law allowed married women to enter the workforce for the first time and provided a legal basis for either wives or husbands to initiate a divorce without parental approval. Neil Diamant, a professor of Asian law and society with expertise in this legislation, describes its framers as young, revolutionary idealists who repudiated the practice of arranged marriage, calling it an "agent of oppression of the young by the old, and women by men." They genuinely longed to reshape marriage into a relationship based on worthier emotional goods, like "love, equality, and mutual respect."

It was all sounding so good. The social reforms envisioned by intellectuals and agitators for decades were finally set down in ink for the betterment of China. What a victory! And yet romantic love would soon be repudiated and attacked by the very people who had done much to introduce it.

In a historical twist both ironic and bitter, the Communist revolutionaries' forward-thinking ideals quickly buckled under the weight of the core mission of the Communist Party. The social reformers of the 1920s and 1930s had fought to reform marriage for the sake of love and personal happiness, but Mao Zedong's motives were not quite so simple. His top priority had always been to establish a socialist economy. (While this might sound like a strange goal for a Communist leader, it is important to understand that socialism is an economic system, while communism is a political system. Thus the mission of Communist China was to instill socialism by putting the means and benefits of production into public hands.) Mao's early support of revolutionary values like individualism and marrying for love had been genuine, but also purposeful. He wanted to break the tradition of arranged marriages and the power of the Confucian family, and inspiring young people to pursue romantic love was a powerful means to those ends. But Mao also wanted people to live sacrificially for his cause, and an intoxicated romantic makes a poor revolutionary.

Thus, once the Communist Party rose to power, Mao had to sacrifice many of the progressive ideals he had espoused before 1949 in order to pursue his primary agenda. Romantic love was not immediately quashed, though, as it was a tool with some use to the party. But love ultimately withered under Mao's watch because it posed too great a threat to a collective society. The party wanted to redefine good and moral behavior as the altruistic pursuit of collective goals. Romantic love was too personal, too individual. Eventually, it had to go.

While the Communist Party never changed its official ideological support for free-choice marriages, its early campaigns for marriage reform were hurriedly cancelled in response to violent resistance from local officials and riots in the countryside. It turned out that peasant men, ostensibly the backbone of Mao's revolution, didn't really like laws that allowed their wives to divorce them. A successful divorce robbed a man of his bride price, his wife's free household labor, and his chance to have a son. Such a blow was catastrophic, for a poor man had little hope of remarriage. In the face of such strident opposition, the party quickly retreated from its radical policies in order to consolidate support for its top priority, the building of New China. By 1953, ideas about gender equality and marriage crouched firmly on the back burner, not to be pushed forward again until the 1980s. Over the 1950s, '60s, and early '70s, Communist policies grew more and more conservative.

Romantic love also fell out of favor because it was associated with the privileged classes. Unfortunately, the people who had heard about and embraced romantic love before 1949 were largely educated, literate, and cosmopolitan. In short, they were the "bourgeois," the new villains of Mao's unfolding class-based social drama. Mao exhorted his peasants to both "struggle against" these oppressors and repudiate their way of life. Good citizens were supposed to strive for revolution, and the revolutionary life was a pressing thicket of goals that demanded complete self-sacrifice. Amusing oneself with a little bourgeois thing like love was therefore very much discouraged in the Mao years.

It may have relented on reform, but the party never loosened its newly established grip on the right to marry and divorce. According to Mao, everything in life was political, especially private family matters. And of course, Mao believed the party should control the political world. Prior to 1949, marriage had been a private affair between families. Under Mao's regime, it became a legal status to be conferred or removed through state approval. Interested couples had to request permission to marry from their work unit, and the party was supposed to approve or reject the union based on the "class background" of the candidates. Anyone who owned land or had wealth before 1949 was stamped "bad class" and was not supposed to marry someone with a "good class" background, like laborers, farmers, and peasants. Similarly, divorces were granted only if "mediation and counseling" failed and the work unit gave its consent.

The party also stretched a long and controlling shadow over married life. Just like the jealous, hovering mothers-in-law it had worked to replace, the party required spouses to continually demonstrate the supremacy of its own needs over those of their husband or wife. People who "joined the revolution" were reorganized not according to family but by work unit. Local leaders told married couples where to live and often housed them in separate dorm areas. Spouses were encouraged to put work ahead of personal life, and many spent only one night with a new bride or groom before returning to work. Some married couples were assigned to posts on opposite sides of the country and had only two weeks to visit in a given year. These separations were not conceptualized as cruel but were instead considered pretty normal. Zhenchao Qian, a professor of sociology at Ohio State University who lived in China until 1989, told me that people felt the revolution *needed* them, and most willingly went wherever the party called them. Whether it was to a nearby village or to an outpost in the Gobi Desert, nobody ever thought about asking, "Oh, can I bring my spouse?"

Committed revolutionaries were simply expected to set their love lives aside without complaint. People were taught to see their natural desires for love and happiness as a moral weakness. If people complained about their separation from a spouse, seemed unhappy about it, or made efforts to visit on unauthorized days, the party literally criticized them for the "sin of putting love first." Mao urged his people to prize the agenda of the Communist Party and to let their noble mission outshine everything else in life. This toxic reordering of priorities did much to silence the fledgling project of romantic love, as all private goals had to be jettisoned in favor of collective ones. As Haiyan Lee put it, people's top priority was never supposed to be finding the right man or having a perfectly fulfilling family life. A good Communist's main concern was always supposed to be devotion to the greater enterprise.

By the end of the 1950s, as the revolution demanded a greater and greater portion of its people's hearts and minds, the popular position on love calcified into an extreme personal and sexual asceticism. Vincent Gil, professor of anthropology at Vanguard University, described the prevailing mind-set of that period for the *Journal of Sex Research*: "A puritanical, if not heavy-handed, sexual 'primness' became firmly established. . . . This included a denial of romantic love, and the affirmation of the absolute role of the collective over the individual. . . . The Great Leap Forward [1958–61] demanded, in Communist parlance, the 'renunciation of the heart.' The Party deliberately created a brand of social altruism in which citizens should work hard every day, directing their affections toward the collective mission without being 'deflected or confused' by love, sexual desire, or any strivings for private happiness."

This brief historical review has only begun to explore what happened to romantic love and marriage in Communist China. The full story is troubling and complex and has rarely been told. The twenty-seven stories in this book are intended to further that narrative, giving voice to decades of personal oppression and illuminating its shuddering impact, which still reverberates through Chinese society today. Opening in a time when romantic love and marriage were largely unrelated, these mini-memoirs trace the lurching efforts of six generations of people to fuse the two together. Beneath each individual tale lies the metastory of a people searching for romantic love in a culture where marriage had simply not been built to include it.

This book captures the perspectives of both men and women, something I very much wanted it to do, as many Chinese memoirs share the voice of only one gender. I faced a human limitation, though, as both my translator and I were women in our thirties. While some men spoke openly with us, I suspect many did not connect with us as naturally as they might have with a male interviewer. Men in the older generations, especially, did not grow up socializing with women or foreigners, and I am deeply grateful to them for their willingness to meet with me and tell their tales. If some of their stories are not as deep or as nuanced as the female accounts, please consider this my own shortcoming, not an indication of their lack of depth.

This book has also been written to honor each story while protecting each storyteller. During each interview, Linda provided a full or partial translation from Mandarin to English while I took extensive notes. As our interviewees were leery of audio recordings, handwritten transcription was my best option. Rather than presenting these exact and imperfect transcripts, I later edited and rearranged each narrative to optimize its dramatic flow while polishing language and inserting cultural explanations as needed. I also tweaked identifying details and created pseudonyms throughout the book. Many people shared very personal things about their lives, indiscretions, and political opinions. They were brave and generous to speak so frankly in a country where most still nurse an understandable paranoia about revealing private information, especially to foreigners. In living memory, countless Chinese people were denounced or even imprisoned for sexual missteps. While the current-day political environment is a great deal looser, the instinctive flinch is still palpable.

China is a vast and varied land, home to countless tales of love and marriage. More than one billion people from fifty-five different ethnic groups live within its borders, and no collection of stories could ever speak for so many. The experiences recorded here are merely a peek into the richly checkered landscape of the heart in the world's most populous nation. I hope they will bear witness to the tumultuous fate of love in this unique country, build our sense of shared humanity, and strengthen our conviction that the freedom to love is a precious thing indeed.

Prologue

Rooster Weddings, Second Wives, and Little Feet

CHANG XING

In February 2012 I had the serendipitous pleasure of sitting next to Chang Xing, a seventy-eight-year-old Chinese woman, on a flight from Hong Kong to Tokyo. As we chatted over tea, Mrs. Chang told me she was returning home to Houston, Texas, after a visit to her Hong Kong–based son. She poked up one black-and-gray eyebrow when I mentioned my interest in the love and marriage stories of her homeland. "Would you like to hear about the weddings of my great-aunt and my mother?" I assured her I would love to hear her family's story. Mrs. Chang's tales of marriage in the time of the Qing dynasty were so curious and captivating that I couldn't bear to omit them. They are sliced from another time, another world. Her illumination of the "rooster substitute," a peculiar Confucian wedding custom, reminded me just how quickly things had changed for my six generations of storytellers, born just a few decades later.

My great-aunt lived in the days of China's last emperor, during the Qing dynasty. She was the second wife of an affluent man, but in practice she was really the first. His first wife had succumbed to illness after bearing a son. Back then, China had no rules about how many wives a man could take. If he had enough money to support a second or third wife and their future children, then he could marry again. This particular man eventually married five wives, though only the first four were his own idea.

The scheme for the fifth wife was hatched among the second, third, and fourth wives, as a pragmatic measure. They had lived together in the family compound for many years, and all had multiple children to cook for and look after. As time went on, their common husband grew older and fell ill. He could barely rise from his own bed. Rather than add the duties of his care to their workload, the wives conspired to bring in a fifth wife. A young, childless woman could more easily devote herself to the care of an infirm husband, they reasoned. They also believed that some happy occasion, like a wedding, might fight off the evil spirits causing his illness.

The wives set themselves to their task, arranging a match with a seventeen-year-old girl from a poor family. When the wedding day arrived, the groom was too ill to stand or walk, so he could not attend the festivities. No matter, the wives furnished the customary substitute: a rooster. It was common practice in those days to use a rooster as a stand-in for an absent groom, since some new husbands lived far away or were sick. Another relative would hold the bird during the ceremony, and as couples did not need to exchange vows or speak to each other during the wedding, a rooster could quite properly substitute for a groom.

This fifth marriage was only a sort-of marriage, as you can imagine. The young bride tended her new husband until his death, but to the knowledge of the other wives, their union was never consummated. It was the family joke that even up to the day she died, this fifth wife was still a virgin. [Mrs. Chang chuckled and shook her head.]

This woman spent the rest of her life in that compound, acting as a maid to the eldest son, according to custom. This son was older than she was, and he had married a woman with bound feet. The practice of foot binding was still popular back then, especially among women who wanted to marry into wealthy families. Tiny feet were considered beautiful, like large eyes or big breasts today. The little feet weren't abolished until the Guómíndǎng, the Nationalist Party, came to power. "How can freedom run with bound feet?" their posters demanded.

My great-aunt's family eventually moved to Singapore, where I grew up. I remember meeting this wife with the special shoes when I was a child. Her feet were even smaller than mine, and she always wore tiny silk slippers stitched in elaborate designs. She had her own personal maid, because she needed constant help to totter around.

You know, my own mother also had a rooster wedding, after the Qing dynasty fell. She was only sixteen when a matchmaker traveled to her hometown in Guangdong province, offering to arrange a marriage to a man in Singapore. He was Chinese but had moved abroad years earlier to further his business as a commodities trader. This matchmaker was his aunt, another great-aunt of mine. Her match was not a hard sell. The villagers were very poor, and the prospect of a stable financial future with food on the table was very palatable. My father did not leave Singapore to attend the wedding, but my mother's family accepted this unseen husband. They prepared the traditional wedding festivities and propped up a rooster in his place.

After the wedding my mother and aunt traveled back to Singapore. It was my mother's first trip outside of China. My aunt furnished the authorities with the requisite official papers, declaring my father's intention to accept this woman as a wife once she entered Singapore. Once she arrived in her new homeland, my father gave a second wedding celebration. The matchmaker aunt was rewarded with *hóngbāo*, a traditional red envelope stuffed with money.

I never met my maternal grandmother, the one who bade her daughter farewell after that second rooster wedding. She could not leave China, because Mao's Communism made it very difficult to obtain an exit visa. My mother was allowed to visit her, but in those days the children of expatriates were not allowed to return to the mainland until they were forty years old. I remember my mother packing for those visits, her suitcases bursting with cooking oil and smoked Chinese pork. My grandmother was on food rations, along with the rest of China, and such provisions were precious. Many people did not have enough to eat, and millions starved to death in the 1960s.

I turned forty in the late 1970s. I was finally old enough to visit my grandmother under Mao's rules, and do you know what happened? The new leader, Deng Xiaoping, changed the rules, saying that expat children of any age could now visit China. Of course, none of this mattered by then. My grandmother was already dead.

PART ONE
The 1950s Generation
When Love Didn't Exist

I was twenty-four when I married my first wife, but I knew
nothing about females. I didn't understand why I had to
marry at all, or what purpose marriage served.
—Tom Liu, b. 1958

The 1950s generation, the first citizens born in Communist China, came of age in a world devoid of romantic love. They learned that life was a high-stakes mission and that their role was critical to its success. They grew up building socialism and fighting class enemies, not thinking about boyfriends or prom dresses. They were taught to care about the causes and teachings of Mao Zedong and to work selflessly for their country. In the harsh light of this grand collective vision, any private desires for romantic love, intimacy, or happiness appeared petty, selfish, even criminal.

Under Mao, public life was purposely desexualized. Men and women dressed alike in drab blue or gray uniforms, cutting their hair in identical bobs trimmed around the ears. Books and movies were heavily censored, scrubbed clean of any reference to love or sex. The married people that the 1950s generation could observe, including their own parents, did not touch or say "I love you." Outside of the bedroom, life was generally sexless. Inside the bedroom it was hardly easier, as many couples shared their sleeping quarters with other relatives.

Interestingly, in the early years Mao Zedong thought of sexual satisfaction within marriage as an effective social pacifier. As Neil Diamant recounts in *Revolutionizing the Family: Politics, Love, and Divorce in Urban and Rural China*, papers on the importance of a good sex life circulated among elite party members in the 1950s. They even handed out a few pamphlets on the subject in big cities. More gripping matters soon diverted their attention, however, and few people ever saw the pamphlets.

Despite being born after the enactment of the New Marriage Law, this generation grew up watching marriages that were more or less arranged. In the 1950s and '60s, parents reacted to the law by allowing their children a brief "viewing" with an intended spouse, and some allowed their children the nominal right of refusal. Very few people did anything resembling modern dating before marriage in the 1950s.

Admittedly, this generation had little time to think of love, buffeted as they were by a dizzying whirl of political movements. Many were also traumatized at a young age by the death of loved ones, other losses, hunger, and violence. In the 1950s, a land reform movement forcibly redistributed the property of landlords and wealthy farmers to millions of peasants. Then the Anti-Rightist Campaign triggered a nationwide witch hunt targeting intellectuals, artists, and religious adherents. Finally, the foolhardy industrial and agricultural policies of the Great Leap Forward culminated in a massive famine in the countryside.

The children of the 1950s grew up in a society tightly controlled by the Communist Party. The elaborate dānwèi, or "work unit," system supervised and assigned the employment of their parents. The work unit also approved things like travel, marriage, divorce, pregnancy, and birth control, while holding the strings to food, housing, medical care, education, and services. Within each work unit, the members of neighborhood and village "committees" peeked through windows and listened on the street, reporting all the local gossip to party leaders. Food and clothing were centrally planned and rationed from the mid-1950s until 1993.

Many in this generation did not experience normal Chinese family life. By 1958 the rural population was reorganized into collective farms known as people's communes, and everyone worked to feed the village, not the family. This style of collective living was calculated to break the power of the Chinese family by raising citizens who cared more about their country than about "filial piety," the duty to care for one's parents. As such, many people ate in communal kitchens, as cooking at home was outlawed in many places. They were often cared for in group nurseries while their parents worked. They aspired to join the Young Pioneers, then the Communist Youth League, and ultimately, the Communist Party.

The 1950s generation spent little time with their parents and observed next to nothing about married love. Their parents were extremely busy "building socialism," attending meetings, and dodging persecution. They commonly worked until 11:00 p.m. or later and slept at their work units. Job assignments took some parents far from their families, leaving children in the care of grandparents or group nurseries. Many parents also faced various persecutions from the party, suffering extreme stress at best and violence, imprisonment, or death at worst. Those who weren't starving were often hungry. Even the strongest marriage bonds will dwindle and fade under constant stress, hardship, hypervigilant oversight, criticism, and lengthy separation. For millions of Chinese parents at that time, such was life.

Many 1950s-born people were deprived of a complete education, as schools periodically shut down during their youth. By 2010, 18 percent had graduated from a vocational or college prep high school and 4 percent had finished university, according to UN statistics. At whatever point their education ceased, this generation did not look for work but received state-assigned jobs that often had little to do with their interests or talents. They knew they would never be fired from these "iron rice bowl" jobs, though, as absolute job security was one of the party's core visions.

The teenagers of this generation did not date. Boys and girls barely spoke to the opposite sex, as such intermingling was discouraged. They learned that feelings of love or attraction for another person were wrong and must be stifled. Unmarried people learned nothing about sex except that it was a dirty activity linked to the reviled bourgeois class. Most remained ignorant about sex and contraception until their wedding day. They were also urged to judge the value of potential spouses by their Communist fervor and class background rather than by personal attributes, personality, education, or looks.

Despite these conditions, the 1950s generation got married in spades. By 2010, 99 percent of women and 97 percent of men born in the 1950s had married at some point in their lives, and 92 percent were currently married. Very few in this generation either had a purely arranged marriage or met their spouse completely on their own. Rather, the introduction of a trusted matchmaker sparked the bulk of marriages. Even if young people did fall in love and choose one another, nobody at that time would have emphasized a couple's knowing each other well before the wedding.

Members of this generation also married quite late by historical standards because of China's budding interest in family planning. In the early years of Communism families had been urged to have as many children as possible. But after the famine, with no end in sight to the ration program, the mood understandably changed. A new focus on family planning came into vogue, but rather than hinging on condoms or oral contraception, policies simply pushed back the legal marriageable age, delaying the onset of reproductive activity in the process. Under the new laws, rural men and women could not marry until age twenty-five and twenty-three, respectively, while urban men and women had to wait until the advanced ages of twenty-eight and twenty-five. (Some regions overlooked these regulations, and thus some of the storytellers in this book married earlier.) In 1980 China replaced the delayed marriage laws with the One Child Policy, and the legal ages for marriage dropped to the current threshold of twenty-two for men and twenty for women. That year marriage rates spiked up 30–50 percent, as ten million people hurried to tie the knot.

Members of this generation generally believe that every person should marry, barring serious illness or mental health problems. They married primarily to start families, and more than 85 percent of 1950s-born wives were pregnant before the couple's first anniversary.

This generation also generally disapprove of divorce. When they were young, divorce was a rare, socially stigmatized, and embarrassing public matter. Divorcees were considered selfish or cuckoo for placing their own meager claim to happiness ahead of social stability. While anyone could apply for a divorce, requests were granted only if mandatory counseling procedures failed and the work unit gave approval. In 2010 less than 2 percent of the 1950s generation were "currently divorced," though some had divorced and remarried and others had informally separated. The majority were still married to their original partner.

Today, this generation is 160 million people strong, equivalent to half the population of the United States and two and a half times that of Great Britain. Surprisingly, theirs is the smallest generation covered in this book, reminding us of the sheer enormity of modern-day China.

Love after Revolution

JACK CHOU (B. 1954)

Jack Chou was raised in Zhejiang province, an economically prosperous region on China's eastern coast. The province is known for its iconic West Lake and a strong green tea called *lóngjǐng chá*, or "dragon-well tea."

Jack and his wife have lived in Shenzhen for nearly thirty years, arriving just a few years after its christening as a "special economic zone." Today he runs a small English school in his home, teaching with a homegrown method he believes can encourage natural speech. Jack is also a freelance opinion columnist who writes about political and social issues.

Jack has a medium build and dark, serious eyes that loom, magnified, behind thick glasses. His black hair is shot through with silver threads and his cheeks and eyes sag slightly. We met in a Beijing-style noodle restaurant and talked for hours without ordering a single thing. The waitstaff proffered menus and brought pot after pot of tea, but Jack kept waving them off, insisting we weren't hungry. We talked over a square wooden table, and I tried not to squirm on my hard, slender bench whose six-inch breadth could barely accommodate me. (Seating in China seems always built for a king or a child, with little middle ground.)

Jack told me that he wanted to tell his story because he hoped the outside world could understand what happened in China when he was young. Jack's story is both difficult and sweet, and he told it in somber tones, leaning toward me on both elbows, his fingers knit in a bony pyramid.

My wife was my first and only date in my life, but not because I am an unromantic man. It was just that there was little room for romance when I was young, for many reasons.

My memory of the country when I was small is pretty gloomy. Our lives were dominated by political turbulence and economic deprivations. Political movements, mainly from inside the Communist Party, came one after another throughout my teenage years. By the close of the Cultural Revolution, this country was on the brink of collapse, and almost everyone, from the leaders of the country to common folks, had suffered a lot. I will tell you of my own bitter experiences.

I grew up in a small city during the nationwide famine triggered by the failure of Mao Zedong's farm communes. Every month the government sent our family a ration booklet containing one ticket for soap, one ticket for oil, one for twenty kilograms of rice, and so on. These "food tickets" were in our lives for decades. We could not buy food freely until the period of "reform and opening up" in the late 1970s, and food tickets persisted in some form until 1993. Some days we had enough food, other days we went hungry. Very often we ate only a thin porridge for our meal. My mother still tells me that when I was small, I always struggled for more food. My three older siblings wanted to take care of me, so at the expense of their own stomachs, one of them would usually share a bit of his or her small meal with me. Most children in those days suffered malnutrition, including my own sister, who still battles a chronic digestive illness developed in those years of hunger.

Urban people like us didn't know that the famine was even worse in the rural areas—much worse. In the cities we had the hùkǒu, a household registration document that ties each family's benefits to a city or town. The hùkǒu entitled us to housing, work, education, and food rations. As such, it was very rare to hear of anyone dying from malnutrition in the cities, but in the countryside people starved by the millions. Since the news was suppressed and censored, we didn't know about their sufferings at the time. Even Mao, who also lived in a city, didn't know the full extent of the famine. His supporters just told him the things that sounded good, instead of the truth. Our revolution was meant to elevate the common man, and Mao himself encouraged the simple, agrarian lifestyle of rural peasants. But his new policies somehow favored urban citizens at the expense of rural ones.

My parents were traditional Chinese people. They never said "I love you" or showed emotion or affection, but then, neither did any other married couple. In their time marriage was more about daily life than about passion or romance. My dad was a forester, and during my childhood his work assignment was far away from our hometown. He could visit only a few times each year, so I didn't observe much of a relationship between my parents.

They never talked openly with us about what was going on in the country, since discussing politics was taboo. The social atmosphere was like it is in North Korea today. And people worshipped Mao. Oh, we were absolutely crazy about him. We all read *Quotations from Chairman Mao Zedong* (popularly called the *Little Red Book* in the West). Most than a billion copies of this book were circulated in China, and we had to carry it all the time and study it, especially during the Cultural Revolution. We also memorized many Red Songs. The teachings of the revolution marched constantly through our heads, and all the while Chairman Mao gazed down, staring at us from the requisite poster of himself that hung inside each home. My parents' worshipful silence over political matters didn't begin to crack until the late 1970s. At that time a man named Lin Biao, Mao's handpicked successor, tried to defect to the Soviets. He died in a plane crash en route, but after that event people began to talk. "Even the handpicked leader wants to leave? Maybe this country is not so good."

Resentment really started to pour out a few years later, once Deng Xiaoping's program of "reform and opening up" took hold. The government still retained censorship powers, but under Deng people had a bit more freedom to criticize the government. Suddenly it seemed like everyone hated Mao and loved Deng. But today I think the supporters of Maoist thinking are growing again. People are turned off by the corruption riddling our party and by the widening disparity between rich and poor. I suppose you could say that the best side of human nature is our short memory.

But let me return to my bitter experiences. During the Cultural Revolution I missed my chance to go to high school. There was no high school anymore. All of the schools were shut down, from primary school through university, for about ten years. Since everyone wanted to join the revolution, there was no secondary school at all from 1966 until 1972. At that time factories also shut down production. The economy was very bad, and of course, millions of earlier graduates from high school and college couldn't get jobs in the cities.

Partway through this time, when I was sixteen, my sisters and I "joined the revolution." Under the leftist craze of that time, every young person was ready to answer the revolutionary call of the Great Helmsman. He called on us to be "reeducated" through farming and manual labor, and no one considered it a painful experience to receive this reeducation. My sisters and I volunteered of our own accord, motived not by force or coercion but by revolutionary propaganda. This point is critical to having an accurate knowledge of these events.

My sisters were both sent to Heilongjiang, a remote northern province famous for a region known as "the big north wild." Countless young people were sent there for two reasons. First, the country was running out of farmland and this province offered vast tracts of arable land. Second, Heilongjiang bordered the Soviet Union, which was Enemy No. 1 at the time. In the event of a war, those young farmers could quickly be converted to soldiers. My sisters' unit was so far from our hometown that they could return home only once a year, during the Chinese New Year festival. My work unit was much closer, so I could take a bus to visit my parents once a month.

I spent the next eight years of my life at that work unit. It was a kind of paramilitary organization called a production legion, and China set up thousands of these around the country to accomplish different goals. Some were armed and participated in military drills. Others, like mine, were unarmed but supervised by officers from the People's Liberation Army.

In truth, I went through unimaginable hardship in this work camp. Early on, my unit was tasked with "reclamation," which meant we had to stop up a nearby river so the surrounding land would dry out and become usable farmland. This business with the river had to be done early in the morning during the winter season, as the water levels ran lowest then. Each day we got up at four in the morning and walked for hours, covering nearly twenty kilometers to get around the river to our work site. We did not have any shoes, and we had to walk through the sticky mud in near-freezing temperatures. Even girls my age had to do this. You can imagine how we suffered.

After we arrived at the camp, we quickly warmed up with the work. We had to scoop out the earth with our hands, carry it up an embankment, and toss it into the river. This hill grew steeper and longer the deeper we dug. By the end, it was quite difficult to scale. We had no tools or vehicles, only many, many workers with handfuls of dirt. It took us two or three months to fill in this river. Once the land was reclaimed, we spent the next several years farming it.

At night the boys would play cards, smoke, and drink rice wine. We slept six to a dorm. Some of the boys befriended the girls and chased them, but I did not.

During this time of mass reeducation, I also sought an education, but on my own terms. I wanted to learn things. I wanted to study. Aside from the Little Red Book, the only book we had was the Chinese dictionary, so I studied that. I wanted to memorize all of the characters. I also studied the index in the back, learning all of the countries and capitals by heart. I taught myself calligraphy, drawing, and singing too. At night I would go outside by the river to practice scales and songs; I could bellow loudly there, since no one could hear me over the crushing noise.

I didn't have grand ambitions for any of these pursuits. I just didn't think I should be miserable all night, since I had to be miserable all day. I suppose I endured those years because I was young and I had an optimistic character. I tried not to think too much about what was going on. I tried to better myself. In some ways, I had fewer worries and anxieties then than I do now.

My life drifted by in this way for years, past the death of Chairman Mao, until Deng Xiaoping announced that China would be offering the college entrance exam almost immediately. I had only a few months to prepare, and since I had missed high school entirely, I knew little of advanced mathematics or history or science. Luckily, my personal studies paid off: I passed the exam and chose Chinese language and literature as my major. The offer letter from Zhejiang Normal College, a teacher-training school in my hometown province, relieved me of my work unit duties. A new chapter had begun for me. I was going to get a college education. And little did I know it, but I was also going to fall in love.

I was part of the very first class of students to return to the university in China. Since they had been closed for so long, universities were quite underdeveloped. The dearth of educational materials was so severe that our teachers actually had to write some of our textbooks by hand. Self-publishing was quite a task, as there were no printing machines. The master copy of each textbook had to be written on wax paper. The teacher would press down with a steel pen to gently slice

THE 1950S GENERATION

through the page. When all the characters had been written out, a sheet of book paper was placed under the wax page and ink was rolled over the top, printing an exact copy through thousands of tiny slits.

Though I was free to visit my family during breaks from school, I didn't go home that first summer. I thought that if China wanted to advance, it would have to open to other nations, and I wanted to be prepared. I decided that I would need to learn English. This language was not my major, but I wasn't worried. It would just require another season of self-education. I spent time hanging around my university's English Department that summer, trying to make friends with professors or students there, with anyone who would talk with me, really. One professor was kind enough to befriend me, and I spoke with him in English at every available moment. Within two years, my English was as good as that of any formal English major at our college.

When I went home to visit my family during later breaks, I devised another system for practicing English. Westerners were few and far between in those days, but some occasionally stayed at a hotel in my hometown of Hangzhou. I would wait outside the gate until a foreigner came walking out, and then I would try to talk with him or her. These were some of the first visitors to China after we opened our borders, and they came for business or travel. They were usually open to talking with me. Perhaps they were relieved to find someone who spoke some English.

After that first year of university, one of my middle school classmates came to visit me, but she didn't come alone. She brought a friend with her, a very beautiful girl. To be honest, I was shocked at the sight of her, and I fell in love on the spot. Soon after, I learned this lovely girl was actually a close neighbor of mine, but we had never met. Can you imagine?

It was the early eighties, and we young people had access to Western books and movies for the first time in our life. This media was very popular, and everything I saw about romantic love appealed to me. I believe love is part of human nature. It got repressed during the revolution, and maybe it got liberated when the country opened up.

I wanted to chase this beautiful girl as soon as I could, and luckily, I found an excuse a few months later. My hometown city was hosting a student arts festival, and I was scheduled to sing at the event. I invited this girl to come with me to the festival, and she said yes. At that moment I knew I had a chance. When the evening drew to a close, I took a risk. "I'd like to be friends with you. What's your idea?" She kept silent, but in our Chinese language that kind of means yes.

It didn't take long for me to win her heart. Do you know why? Yeah, I was a bit handsome when I was young. But much more significantly, I would soon be an educated man. At that time there weren't any rich people, so the most ideal marriage partner was a college graduate. Such men were a rarity, like diamonds, and it was every girl's dream to marry one.

My girlfriend's parents were very open-minded people. Her father thought that as long as a couple felt some àiqíng (romantic love) and had a lot in common, this foundation was enough for marriage. He didn't intervene in our love. Actually, neither of her parents said anything at all about our relationship from our first date through to our wedding. So, of course, I knew that they liked me. They didn't treat every son-in-law with such favor. My wife was one of three sisters, and her oldest sister made the mistake of marrying a factory worker. Her parents strongly opposed her choice. They were so upset that they didn't attend the wedding and didn't allow their daughter and son-in-law to enter their home for many years afterward.

I didn't give a bridal gift to my wife's family, and we didn't have a formal wedding ceremony, or even a simple lunch with both of our parents. At that time the old customs were considered "not revolutionary enough," and my wife's father was the editor of a publishing house devoted to state books, so he was especially opposed to any old ways. Since China hadn't developed any new customs to replace the reviled old ones, my father-in-law just accompanied his daughter to my parents' home on our wedding day, had a cup of tea, and left.

Afterward my wife and I went to get registered with the government, and then we used our two-week wedding break to travel to Shanghai, Qingdao, Nanjing, and other places. In those days the government wanted to encourage people to marry later than the legal age of twenty for women and twenty-two for men. If a couple married at any age beyond that minimum, the government granted them a two-week wedding break. If they married at the minimum, they got only three days. Since I was close to thirty and my wife was twenty-four, we enjoyed the full two weeks.

After our wedding we moved to Hangzhou, where I was assigned to teach in a middle school. We didn't have the freedom to choose our own careers then, we just went where we were told. A few years later recruiters from the Nanhai Hotel in Shenzhen came to my city to find some new managers. Shenzhen was one of the new special economic zones, a place where people were free to accept a job if they wanted it.

I took their exam, which was just an English test and a composition in Chinese—my cup of tea. [Jack smiled at his use of this English idiom.] I passed, so they sent me to Shanghai to interview for the job, even though I myself had never set foot in a hotel! I did well, got my acceptance letter, and my wife and I moved to Shenzhen. I was even sent to Hong Kong for additional training, with three hundred other colleagues. This was the first time since the Communist Revolution that regular Chinese people had gone in such a large group to a capitalist-world place like Hong Kong. We were overwhelmed and dazzled by everything: the shops, the neon signs, the variety of goods, the clothes. All that color! I had grown up in a monochromatic world, where everything was dull and everybody wore the same gray and dark-blue clothes. I was dizzy. Everything was amazing to me.

My wife and I began our married life just as China was opening up, and we have grown up together alongside our nation. Our son is almost thirty years old, and my wife and I are still together. These days, I hear that divorce rates are climbing among the post-eighties generation. In these very young age groups, maybe as many as 40 or 50 percent of couples get a divorce. Among my own peers there are some divorces, but not so many as this. My wife and I have learned to cherish each day together, to practice qīnqíng (family love), because life is short. I wish everyone could understand that. If you don't cherish what little you have today, how can you expect to cherish whatever more you can get later? If you don't have a good and kind heart now, you'll likely have the same problem after you marry and remarry.

My brother-in-law was a man who knew how to love his wife. She fought leukemia for eight years and was nothing but a shriveled bag of bones by the end of her battle. My brother-in-law cared for her until the very last minute. [Jack's expression grew serious. He was obviously touched by this memory.]

Chinese tradition stipulates that we cannot tell cancer patients that they have cancer. We must tell them they have something else, some other problem that requires treatment. The wider family is told, but not the patient him- or herself. It is very painful to watch the result. On many occasions the patients know they are dying, but they pretend they don't know, while the families pretend they aren't worried or sad. As long as a loved one lives, that family will know what happiness is, even if they couldn't recognize it before.

During that season, I said to my wife, "My dear, this is why we must cherish every day. I want us to treat every day like these last days." [Jack's eyes filled with tears as he shared this exhortation with me.]

We Didn't Know What Love Was

LUCY LAI (B. 1957)

Lucy Lai was born in Beijing, the capital city of China. At fifty-five years of age, Lucy is an attractive woman, with full lips, a bright smile, and short black hair that puffs in gentle waves. We met in Portofino, a neighborhood where shops, Western cafes, and Laurel, a famous dim sum restaurant, ringed a picturesque lake. Lucy asked if we minded cigarettes and then methodically smoked an entire pack while she unfolded her delicate memories. She has two sons and runs a successful business with her second husband. But Lucy feels disoriented in life and wishes for more. Her story reaches into the past, tracing the murmur of things both experienced and left undone.

My first love story is not really about my own feelings but about the boy who loved me. Over the years I have often thought, *If I had married him, we might have been very happy*. But my generation didn't know anything about love. I think we are the most miserable and tragic ones. We didn't even know to *want* to try. We had no system, no time, no opportunities.

I was born into a religious family and grew up with my grandmother because my parents were not there. My great-grandfather was a Christian pastor and he founded the first branch of [a Protestant denomination] in China. His son, my grandfather, continued the ministry and planted churches in over twenty new provinces.

We were also a well-educated family. My grandmother was a teacher, my father was an engineer for the Beijing Civil Research Ministry, and my mother was a doctor. After the Communist liberation, not many people in China had religion, and my grandfather was arrested for his leadership in this Christian group. He was imprisoned for much of the 1950s and died in Qínchéng Jiānyù, China's infamous maximum-security facility for political prisoners.

Before the liberation, Zhou Enlai, second in command under Chairman Mao and the future first prime minister of New China, asked my grandfather to join the Communist Party. My grandfather was a well-known figure in China in those days, because of his Christian organization, and the CPC (Communist Party of China) wanted powerful and famous people to join its ranks. But my grandfather refused Zhou Enlai's offer, saying that God was his leader, so he did not need to join any party. In truth, he supported the Nationalist Party, because they had funded his organization's project of building Christian schools and hospitals across China.

Soon after his refusal, everyone could see that the Nationalist Party would lose to the Communists. My grandfather's political contacts offered our family tickets to escape to Taiwan. It was 1948, and such tickets were almost impossible to get, even for wealthy families. Most people were simply not able to escape the mainland, so our family was one of the lucky ones.

Or we would have been one of them, if my grandfather hadn't changed his mind on the very morning scheduled for departure. He felt a deep responsibility to his life's work, to all those schools and hospitals that he feared would be destroyed in the coming liberation. He held our family back and sent the organization's secretary and president overseas instead. This pair went on to plant many churches in their lifetime, across Taiwan, Malaysia, Australia, and America. Meanwhile, our family suffered tremendously because of this pivotal decision.

For the next twenty-six years, my grandparents and their eight children, including my own parents, had no dignity or peace. After the liberation our family's personal property in Beijing and the property of the church organization were seized, just as my grandfather had foreseen. The revolution supported the worst kind of poor people— the grabbers, the lazy poor. Some people in China were poor because of bad circumstances, but other people just wanted to grab things from wealthy families. They didn't want to work hard.

Overnight my family's life changed from wealthy and comfortable to very poor. The big house, our chain of silk shops, everything was taken. My grandmother sold her remaining jewelry and nice clothes to support the family. In those days nobody could run a large private business, but small shops selling everyday items were still allowed. My family opened one such shop to sell and repair sports equipment.

I was born during this season in our family's life. It was 1957, eight years after the establishment of the People's Republic of China, and the beginning of the Anti-Rightist Campaign. My father was arrested and chucked into the same prison as my grandfather. Right after giving birth to me, my mother was exiled to Sichuan, assigned to a small suburban hospital. My grandmother stayed with me in the capitol, and many years would pass before I saw my parents again.

Despite all this turmoil, I felt much warmth in my family when I was small. I didn't understand the things that were happening in our country, but I knew that my relatives were happy in their hearts because they had God and each other. On the weekends my aunties and uncles would sneak secretly into my grandmother's house, and we played the violin and drums, sang Christian songs [she sang a few bars of one of her favorites], and prayed together. My aunties and uncles would greet each other with a hug, and they would say "I love you" to each other, which is quite unusual in China. I remember those happy times so well.

We could invite only family members to our gatherings, and we had to close the windows and doors to muffle the lyrics. If our neighbors heard only distant music, that wasn't so bad. But if they heard the words, they could have made serious trouble for us. Luckily, nobody cared very much, because we were no longer important people. We were just poor, like everyone else.

Even still, our neighbors were afraid to befriend us directly because of our political status. The government classed our family as *fǎndòngpài*, "reactionaries," because we were Christians and landowners. Our class label literally meant "against the group," and it was a terrible mark to bear. Close neighbors knew we were good people, but the government was watching everything and controlling the family environment. Every week our neighborhood committee had to make their report to the Communist Party. The local party leaders pressed our neighbors about us. "What about that Lai family? What did they say this week?"

In the early sixties our already-impoverished nation was stricken with famine. Beijing fared a little bit better than the other cities, and four of my aunties and uncles still had jobs, so my family had enough to eat through those dark years.

Then, in 1966, the Cultural Revolution began. This was a very bad time for my family, the very worst time. One day the new Red Guard soldiers, who were primarily very young students, rushed into our home. They took all the books and everything they could grab. My grandmother managed to hide one small copy of the Bible, an old gift from an American pastor, by slipping it onto the roof over our toilet. After the Red Guards left, she hid it permanently in my clothes. She thought no one would search me because I was only a child. To this day, I still have it.

Every day my aunties and uncles had to wear high paper hats and large placards on their chests, both of which proclaimed their "reactionary" status. Many times the Red Guards pulled them out of their homes to humiliate them in public struggle sessions. Our neighbors and friends would gather around them in a large knot, raising their fists. "Struggle! Struggle!" they cheered. [Lucy raised her own fist to demonstrate. Her eyes were wide and wet.] Then they would beat my relatives with their fists or with wooden sticks or anything they could find, until they bled. I was only nine years old, but I had to watch them. These struggle sessions happened all the time, and all the "rich peasants" and "rotten elements" and other bad-class people suffered continually. I felt scared all the time in those days. I didn't understand why these things were happening. I just felt blank inside my brain. I think these scared and blank feelings went together.

The next year my grandmother and I were kicked out of Beijing, and for two days we wandered homeless. We went to find one of my uncles, a middle school teacher. He lived at the school, as was common in those days, but that year there were no classes. School was not closed, though. To the contrary, they opened the doors wide, but for "making revolution," not for learning. We found my uncle but realized he was wearing the tall paper hat in struggle sessions too. He had not escaped our family's political status, so we could not stay there.

We continued on, traveling to another one of my aunties, a professor at an agricultural university near Beijing. University classes were not in session either, and we discovered my auntie detained in the school's "cow pen," the makeshift jail of that era. The cow pen was for reactionaries and other bad-class people, and this auntie also suffered under the paper hat. Her Red Guards didn't want us to stay either, but my auntie kneeled at their feet and begged them to let her mother and niece stay with her. The guards relented.

Two days later, the very worst thing happened. The Red Guards came to our cow pen and dragged my grandmother away. They arranged a struggle session just for her, because she was a religious lady. "Struggle! Struggle!" everyone chanted fervently. The guards found a horse and bound my grandmother's wrists with its tail. Then they beat the horse until it panicked and galloped away, pulling my grandmother through the city streets for a long time. She almost died.

That evening my grandmother felt no more hope in China, no more room to believe in God. She wanted only to die. And that cow pen was near some railroad tracks.

At midnight I felt my grandmother get up. She put on clean clothes. I was only nine, but my sixth sense told me something was very, very wrong. I held her legs and would not let her leave the room. I cried and cried. I did not have anyone else, I sputtered. She simply could not leave. [Lucy's eyes filled with tears.] Finally, after an hour or two, my grandmother stopped struggling.

"Okay, Lucy," she sighed. "I don't want to die. I will stay."

We lived in the cow pen for six months, until we were ordered to return to my grandfather's original hometown. The government wanted us to learn to be farmers again, to return to an agrarian lifestyle. We didn't know a single thing about farming, but it was safer to live away from the big cities, so we accepted this reassignment gladly.

When we arrived in this village, my grandmother and I had nothing, no food, no clothes, no door to knock on. All we could do was stand in the village square while the local farmers gathered around us, staring like we were pandas escaped from the zoo. Most of those villagers were also Lai people, and they were good to us. One family took us in, giving us food and a room for sleeping. There was no bed, but we built one from available wood scraps. The government also gave us a piece of land to farm. I had never so much as planted a seed, so we had to start at the very beginning. There was no other place to start. And those Lai farmers helped us.

The next month my two uncles from Beijing arrived in the village.

One had been a university student, so he was sent to the countryside. The other uncle was a steel factory worker, but in those days the steel factories were making only revolution, not any steel, so he was sent to the Lai's traditional hometown as well.

After some time my grandmother began to worry about my education. I had completed the first grade in Beijing, but for the next two years all schools were closed, and I was not learning much in the countryside. My mother still worked in Sichuan province, so my grandmother contacted her to see if any schools were open there. "Yes, classes are in session," she replied. "Send Lucy to Sichuan."

I had no memory of my mother, but I was sent to live with her right away. It was very hard at first, because my mother was a stranger. She had lost contact with my father, so she had married a second husband and had two new children by that time. My mother was stunningly beautiful, and I know she really loved me, but she did not know how to express her feelings. I often felt I did not belong. I didn't want to be close to her, because I did not have the mom feeling toward her.

I missed my grandmother terribly. She stayed behind in that Lai village, where she lived until 1975, the year Deng Xiaoping exonerated the Rightists. He declared they were not Rightists anymore and they could all go home.

I really needed good feelings in my teen years, and I finally found them in books. I devoured English literature, with all its beautiful love stories about royal ladies, dashing gentlemen, and regal white horses. I was also very lucky, because many excellent Shanghai teachers had been labeled Rightists and sent to Sichuan. As I grew older, I swallowed myself up in reading and homework, blocking out the rest of the world.

My mother was very strict with me about boys. "When a girl grows up, she must be like the rose flower with many thorns," she told me. "She should protect herself. She must not open to a man." In my generation everyone was so pure, so innocent, that we didn't even know how a girl could open to a man. We didn't know how men and women were supposed to feel with each other. Some boys liked me in high school, but I didn't understand such inklings. I thought a boy liking a girl was an evil thing. *He must be a bad boy,* I would think dismissively. Every girl I knew thought the same way. We agreed that anyone who sought love must be a very low-quality person.

I remember the first time I noticed a boy. We were both top students, and I had the simplest sort of feeling for him. I just wanted us to be together in the same room. I didn't want to talk to him, since girls and boys didn't really talk in those days. I just knew I felt strangely happy when I could see him. I didn't love him—we didn't even understand what love was back then. I just admired him.

This ignorance about love was not just a problem among young people. I think very few couples of any age understood love feelings in those days. Traditionally we Chinese did not express our emotions. I think the middle and lower classes probably never knew about love until recently. If they said "I love you" to their spouse, their village and family would think that was a bad thing. But the higher classes did not always think this way. From 1911 to 1949, under the Nationalist Party, higher-class families had a good situation. They were very open, embracing early capitalism, industrial establishment, and a budding military. Big port cities like Shanghai, Beijing, and Nanjing were open to foreigners and the people wanted Western education. Over time, they admired the Western system and adopted some of its culture. They knew about love and they could express their love feelings. Many people from Shanghai or Beijing even studied overseas and learned about romantic love.

But after Mao's liberation, this kind of love was suppressed. Romantic feelings were stamped out of Chinese society. Everyone was suspicious of each other, and they understood only two feelings: stress and scorn. If anybody said "I love you," we all thought that was a bad thing. There were no healthy social relationships in China. Nobody talked about love, not at school, not in university, not in society. My mother was so busy, she didn't tell me either. It was as though love didn't exist.

But I knew something about love. I learned about love feelings quietly, through Western books, and I knew love involved a white horse and a tall man. But I had only the faintest sort of picture.

In 1977 I was among the first group of students to go back to university. I got a very good score on the college entrance examination, but I was barred from attending the best university. The specter of my family's black "reactionary" status, stamped three decades earlier, haunted me still, so I was sent to a second-tier college.

My school did not permit students to have love relationships, of course, but as my class had only eight women and forty-two men, somehow even the ugliest girl was chased by many men. I myself still gave no thought to boys, but I felt very lonely in my heart, and I didn't really know myself. I didn't know if I was beautiful; I didn't know anything. I ignored my feelings and focused on my very high standards. Because I was from Beijing, from a well-educated, religious family, I thought nobody in this small city school could be suitable for me. I was very confused about my future.

After graduation my university leader asked me to stay on as a professor. One boy, a classmate of mine, received the same invitation. During our student years, he was always the top student and I always took second place. After graduation this boy told me he loved me. He started to write letters to me every day. I did not feel sure about this boy, since he was very short and not particularly handsome. Actually, I liked to read his letters very much. I just didn't like to see him! [She chuckled.]

The following year I learned that my father was still alive. He was living in a northern city, not far from the border of North Korea. I was twenty-one years old and had no memory of my father, so I moved to that city to get to know him and to teach at the local university.

For the next three years, this boy who loved me continued to write letters every day. And each year when I went to visit my mother in Sichuan for the Chinese New Year festival, he traveled to visit me. I still didn't understand that it was natural for men and women to feel love feelings for each other. But sometimes a little thought floated through my mind: *If I married this short man, I might be very happy.* Bolstered by this idea, I would permit him to come just inside the door of my mother's house. I didn't know what love was, but I still remembered about the tall man with the white horse.

This boy knew my family was a religious family, and he also understood my love for English literature and culture. He wanted everything to be suitable for me, so after three years of letter-writing and annual visits, he announced some special news. He had been accepted to a master's program in Shakespeare. He would begin his coursework in the fall, at a university up north. Incidentally, his university was right next door to mine, separated from my school by only one wall! Of course, I knew he was coming for me.

It was 1984, and I was twenty-seven years old. Every day my father said, "You should find a husband." He arranged a friend to be my matchmaker, and that friend introduced me to a man from the local TV station. In my heart I wanted an older man, perhaps because I grew up with my grandmother. This TV-station man was tall, a little handsome, smart, and six years my senior. We did not love each other, but my father had arranged it for me, and I trusted this traditional method of introduction. I agreed to marry him.

In truth, I gave very little thought to marrying that letter-writing boy. I knew he loved me very much, but it was all folded up inside his brain. We had never held hands, never kissed, never had anything together. One day I wrote to tell him of my engagement. Before he began his Shakespeare studies that fall, I was already another man's wife.

Even my marriage did not daunt this boy. He continued to wait for me. More than ten years later, he visited me in Shenzhen, where I had moved with my first husband. My first husband's parents hadn't known anything about love, and neither did he. He didn't respect me. He didn't care about my emotions or understand my thoughts. Never once did he ask me, "Lucy, how do you feel?" He understood only one thing: "I buy you the television; I get a fridge for you. That is love."

During our visit I told my old friend that I was planning to divorce my husband. He was a professor of Shakespeare at Sichuan University by then, and he had never married. As soon as I said this, he confessed that he still loved me. He had always loved me, he said, for all those intervening years. If I would only accept him, I could come to live with him. We could finally be together.

I felt very sorry for this man because he had loved me for so long. I tried to express my feelings by buying him some clothes and inviting him to dinner. I tried to say thank you for your deep feeling for me, for all of these years. But I told him gently that I must refuse his feelings. I told him not to hope for me any longer, not to wait anymore. Years later I learned that he did get married soon after this visit.

I had not yet had my own first love. Even when I thought I had found it, my second marriage did not turn out like I hoped. This second husband was my auntie's classmate. He was thirteen years older than me and also divorced, because his wife had gone to South Africa and found another husband. It was 1998, and he came from Harbin to Shenzhen to meet me. For me, it was love at first sight. It was my first time to experience those excited feelings. This man was very handsome and gentle. I thought he would be a romantic husband, because we dated for one year and had these good feelings for each other. I imagined this romance was love, but he did not turn out to be a loving or romantic man. Within two years his northeastern culture came back to him. He grew selfish and didn't care about other people, only himself.

We have been married for fourteen years now, and I only stay with him out of responsibility, out of pity. He is a poor thing, but he is old and I am old, so I think we must stay together to move forward. If I leave him, he will think I have abandoned him. In all these years, he has never said, "Lucy, I love you." He's never said that. I really, really need to hear him say that he loves me. Sometimes I am strong, but other times I think maybe my desire for romantic love is wrong. I've never said "I love you" to him, either. I feel too shy. I have so many feelings in my heart, but I can't speak them aloud. My husband knows that I love him. With everything I do for him, he must know. Do you think so? I have written "I love you" in letters before. Sometimes he says, "Lucy, I miss you," if he is on a business trip. But face-to-face, we cannot speak.

My whole life, I was always so afraid to say "love" because this is a very deep word. During all those years when my own sons were growing up, I could never say "I love you," and I felt too shy to hug them. I love them very much, but I could never bring myself to do these things.

By the time my youngest son was twenty, I knew I had been wrong not to express myself. So I started to write, "My son, I love you," in emails. He went to Australia for school, and when he came back, I somehow found the courage to say "I love you" to his face. I can

THE 1950S GENERATION

hug him now, too. I visited this son for three months, and perhaps I learned from the Australian people. Every day they express their love; they can speak those love words so effortlessly. I have very strong feelings, and I am trying to learn to express them now, step by step.

I don't have sex with my husband anymore, because we don't have those love feelings. We only have qīnqíng, the family feeling. I want very much to look for another lover! [Her face brightened tremendously, and she smiled.] I would love to meet someone, to have that spark, more than anything else. I hope one day this will happen.

I think my heart is becoming younger and younger as I grow older. Last year I went to Beijing to study philosophy, to explore the meaning of life, because I don't feel that sense of happiness right now. Objectively, I have a lot of wealth, but I have no deep sense of beauty. I want to explore happiness. Not even just romantic love, but the kind of society-wide happiness that I felt in Australia. People respected each other there. Even a man who collects the garbage can work diligently and be well respected. In China our respect is only on the surface, and it is triggered only by status, power, and money. Even within the family, the older generation can only understand and respect money. Relationships are based on benefits, even between friends, maybe even between a wife and husband. I feel desperate for respect and dignity and love and happiness, from both my husband and my society.

Sometimes I still remember this first boy who loved me, and I feel some regret. If I had only understood what love could be, if I had only accepted his love and companionship, would I have found the happiness that eludes me still?

The Three Wives of a Former (Teenage) Intelligence Operative

TOM LIU (B. 1958)

Tom Liu was born in Dalian, a major port city in Liaoning, a northeastern province. He described his home city as a "very nice, romantic city, influenced by traditional Russian and Japanese architectural styles." Dalian is China's northernmost warm-water harbor and was home to foreign traders and businesspeople in the early twentieth century. It was also the entry point for occupations by the British, Russians, and Japanese.

Tom is a trim, good-looking man with an easy smile and thoughtful eyes. He invited us to talk in his home, which was immaculate, pleasantly Spartan, and decorated exclusively in black and white. He lives there with his third wife, whom he met through a local dating service, and her teenage daughter.

Tom offered tea and coffee, and after settling us at his kitchen table with our cups of green tea, he mixed instant coffee for himself. Few Chinese people I know would choose coffee over tea, so I expressed my surprise at his beverage choice. "I am a typical American," he smiled broadly. "I drink four cups every day."

Tom leaned back in his chair, lit up a cigarette, and asked us what we wanted to know. He drank coffee, smoked, and told us his story for several hours. Despite his many losses and difficulties, Tom spoke in an upbeat and jovial manner. He seemed like a contented man.

Tom's experiences made me see that despite the revolutionized atmosphere and the push to do away with "feudal" customs during his youth, much of China's social and moral life was still dictated by ingrained Confucian traditions. Tom doesn't recall any direct teaching on the subject of men and women, but his first marriage was likely motivated by remnants of the old teaching of *nán nǚ shòushòu bù qīn*, which means "it is improper for a man and woman to hold each other's hands, or pass objects from hand to hand." This concept, which is responsible for some of the Chinese people's traditional physical reserve, just came to Tom through social osmosis. It was in the air—it didn't need to be taught.

The first time I saw her, I loved her. I was twenty-one years old, and she and I were assigned to the same college entrance examination location. I fell in love on the spot, and a tiny, secret idea unfurled in my

48

mind: *If she could just be recruited by the same university as me, then I would be very happy indeed.* My imaginings wandered no further than that.

In all my youth, I never saw anything about romantic love. Can you believe it? Not one reference. During that time China was just focused on politics. My mother and father were both high-ranking officers in the People's Liberation Army, so my younger sister and I grew up on a military campus. My mother was a gynecologist and my father was one of China's earliest pilots. His unit spent five years training with Russian experts in the 1950s, building an air force for China. Because of our high status, my family had more money, food, and resources than most people in China.

Nobody taught me anything about love—even my own parents never broached the subject. They thought romantic love was capitalist, so it was wrong. They thought everyone should be "red," or very pure. In that time of high-pressure politics, anyone who talked about romantic love was considered "black," a rotten element. Consequently, romantic love was a sealed subject. China wasn't always this way, before Mao. And after the "reform and opening up" of late 1970s, we were again very interested in love. But while I was growing up, if you so much as listened to foreign music, you must be a capitalist! If even a simple song was bad, imagine what we thought about love.

When I was fourteen years old, I became a monitor at the PLA air force academy. I worked like a CIA operative, collecting information, detecting radio signals, and listening to conversations for military purposes. I studied English for eight hours every day, and afterward I would tune into the BBC, NBC, and other main news agencies. My unit primarily listened to America, while other units focused on other countries. We even listened to the big Soviet news agency in Russia.

In 1969, when the United States landed on the moon, they announced, "The whole world can watch Apollo's landing, except for China." But really, we were watching. We had already built a secret satellite that very same year. In 1972 Nixon set up a satellite during his visit to China. We called it Qībǎo, the "Seven Treasures," and let the Americans think it was our first satellite.

We did have girls at this air force academy, but I remember we had to seal our mouths! We could not say "I like you" directly. We had to go a long way around to reach our real meaning. I worked as a monitor for the Chinese air force for seven years, until China opened its universities again and I was allowed to take the entrance examination.

It's hard to believe, but my secret wish was answered: that girl from the testing center *was* recruited by the same college. I allowed myself to expand my dream, whispering, *If she was in the same class with me, then I would be very happy*. Well, on the first day of class, there she was. We were both majoring in English.

I loved her for the next four years, but I kept my distance. I decided purposely to do this, but I don't know why. I suppose I didn't want anyone to know I loved her. Since I was the top student and the class leader, sometimes she needed to ask me something about schoolwork. It was my job to help her, so I did, but we never spoke of love.

Then, in the third year of university, I got a new desk mate. She was a girl, and one fateful day, I brushed her hand in class. It was just a very shallow touch, maybe a ghost bumped me. I had never touched a woman before in my life, not even a simple touch like this, because I believed it was improper. One day after that, I visited her privately at her dormitory and held her hand. I had only a very plain feeling for her, and I didn't know what love was or what marriage was about. I just knew that we had to guard our secret or I would have big problems. This girl and I could not go on dates anyway. We were too poor.

A few days before graduation, an extraordinary thing happened. I was sitting outside alone one evening, and the girl that I loved came to find me. She looked at me for a long moment. "I like you," she said. "I want to be your girlfriend. Will you date with me?" I was amazed. I had carried this secret love in my heart for so long, and in a handful of days, we would all be reassigned. This girl and I might never see each other again. It was her last chance to try, and she took it. It was also my last chance to tell her I loved her too, that I had loved her for many years.

But I didn't.

I opened my mouth to tell her, but what came out was, "I have a girlfriend already."

The girl that I loved waited for more, but I didn't say anything else. Her narrow shoulders slumped a bit as she turned to go. She had been so brave, and I was so cowardly. I couldn't speak of my feelings, couldn't tell her I had loved her from the start. I felt very sad after that day. [Tom's normally jovial face grew grave.]

Do you know why I refused her? I was cornered by a very ridiculous idea. Since I had already touched my desk mate's hand, I believed I could not accept another woman. I thought I must marry this first girl because of our shallow intimacy, or I would be making a big mistake. I imagined I would be blamed by my parents and other adults if I stopped my relationship with this first girl. My thought was just an instinct, since no one had directly told me any rules about romantic love or about breaking up. At the time, I thought I was right. But now I think I was wrong! [He chuckled good-naturedly.] If I could tell that girl now how I really felt, then I would. And I'm sure she would ask, "Then why did you refuse me?"

Actually, this girl was not the only girl who asked to date me toward the end of college. At that time I had another privileged condition: I would be assigned back to my hometown of Dalian, a better place than most. If I married quickly, my wife would be assigned along with me. Since husbands and wives were commonly assigned to work units in different cities or provinces, this guarantee of coassignment was a significant benefit. Many girls wanted to marry me because of this privilege and my family background. In those last few days before we graduated, at least five of my classmates asked to be my girlfriend, and I refused them all. I don't know why. Maybe I was controlled by a ghost.

Right after college graduation, I requested permission to marry from the governmental department in charge of social life. After checking my girlfriend's class and family background, they approved my choice. On the surface, the government told everyone, "You can marry freely." But really, they needed to check, and check again, before your choice could be approved. Especially in the party-controlled environment of the PLA, class status and political background had to be checked thoroughly to ensure that only "good-class" marriages occurred. For simplicity, marriages were often arranged by government officials who had already considered each person's status. If an air force leader had introduced a girl to me, for example, I would have known our marriage could be easily approved.

I was twenty-four when I married my first wife, but I knew nothing about females. I didn't understand why I had to marry at all, or what purpose marriage served. Two years later, in 1984, our daughter was born. By the time she turned eight, we were divorced.

In China we have a proverb about the most suitable kind of marriage. We think if you want to marry, you had better find a *méndānghùduì*, a "marriage between families of equal social rank." My first wife and I were not equal in this regard. I came from a family of high-ranking soldiers, while my wife's parents were just common workers. Consequently, we were used to different family lifestyles, and these conflicting expectations caused some difficulty.

I had a habit of saving some money. But my wife, well, she was a compulsive saver. She would only spend money on her own family, and after a while, I concluded that she didn't love me, just our money. Things got particularly bad when I was working for a human resources company. For some reason, I couldn't make enough money. My wife was in charge of our account, and she signed all the banknotes. I didn't know where our money was going, just that we didn't have enough.

One day, before a business trip, I went to the local police station to complete some business regarding my passport. By chance, I caught sight of my wife's brother's passport. I was curious, since I hadn't heard he was planning a trip. I knew the police officer on duty. "What was the purpose of his trip?" I asked.

"He is a student in Australia," he replied.

I went home and asked my wife why she had never mentioned her brother's studies in Australia. She kept silent. I found out she was spending all of our money to secretly support her brother. This expensive deception lit the fuse for our divorce, since we had no foundation of love or romantic feelings to help us endure. After our divorce my wife moved to America with my daughter and ceased all contact with me. My daughter is twenty-seven years old now, and I don't even know where she lives.

My second marriage started with a bet. [Tom chuckled and lit a fresh cigarette.] It was 1993, and China's newly expanding private sector was generating fistfuls of money for some people. Everyone wanted to invest in real estate, so I got into the business. I was the deputy manager of a joint venture corporation. We spent our own money on development, and the government provided land in Guangxi, a coastal province in southeastern China.

One day my colleagues and I were watching an entertainment show broadcast by the local television station. The show's hostess was a good-looking woman who spoke fluent, standardized Mandarin in a place where most people spoke only Cantonese.

One of my friends joked with me. "Tom, okay, I'll bet you that you can't get this girl to go out on a date with you." He wasn't betting much, only enough money for the proposed dinner, but I accepted. I actually knew this woman already, through some business connections. She was a TV hostess as a hobby, but during the day she was a teller at a bank that handled some of our company's investments. I picked up the phone and called her station. She had just finished her broadcast, so she answered.

"You want to go to dinner tonight?" I asked. "Do you have free time?"

"Who is this?" she replied.

"Mr. Liu."

"Okay, sure." One year later we got married.

My first marriage had been very dull and boring. The second time around, I thought, *Okay, I want to have a change.* I wanted to taste the new wine. This girl worked in television, everyone could see her good-looking face, and the audience respected her. I thought if I could get a girl like that, then I would feel a little proud. It felt like a game. I didn't really have a purpose for our marriage—I just wanted to show off. Unfortunately, it worked.

This second wife and I had one son together, and we also had very different personalities. I had judged her only on looks, but this had not been a well-reasoned decision. After a while I had what we call *shěnměi píláo*, the "aesthetic fatigue." You know, if you look at your wife very often, even though she is beautiful, you will sigh and think, "Ah, she is so common. So tiring."

Our real problem started when I needed a new job. I felt I could find the right kind of work only back in Dalian, which was quite far from Guangxi province—over three hours by plane. I asked my wife many times to move to my hometown, but she refused. She had graduated from *yì xiào*, a type of vocational high school for arts and performance, and it was a poor education by big-city standards. It would be hard for her to secure work as a bank teller or any similar position, and she didn't want to be a housewife. In the end, I worked in Dalian and she stayed in Guangxi, and we saw each other once a year. This kind of long-distance marriage is very common in China. In the army, for example, you have to serve away from home for years at a time, spending maybe one month with your wife in a given year.

We Chinese have another saying: Ài měi zhī xīn rén jiē yǒu zhī, or "Everyone loves beauty." It doesn't matter if a beautiful person is married. Even if she is, she will likely be chased by another man, since everyone loves beauty. After I had been working in Dalian for one or two years, other people began to tell me romantic stories about my wife. They whispered that she had a boyfriend, my good friend from our old real estate group. But I didn't want to believe them.

I have to take some responsibility for this problem because I saw my wife and son so infrequently. I suspected her, but I didn't have any hard proof. I would never have brought it up with her myself, but one day she raised the subject of divorce. During the proceedings, that friend of mine appeared with her in court. I was absent. I didn't want to be in the court, because I am more traditional and I didn't agree with the divorce. We divorced almost ten years after our wedding, and when we separated, the courts ruled that I owed her nothing. They said I had already paid it all.

This second wife still lives in Guangxi province, but she does not allow me to see my son. When I think about this, I feel very sad and upset. She is the one who cheated, after all! I could have forgiven her affair. I could have contained her shortcomings. I could have borne it all. In family matters, it is not about who is "right," because usually there is no right. If she hadn't asked for a divorce, I would still be with her. My wife has already changed my son's name to her family name, and this affront means a great deal. You see, China has this bad habit, not like Western people: our descendants must continue the family line. Usually this descendant has to be a son, though I don't care about that very much, maybe just a little bit. I have saved a large sum of money that I want to give to my son as an inheritance.

Maybe when he is older, our relationship will be restored. But I have little hope. [The twinkle left Tom's eyes as he spoke of this separation from his son.]

I met my third wife through a marriage-making agency in Shenzhen in 2004. For a fee, they take your requirements and match you with the right person. In truth, they are not very good at this, as their success rate is less than one in ten thousand. But my wife and I fell in love at first sight. It was her second marriage, and my third.

After we met we founded an English school together, as we had both studied the language for many years. We have a patriotic duty to train up kids for our motherland, but actually, my motivation is just to educate children with excellent, advanced ideas. I want them to think with Western philosophy and knowledge, not with backward ideas. Today our school is successful and growing, and we offer classes from primary school through high school.

My third wife and I have also had many conflicts because of personality. We are both stubborn, and we want to stand by our own ideas. Since we are also both well educated, we think we know how to fix a problem. Sometimes when we try to solve something, though, we just end up arguing. We must try to get used to each other's character, try to bear with each other's difficult points. We are also getting older and more mature, so now we can think before we jump. We will not give up on our marriage. Even if we think we have gone to the end of one road, we will find a new way.

Neither of us ever made romantic gestures in past marriages, but this time around I made an effort to arrange some surprises for her and she also tries to find romantic things to do. One time my wife had to have surgery on one of her breasts. Before she came home, I set six very beautiful flower baskets by her windows. They were all different shapes and colors, and she was very touched.

This third marriage is much happier than my second one. It is not perfect, we still have some conflicts, but my only important regret is that we are not allowed to have a child together. My wife has her daughter, and I have my children, so we must follow the One Child Policy.

My wife's teenage daughter lives with us, and we have fostered a democratic environment, like a Western family. If she has any experience with a boy who likes her, she will talk to us about it. We give her some advice, but we also allow some of her shortcomings and not-so-well-thought-out ideas. It doesn't matter, as long as we can talk together. No matter how many boys chase her or pass her love letters, she tells us about each of them. She will even tell us about private things that happen between men and women. This kind of frankness is unusual in China. Usually we don't like other people to invade our privacy. Shenzhen is more open, though, and more democratic, more Western, than other places in China. We have suggested that she wait to have her own love story. We don't think it's the right time to have a boyfriend, because maybe he will interfere with school or her health.

When she was in junior high, she was hurt by a boy that she loved and felt very sad. She got some life experience from her loving, and from then on, she has agreed with us. Even now she feels too young to have a boyfriend. She doesn't know about condoms to prevent pregnancy or disease, and we don't think it's the right time to tell her. Her mother is a doctor, so she will guide her later, in college. I do believe she will wait to have sex until college.

In the end, I have not learned very much from marriage. Why should I learn? I have just tried to test life, to taste and feel it. I did learn that marriage is not easy. Sometimes I am afraid of marriage. But it is our responsibility to carry on the human race, to give birth to the younger generations. I never think of marriage as so romantic, so loving, so exciting, like some writers say. It is a human task. We have to carry on.

The First Group Wedding in Zhengzhou

MA YAJING (B. 1959)

Ma Yajing is fifty-three years old and came of age during the tumultuous Cultural Revolution. She was raised in a village in Henan, but she and her husband now live in its provincial capital, on the southern banks of the Yellow River. For the past year, Ma Yajing has been living with her daughter in Shenzhen to help raise her new grandchild. It was this daughter who introduced us.

Linda and I talked with both Ma Yajing and her daughter at a Starbucks next to the Hongshuwan metro station. Mrs. Ma's lined face is still quite beautiful, and she spoke with animation, often arching her eyebrows, smiling, laughing, and puckering the single dimple on her left cheek. She wore a nice dress and a hint of lipstick and paused easily each time her daughter patted her arm to break in and translate. I think she is a happy lady.

Ma Yajing's story sketches the austere social landscape of her youth, in which girls understood that their reputation was critical but were given little direct guidance about love or marriage. In the absence of formal instruction, they learned what not to do, think, and feel largely by avoiding whatever brought gossip down upon other young girls. Mrs. Ma has witnessed the rapid social changes of the last several decades and had both praise and caution to offer.

I never thought about marriage before getting married. When I was growing up, nobody ever talked about marriage. I never even raised the subject with a friend, and I think everyone else was too shy to bring it up. One time a colleague tried to introduce me to a boy, but I ran away! Because of the social environment, you really could not think about marriage, and certainly not about dating. People could not date. They could not even hold hands. When I was single, my only thoughts about love were *I cannot date; I cannot fall in love*. I knew these were bad things. I was a lady, after all. I could not just go out and find a man. It wasn't right!

Nowadays, China is completely different. Young people have so many things to guide them, so many books and movies and conversations to stoke their curiosity. Once they are exposed to these ideas

57

about love and marriage, then they want to know more, they want to think more deeply. But when I was young, the lack of media about love created an environment that repressed our thoughts. People talked about work, and maybe a little about politics, but mostly just about work. I think people were too simple back then.

Now back to this boy I ran away from. I was twenty years old when I started my first job, and China was just starting to open up. My older colleagues wanted to introduce a boy to me, but I refused. I was very shy, and also I did not think that meeting a boy was a good thing. Even if I liked a boy my colleagues picked, and even if we got along very well, it was not okay. He would still become only a boyfriend, not a husband, and I knew that a good woman should go from single to married.

In my hometown village, anyone who had a boyfriend or girlfriend was always discussed in a negative light, and that was the last thing I wanted. My father was a supervisor at the local hospital and he had a good reputation, so he was very strict with his two girls. If I accepted a boyfriend, I would get a bad reputation, and that was not allowed. Even if I had wanted to go on a date, there was nowhere to go. We had a movie theater, yes, but if you went there with a boy, well! Everyone would talk, and you would never live it down.

Actually, my parents had already introduced me to my husband, but they hadn't told me. He was quite good with machines, always tinkering with engines and parts, and he fixed the equipment at my father's hospital. One day, when I was sixteen, my dad invited him to our home for lunch. He was composed, calm, relaxed. At that time people were very simple. The first time we met, I didn't have any feelings for him. I didn't even speak to him, because he was a boy. Since our eating room was very small, I ended up sitting outside to finish my food. I suppose I thought he was honest and down to earth, but I didn't notice his appearance. I wasn't thinking like that.

When I was young, I only knew two things about marriage and one thing about love. I knew that you had to marry at the right age, before you were too old, and I knew that your family had to introduce you to the man if you wanted to avoid gossip. All I knew about love was that it was wrong, and young people should àn lián, "hide their feelings."

I didn't know exactly what was bad to do until people gossiped, and then I knew that thing was wrong.

This was during the Cultural Revolution, so we didn't have any media about relationships between boyfriends and girlfriends. We did have movies, but they never told a love story. They were just about war, politics, and how to defeat your enemy. Before the Cultural Revolution, maybe movies could have a little bit of love in them, but once it started, no one could make this kind of movie. It was considered a crime. I remember two actresses who made a love movie in those years, and they were actually sent to prison. The young generation today cannot understand these things that happened in our time. We can hardly understand them ourselves! People were too simple when I was young.

Eventually I found out that his parents had approached my parents directly about our match. Our lunch meeting was orchestrated soon after, though of course my future husband's parents didn't tell him either! [She chuckled.] His parents knew of my father's good reputation and they liked me. Since they already knew each other, no matchmaker was needed. My dad thought the match was a bit unorthodox, since the ideal husband should be two or three years older, and this man was a full six years my senior. My mother accepted readily, though, because she thought my husband was good. Back then, usually the two families arranged the engagement, while the intended couple was not in love at all. Afterward, as the couple got to know each other, then probably they would fall in love.

It might surprise you to hear that I already knew this man. Well, I knew *of* him, because he was quite famous in our area. He had been very good at his studies, and by the time I was in primary school, he was already something of an educational legend. All the teachers spoke of his scholastic achievements and urged us to learn from his example. My husband was delayed in going to college because of the Cultural Revolution, but after it ended, he got to take the first college entrance exam. He was accepted into Peking University, a very good school. We didn't have a lot of chances to get to know each other before we got married, since we saw each other only a few times each year. He could come visit me in my home during summer breaks, but I could never visit him.

Gradually, the whole village knew we had been introduced. Five years later, in 1980, the people around us started saying, "It's time." So I also began to think it was time. Since we had been introduced, my grandma had always spoken well of this man. Of course, our teachers and classmates always said he was exemplary too. I thought this man was probably a good person.

Our wedding was a little bit interesting. My grandpa wouldn't allow traditions—no wedding party, no firecrackers. It was still too soon after the Cultural Revolution, which had tried to blot out all such old habits. Instead, one day my husband-to-be picked me up on his bicycle and took me to the train station. We didn't really have luggage, so there was little to bring along. We were moving to Zhengzhou, the capital city of Henan province, and we were going to participate in the city's first group wedding. It was the first time those kinds of things were happening. The party had issued an appeal for people to live a simple life, so this group wedding idea was one solution for nuptial simplicity.

More than ten couples got married at the same time that day. Nobody wore a wedding dress; we just wore something clean that we already had. Couples stood in a line while someone read the wedding registration paper. Then the local leader of the Young Pioneers gave a speech about politics and nationalism, tacking on a few words about marriage at the end. I didn't have many thoughts about this group wedding. I just thought it was a new thing, and it felt nice to join in.

At that time our thinking was simple, so different from today's young people. Now they date so many boyfriends and girlfriends that when they get older, they think too much and feel too much pressure to make a choice. Once they do finally plan to marry, they spend so much money on pictures, the ceremony, the special clothes, only to get divorced a few years later! When I was young, you got engaged because of your family and then you never, ever divorced. Recently, many of my same-age friends have divorced, but I have advised many others not to think about divorce so much or to speak of it aloud to their husbands. No matter which man a woman marries, she will have problems. Even if you divorce, how can you know that your problems will be solved in the future?

I also think young people should calm down and be realistic, instead of focusing so much on their hopes, wishes, and dreams. Nowadays people can marry for love, and love is important. But daily life is more important. If young people focus so much on love, only love, they will forget about the many years of daily life in a marriage. When they encounter any problems, they will want to escape immediately. My advice to young people is this: you married a person of your own choosing, so don't be so quick to divorce. If you divorce, you will hurt yourself and your parents. Chinese families are very close, so a divorce will hurt emotionally, and it will also hurt the family's reputation. Marriage is not so complicated; it is dependent on what you do. If one person behaves well, it will have a positive effect on everyone.

My husband and I have enjoyed a happy family life for many years now. He is a very good man, a better person than me. He is very tolerant and good to his children and his parents. When I am with him, I feel secure. He is a gentleman, so he doesn't go out to play with girls. Even during this year that I have lived in Shenzhen to help with my granddaughter, we have maintained a good relationship. Today, for example, I had planned to return to our home to care for my husband's mother, since she is sick. My daughter's baby has a fever, though, so I said to him that maybe I should delay my return. He didn't complain. "Don't worry about it," he said. "I can help with my mom."

Also, while many couples might argue about how much to give to his parents or her parents, we do the opposite and always try to give each other's parents more. My husband will send me to buy clothes for my mother, insisting that I not worry about his mother, as she doesn't care so much about fashion. But while I'm there, I'll pick out some things for his mom too. [Mrs. Ma smiled conspiratorially.]

My daughter married not too long ago. She studied in Canada and met her husband there, a Chinese man with a Canadian passport. At first I did not approve of him, since he was interested in business. In my family we prefer stable professional jobs, something in a hospital or with the government. We think businesspeople are too unstable, so I didn't like him. "Marriage is not only about you and your boyfriend," I told my daughter. "It is about joining two families." She listened to me and ended things with her boyfriend. But he kept pursuing her—

for the next eight years! They both ended up back in China, and he kept trying and trying until, in the end, she accepted him.

Before they married, this man's father came to meet me and asked how much money I wanted for their engagement. "We don't need any money," I said. "We only hope our daughter will have a happy life." This response made the new family very happy and appreciative, and now they respect me very much. My daughter is happy in her marriage. She has a good relationship with her husband's family, and especially with his sister. I am happy with how things have worked out for her. [She smiled warmly at her daughter and patted her arm gently.]

The "Old Hand" Man

MR. YANG (B. 1959)

Mr. Yang grew up in a small city in Guangdong province and moved to Shenzhen in the late 1980s, as the special economic zone picked up steam. Linda and I interviewed him near his home, at a Starbucks in the Sea World neighborhood. If "Sea World" sounds like it should involve dolphin shows and the iconic Shamu, picture instead a neighborhood several blocks back from the water, featuring little more than an enormous landlocked boat to claim its name. Sea World is best known for its huddle of somewhat dated international restaurants and bars, and the area is home to many expats and international businesspeople.

Mr. Yang waved us back to seats in the far corner, out of sight from the door. His sunglasses were slung behind his head, resting on the nape of his neck, and an expensive watch and diamond ring glistened below his cuffs. He was stylish and masculine, with a crew cut that actually worked. Mr. Yang was a cool guy— there was no way around it. He spoke with a mixture of confidence and aloofness, a sharp contrast to the younger colleague he brought along. This man fixed me with a jubilant and near-constant grin throughout the interview, taking every opportunity to say something to me. He only knew words like "Cheers!" but found plenty of opportunities to apply them. Mr. Yang spoke no English, but he gestured toward me as he told Linda, "I wish I could talk to her. She is so beautiful!"

Before the interview, Linda's friend had described Mr. Yang as lǎoshǒu, literally "old hand," a term for mature, sexually experienced guys, similar to the term playboy. While his demeanor and general vibe certainly supported this description, Mr. Yang spoke guardedly about his life, espousing a more traditional set of values than I had expected. For example, he was the first to mention yuánfèn, the complex, deterministic force that brings a couple together at a particular moment. Yuánfèn is similar to fate or destiny and has roots in Chinese spiritual beliefs, but the term cannot be perfectly translated into English. Essentially, it means that certain love stories are meant to be, and the universe might use a happy coincidence to bring you "the one."

Mr. Yang described growing up in a time when men had virtually no opportunity to meet women before marriage. Those circumstances, coupled with the explosion of Western ideas and media in the 1980s, left his generation curious and hungry for sex and love. At the same time, their nation was increasingly full of options to experience both. Such conditions led to the development of Shenzhen's "Second Wife City," a neighborhood famous for housing the well-kept mistresses of wealthy Chinese and Hongkongese men. I am told that the city peaked about ten years ago, but interest in second wives is not gone. I have personally seen advertisements for "second-wife matching services" in the metro station of Shenzhen.

This interview unfolded in more of a Q and A style, probably because Mr. Yang didn't feel comfortable sharing his full story with two younger ladies. I also got the sense that he did not trust Americans. Nonetheless, I think his answers are both interesting and revealing of the old generation.

I was introduced to my wife in the mid-1980s. She was the sister of one of my classmates, and I agreed to our match. While most people in my generation needed to consider their parents' approval, I did not because my parents were dead. They both passed away when I was very young. When I moved to Shenzhen in 1987, I brought this woman with me. We got married, had our daughter soon after, and I've been running my own business ever since. I'm a wholesale agent, dealing in packing tape, boat parts, that sort of thing. I've been working hard for many years, so I'm a lǎoniú—an old working cow!

Q: Many people tell me that after a couple has been married for a long time, only qīnqíng, or family love, remains. Do you agree?

A: We Chinese are not like the foreigners, always kissing and hugging, but this doesn't mean we don't have love. We always have our qīnqíng. Chinese people are more realistic about marriage, not so romantic like people in Europe and America.

When I was young, relationships were even more different than they are today. We were still very traditional then. Even in the factory, a couple holding hands was not an acceptable thing. Starting in the 1990s, some Chinese became open with their affection. Even though we are changing and becoming more open nowadays, still we are traditional.

Q: I have heard that Chinese men can love their wives and also have an affair. Do you agree? Is this a modern idea or a traditional idea?

A: A husband will still keep his wife, will still love her, but since China opened its doors, more men like to have affairs. Even if we do this, we still care for our wives and carry out our responsibilities. If we were like the Americans, who do not care, then maybe we would have divorced already.

Actually, this social situation won't last a long time. Having an affair or getting a divorce is a new thing, borrowed from Western ideas, but this situation won't last forever. In my generation, men had no relationship experience in their young life, no chance to date or meet women. After the period of "reform and opening up," things happened too quickly and people got overexcited. As they grew a little bit older and made their money, then men finally had the time to have more opportunities. As we say, "Now we can see so many flowers. Before, we saw only one flower, at home." In the end, China will go back to its traditional ways.

Q: Have you heard of Second Wife City?

A: Society was developing, so Second Wife City sprouted up, but it doesn't mean that all of China is like that. It is only a small group, and they were exposed too quickly to lots of Western ideas. Nowadays I think second wives are getting less and less popular because they cause too many problems. I think it is better for a man to cultivate a "deep-heart friend," a woman with whom he can unburden his mind. Maybe they also have sex, but he doesn't have to pay for everything. They can just be friends.

Q: Many other men have mentioned this idea as well. They want to speak intimately with a woman, they want to unload their troubles. Is it difficult for a wife to fill this role?

A: It is difficult to explain. Things change after we get married. When we have a baby, then our wife is very busy, and she gives her husband much less love. When the husband is tired, then maybe he wants to communicate something, but his wife is also very tired, so he does not. Also, she stays home while he works, so gradually her opinions change because she is in the house. Over time, when a man tries to talk to his wife, maybe she doesn't understand him anymore. A Chinese man can go out with his friends, and they can talk and relax over tea. But with his wife, he cannot do this.

Q: Let's say that a wife could understand her husband and could make time and space for the marriage. Would husbands still want these "deep-heart" friends?

A: Maybe, but the percentage having affairs would be much less.

[At this point Mr. Yang turned to Linda, my translator.] "Look, does your husband tell you everything?"

"Yes, he does," she smiled.

"Then you are special," he conceded.

"Well, he is also a foreigner."

"Oh, well, then that's why." They both nodded knowingly.

Q: Do you think Chinese spouses could do something to maintain their initial romantic love? If they went on dates or spent some time alone to strengthen and maintain their friendship, would such efforts help?

A: I think these steps could be a very good approach for maintaining the marital relationship in China. When my generation was getting married, of course, their family's financial situation made such activities impossible. Also, our philosophy is to care more for the family as a whole. We always want to be with our parents and our children, not just with our wife. Even now, if I travel, I go with my entire family.

Q: If you asked your wife to go on a date, what would she say?

A: Because our daughter is an adult already, my wife and I very often find ourselves out to dinner alone. But the feeling is different. If we go to Macau or Hong Kong, for example, and I am very tired and want to stay overnight, my wife will complain. "Why do we need to spend money for a hotel? We are so close to our house in Shenzhen!" Even if she did encourage my idea, I would not exactly be happy, because these days our relationship is more like the one between relatives. Now, if it were a mistress who agreed to stay over in the same situation, then I would be very happy indeed!

Q: Some women tell me they think a mistress is a good thing for marriage. Do you agree?

A: I think a mistress is not good for the marriage. If other wives claim a mistress is acceptable, then they either need more sex, or their relationship with their husband is not really like lovers but more like friends.

Chinese people are better because we are more responsible and traditional inside. I think sex should be a little bit serious. If you fool around with too many people, that is not good. But the situation in old China, when you could not express yourself very much with sex, that wasn't good either.

Some people say that sex leads to love for men, while love leads to sex for women, but this is not completely accurate. Chinese men are changing, we are becoming more mature. We are not so emotional and overly excited to try sex these days. Many men also care about love and feeling close, they care about the mind of their partner. Sex with a woman you love and can talk with is always preferred.

Q: What is the best way to find this kind of relationship?

A: Just by fate, just by a chance meeting, like this conversation. We call this yuánfèn, it's the idea that some couples are meant to meet each other and maybe destined to stay together. Chinese men also meet women in other ways. They may use pickup lines, but this is becoming less popular. Maybe they meet women at a bar or at KTV [Chinese-style karaoke bars, many of which double as brothels]. But connections like that are only for fun, for business clients. There is no deep feeling.

Q: What kind of man do you hope your daughter will marry?

A: I hope she can find a man who loves her. He doesn't need to be so special or different, just someone who leads a normal life. If they can get along well together and he has a job, that is enough.

Q: I have one last question, but if it is too personal, we can skip it. You mentioned your parents passed away when you were very young. Did something happen to them during the Cultural Revolution?

A: At that time I was small, so I don't remember much. But you can ask if you want. I grew up in a city. [He paused, his face darkening.] I don't really want to talk about it. It's too much, and it's in the past. It is already past! Americans can't understand. The situation was similar to North Korea today, the same kind of politics. No American will ever understand.

After our interview wrapped up, Mr. Yang and his friend invited Linda and me to dinner several times, with beaming smiles. They were very anxious to talk with me, but their approach was flirtatious and rather off-putting. When I cited previous plans with my husband, Mr. Yang said, "You can bring him!" But then he looked at his friend, laughed uproariously, and said, "No, maybe it's better if you don't!"

Despite my protestations, Linda and I escaped dinner only narrowly and only by accepting a ride home in Mr. Yang's extremely swanky sports car. He rolled the top down, blasted pop music, and drove at maniacal speeds through crowded streets, stopping for this errand and that, before finally depositing us at our homes. I felt entirely unprepared for the unwanted pressure that followed this interview, partly because no other Chinese man had tried anything like it.

PART TWO
The 1960s Generation
Forbid the Early Love

Marriage is mostly just firewood, rice, oil,
salt, soy sauce, vinegar, and tea.
—Chinese proverb

The 1960s generation grew up in the shadow of the worst famine in human history. Between 1959 and 1962, as the nation implemented new agricultural policies and a foolhardy iron-ore production scheme, farm output plummeted and tens of millions of Chinese people starved to death. The nation's official estimates place the death toll at seventeen million, while independent scholars argue it was thirty or even forty million. This staggering loss of human life is almost incomprehensible, equivalent to the decimation of the entire population of Canada or Afghanistan. To put it in a modern context, nearly one hundred times more people died in China over this three-year period than perished in the 2010 Haitian earthquake or the 2004 Indian Ocean tsunami.

The nation had barely emerged from this catastrophe when "sending down" began in 1963. This social movement relocated millions of urban youth to the countryside to be "reeducated" by peasants. Then, in 1966, Mao kicked off the decade-long Cultural Revolution, a terrifying effort to destroy the "Four Olds": old ideas, old culture, old customs, and old habits. Violent bands of young Red Guards menaced communities, persecuting millions of artists, intellectuals, religious adherents, "bad-class" folks, and "sexual deviants."

For good reason, nobody dared talk to the 1960s generation about love, romance, attraction, or sex. During the Cultural Revolution romantic love was mangled in the jaws of radical collectivism and then essentially condemned. This extremist philosophy urged each person to lose him- or herself completely in the cause of "building socialism." Anything that brought attention to personal feelings and desires was shameful, so romantic love was completely off-limits.

Haiyan Lee of Stanford University, an expert in Chinese literature and culture who also lived in China until the 1980s, explained the taboo against romantic love in this way: "If a boy showed interest in you, it meant he was not showing interest in bigger things, and he was also singling *you* out from the masses. It was a clue about his values. It meant that he thought a great deal of himself. He wanted to be recognized as an individual by another person, instead of being recognized as a member of the masses by the party, which is a very different kind of recognition."

As this generation came of age, all public discussion of sexual matters was forbidden and the retribution for sexual missteps grew especially harsh. Physical contact between an unmarried man and woman could lead to social condemnation, "struggle sessions," imprisonment, or even death. Consequently, this generation also grew up without any examples of physical or verbal affection between spouses. They had no access to stories about love or sexual attraction either. Since reputation was everything and frank discussions were taboo, this generation learned about morality indirectly. They watched punishments being rained on people who fell in love and learned that such feelings were wrong and must be stifled.

Dating barely existed among this generation. Generally speaking, rural women who chose a boyfriend independently were skewered by local gossip. An unexpected pregnancy, however, could be covered up with a hasty wedding. Urban society offered a bit more privacy, and a bold minority in this generation risked secret dating relationships after the "reform and opening up" of 1979.

Despite the nationwide clampdown on discussions of love or sex, the institution of marriage changed slowly but inexorably throughout the Mao years. By the end of the 1970s, purely arranged marriages were declining and terms like "match by introduction" and "free-choice marriage" showed up in everyday conversation. While most people born in the 1960s believed an introduction to a "good match" was the best way to find a spouse, a growing minority chose their partner on their own.

Having some say in the matter and marrying for love are two different things, though, and marriage remained a practical and near-universal institution for the 1960s generation. By 2010, 99 percent of women and 96 percent of men from this generation had married at some point in their lives, and 94 percent were currently married.

Almost everyone in this generation also bore their children after the start of China's infamous Family Planning Policy, better known as the One Child Policy, which took national effect in 1980. In actuality, "one child" is a misnomer, as multiple children are allowed in many circumstances. Twins are a natural exception, and China's population of ethnic minorities faces no restrictions on family size. The policy also allows rural parents to try again if their first baby is a girl, in order to curb infanticide rates in a country where having a son is considered a filial duty. Mercifully, attitudes toward daughters are starting to change, but the preference for sons is not yet stamped out. Finally, later amendments allowed some couples to try for two children if they were both only children themselves. In late 2013 the Chinese government took things even further, announcing that couples could have a second child even if just one spouse was an only child.

The 1960s generation suffered some educational disruption, as schools and universities were closed during periods of the Cultural Revolution. According to UN statistics, 22 percent graduated from some version of high school while a scant 7 percent finished university.

In 1983 China's "radical collective" era was coming to an end, a shift demonstrated by the dismantling of the people's communes (Mao-era collective farms). While ultimately a positive change, the termination of the collectives created a power vacuum that fostered the rise of local bullies. My 1960s-born interviewees were the first to mention the "black societies," or local gangs, that sprang up in those days. The word black refers simply to darkness and crime, not skin color.

Most 1960s-born people took government-assigned work, though independent career-seeking emerged in the 1980s and 1990s. For those with government jobs, work units continued to have the power to influence personal life choices throughout the 1990s, though much of that power has been dismantled today.

All but the wealthiest members of this generation are still working, but most will retire soon. China's official retirement age is fifty for women and fifty-five for men, after which point most people move in with their children and care for their grandchildren.

Today the 1960s generation numbers 230 million people. If they were a country unto themselves, they would be the fifth-largest nation on earth, dwarfing Brazil by nearly forty million people.

Marriage Is Nothing Special

ZIU SHOUHE (B. 1960) AND LIN CHUNJIAO (B. 1962)

This interview, conducted with a Hunanese couple in their early fifties, was one of the few we did with both husband and wife present. Their daughter May and their baby granddaughter also joined us. In the beginning of our project, I expected some people would bring their spouse or partner along for the interview, but very few did.

Ziu Shouhe and Lin Chunjiao struck me as squarely from "the old generation," the generation raised with Mao-era thinking and values. They were introduced by a matchmaker in 1977 and married in 1978, tying the knot on the cusp of Deng Xiaopeng's era of "reform and opening up." They spoke the Hunanese dialect and had never learned standard Mandarin. They spent their working years laboring for the government and had moved in with May and her husband just before the birth of their granddaughter. May is twenty-nine and sees her husband just three or four times each year, as he works abroad.

On the day of the interview, May and her parents invited us to share a meal in their home. May's mom, who does most of the family cooking, prepared nine dishes! It was some of the best Chinese food I've ever had: spicy pork, sweet-and-sour fish, cabbage and peanuts, garlicky kale, string beans and chilies, a tomato and egg soup, and many other delicious things. I am told that a traditional meal includes four dishes, so I felt deeply honored by this sumptuous culinary gift (and very full afterward). May confided that her mother had worried for days about the menu, afraid that my foreign taste buds might reject her cooking.

As I was praising the delicious lunch, May laughed and said, "I always criticize my mother's food and now here you are praising her, so her confidence will be very high!" May translated the discussion for her mom and they shared a side-splitting laugh while I tried to get my mouth to close. May's criticism didn't seem to be a slight of any kind, quite the contrary, but I could only imagine what my own mother would have said!

After lunch, May's father, Ziu Shouhe, smoked outside on the porch while everyone else settled in the living room. Throughout the interview Lin Chunjiao held her squirming granddaughter, jostling her or taking short walks around the room. Ziu Shouhe played with the baby only once, but he broke into a huge smile when he did. The family living room contained no baby toys, mats, nursing pillows, rocking chairs, blankets, or other signs of infancy. Rather, someone always held the baby, who smiled, cooed, pulled off her socks, and was generally fat and adorable.

Weeks after the interview, May said to me, "I think my mother wanted to say more to you, but my dad didn't want her to, so she kept quiet." Hoping to perhaps hear the rest, I reached out to May and her mother independently two more times, several months apart, to see if we could meet again. That interview never came together, as each time May replied that her mother was ill or needed to help with the baby. I even asked to meet for cooking lessons, but to no avail. I assume this was May's way of indicating that her mother didn't want to revisit her story.

Ziu Shouhe: I grew up in a town family, with my parents, my brother, and my four sisters. That might sound like a big family, but my paternal grandmother bore even more children, ten babies in all, between 1930 and 1960. When her first daughter was only six months old, my grandfather joined the Nationalists. He was later decorated for his many military achievements. Those were the years of the Japanese invasion, and Shaanxi province, our ancestral home, was an area of heavy fighting. My grandfather eventually migrated south, to Hunan, and his family followed. Many of my grandmother's babies died from starvation and sickness in those years, while the family fled the Japanese.

My own parents did not marry because of romantic love. Back then China had many other strategies for creating a match. My mom was a *tóngyǎngxí*, which literally means "baby, raise, wife," or child bride. When she was a baby, my paternal grandparents took her in from a poor family, raised her themselves, and then married her to their son—my father. One of my aunts, my father's oldest sister, had another kind of marriage called *wá wa qīn*, or "baby-managed marriage." When she was very young, my parents promised her to a man from our hometown. She did not have to live with his family, just marry him when she grew up. After Mao's liberation, my grandfather pushed my aunt to return to Shaanxi and fulfill this promise. She did it, although she didn't want to marry that man. Back then marriages were arranged by a matchmaker, so couples only had *qīnqíng*, or family love.

After the war my dad worked for many years in a government restaurant. It was a public company catering to travelers and visitors, not really to local people, since families always ate at home. My mom was a housewife, and she bore her six children in this order: a son, then four daughters, then a second son—me. They wanted a second boy, so they kept trying. Every family had four or five kids in those days. Everyone wanted sons, since they would continue the family line, and it was better to have more than one if possible.

In 1967, when I was very young, my father had some political problems. As I mentioned, my grandfather initially served with the Nationalists, but by the end, he surrendered and joined the CPC (Communist Party of China). He helped the Communists fight the Japanese, and they gave him a good pension until he died. [Ziu Shouhe didn't go into detail, but his father's "political problems" probably came about because of his grandfather's Nationalist affiliations.]

Lin Chunjiao: I also grew up as one of six children, but in a big village, not a town. We lived with my parents, but not my grandparents, since they died before I was born. We lived on a street in the village, not on a farm. My parents had government jobs and also ran a shop selling knitting supplies, drinks, and that sort of thing. Food rations were centrally controlled by the government back then, and my father worked for the local company that oversaw our town's oil, rice, and household goods. This was a very powerful company. They went into the village to collect the food from farmers. Farmers didn't have a quota and could sell as much or as little food as they chose, keeping the extra. But they really needed to sell as much as possible to get money for other things. Of course, they used ration coupons to buy food and clothing back then, since money could not be used for those items.

My parents did not have romantic love either, just qīnqíng, the family feeling.

Ziu Shouhe: I wasn't thinking about romance when I got married, because I was poor. If a couple knew each other directly and picked each other by themselves, then they could have romance. If you married by a matchmaker, like we did, then romance was not important.

Lin Chunjiao: We never thought about romantic ideas. Only the family kind of love seemed important to us. Back then we had no TV, no examples in the media, and no books about love. We would not have been allowed to read them anyway, even if they were available. Books were just about war or history, to encourage us to build our country and make the future better. We read the Red Book, of course, but there were lots of other famous books too.

We met each other in 1978. [They exchanged a playful smile, and she stuck out her tongue at him.] He had gone to fight with the army, and when he came back, a friend from the factory introduced us to each other.

Ziu Shouhe: I had just returned from a year of compulsory service with the army. I fought in Vietnam with China's ground troops, but the war ended just ten days after we got there. So we came home. People were very pure then. I didn't think about fighting; it was just my duty. If it was your duty, then you just did it. You didn't think about how you felt.

When I came back from the war, I worked for a government trading department, which was operated by the lowest level of government. We collected leather, animal skin, hair, local specialty food products, and traditional medicines, all for export. I'm not sure where we sent them.

Lin Chunjiao: I worked for another government company, one that collected cotton. Later on I switched to working for a cigarette company. The government assigned all the jobs back then, based on your hùkǒu [regional registration document]. If you were not from the village and not a criminal, then the government arranged your work. It was just random, not based on your education or any special skills. When we met, the matchmaker just brought me to Ziu's company for the introduction. It was very simple.

Ziu Shouhe: I took a few minutes off from my work to meet her. We drank some tea and chatted a little bit. Afterward the matchmaker asked each of us how we felt. We both said, "I feel okay," so we continued to try it out. At that time we worked seven days a week. There weren't any breaks for weekends or holidays. If something urgent happened, then you could take leave, but many people just worked 365 days a year. [When I expressed surprise that no time was reserved for rest or family life, Ziu replied sharply, "You should learn something about Chinese history!"]

Lin Chunjiao: Before this introduction, I hadn't met any other man in person. Various matchmakers had tried explaining a potential man to me, but I always said "not suitable" based on their description. It was normal to be introduced to a few people before you met the right one. Everyone did this.

Ziu Shouhe: She was my first introduction, too. But I was very busy.

Lin Chunjiao: At that time it was completely different from now. Now people think more about romance.

Ziu Shouhe: I didn't think too much about what I wanted in a spouse. I just wanted to feel okay about the person. In those days we didn't really use complicated language for our feelings, and we didn't have so many love words. We just said, "I feel okay." Of course, I cared something about physical appearance, but that wasn't the only factor.

Lin Chunjiao: I wanted someone I could communicate with easily, and it felt very natural to talk to him. The physical appearance was one part. Maybe his looks were 50 percent important. [Her husband nodded his agreement at this figure.]

Ziu Shouhe: After that first introduction, we were both very busy, so we just met sometimes to have lunch or dinner and chat. Only that. After more than one year, both of our parents agreed to the match. My family gave her family ¥150 ($88). It is a custom in China for the man's side to send a person to talk with the woman's side. Since my mom had died by that point, my older brother's wife went to meet her parents and give them the money. We got married a few months later. The wedding was very simple; we just invited friends and relatives to my home. After we were married, we lived with my father and brothers.

In those days everyone got married when it was time to marry. Except for people who were very sick or had mental health problems, maybe they didn't marry. In my opinion, people who never marry, or who don't want to marry, must have some reason. Everybody wants to marry, of course. In the whole world, I don't think anybody doesn't want to marry. Maybe if they had a bad experience or too much pressure? I think some married couples don't want to have children because of financial problems or life pressures. Or maybe they just want to enjoy their life.

Our daughter got married last year. We were quite open, letting May make decisions by herself. We didn't request too much of her husband. Then we moved in several months ago, after she had the baby. Most Chinese parents are willing to do this for their children, to help them. I think 99 percent of my peers have moved in with their children and are taking care of their grandchildren. But I think another reason they do this is because maybe they have some dreams that didn't come true. So they hope their children or grandchildren can make those dreams come true. [I gently asked if he himself had any such dreams, but he said, "I don't want to talk about this." Later on May explained, "My dad really wanted to have a son but had only me, a girl."]

We are raising our granddaughter very differently than we raised our daughter. So many things have changed. For one thing, we talk to her a lot. When we were raising May, we very rarely had any help. We were very busy, so we didn't talk with her much. Another thing is that with our granddaughter, we have to care about so many more things. When we were raising May it was very simple. We only thought about her food or her clothes. Now we have to think about education, which school she will go to, that kind of thing. [At this point Lin Chunjiao stepped out to help with the baby and didn't come back for several minutes.]

Life is growing more complicated because society has developed. With so much competition and pressure, today's kids need to learn many things to get ahead. This competition pushes us to want to give our granddaughter many kinds of education, to help her learn many things. [I asked Mr. Ziu to describe something cute his granddaughter does. He positively beamed at this question, his face compressing instantly into hundreds of happy wrinkles.] If our granddaughter is happy, we feel happy. If she smiles, we smile.

Lately the Chinese family has another new problem: divorce. Around 2001, divorce rates began to increase. I think now there are so many divorces because people have forgotten our traditional culture. They care more about money, beauty, all of these things. But these things are transient and too easily changed. So when one person loses his or her money or beauty, then the other side will seek a divorce. Now couples even meet on the Internet and have sex the first time they meet. They don't know each other, so their intimacy is not real. They have no foundation.

If my own daughter or granddaughter ever had marriage problems, then I'd like to advise them to remember our traditional culture. I would encourage them to understand the difference between real love and fake love. If the relationship is short-term, and people just meet and know each other very quickly and then marry, that is fake love. It is not from the heart. Couples need to respect each other. This is the most basic marriage principle. If they have problems, then they need to communicate, to talk about their problems honestly. I hope that my girls will be people who know how to behave.

I recently read one book that a Chinese artist wrote. It was his story, his memoir. When he was young, his relationship with his wife was closer to àiqíng (romantic love), but as they grew older, they felt more like friends, and they needed to respect each other. Their love is changing, and the meaning of their love is changing. He writes that romantic love is only one kind of emotion. If a person can think like that, then he will understand more. Romantic love is not all there is to experience with love; it's not the only love in the world. Also, nobody can understand romantic love completely. Since everyone experiences a different feeling, there is no standard, no consensus. Romance is only one kind of love, only one kind of feeling. [His wife returned at this point.]

Q: Can you tell us the story of a happy day you remember with your husband?

Lin Chunjiao: I don't have feelings like this about a particular day. Our generation doesn't think about whether a marriage is happy, so we don't think about this kind of special feeling. I really don't have any romantic feelings about marriage. Marriage is about family, about making children. It is nothing special.

Wearing White for Chairman Mao

XU KIWI (B. 1966)

Xu Kiwi is forty-six years old and came to Shenzhen in search of a new life in the special economic zone nearly twenty years ago. She moved here against the wishes of her family and ex-boyfriend, which shows some remarkable independence. At the time Shenzhen was one of the only places in China where she, a university graduate, could search independently for a job. Kiwi wanted to make her own way in the world.

Kiwi is still a stunning woman, trim and fashionable, with creamy skin, piercing black eyes, and long hair that falls in gentle ringlets at her elbows. She smiled easily, carried a fashionable clutch purse, and wore a black skirt over tights and high boots. She didn't look a day over thirty-five. Linda was rather taken with Kiwi and pressed for her age-defying beauty secrets. The two of them ended up going to dinner later that week, and Linda mentioned afterward that Kiwi had wanted to know all about how to catch a foreign boyfriend. (Linda recently married a European man after dating him for several years.)

Toward the end of our conversation, I asked Kiwi if her marriage had been happy. She paused for a few moments, a bit puzzled by this question, before answering that she hadn't really thought about that. Her response was illuminating and reminded me, as did so many of my storytellers' comments, that my own perception of what matters in marriage is not universal.

My family lived in Beijing when I was born. It was 1966, the start of Chairman Mao's Cultural Revolution, and the streets were always packed with exuberant men, spilling out of Tiananmen Square, shouting the slogans of the revolution. When it was time for me to come, my mother had to walk to the hospital, pushing and elbowing her way through those fervent throngs. None of them noticed her round belly or tried to help.

In those days we were on the wrong side of politics because of my grandpa. He was a Nationalist, the group that lost to the Communists in 1949. Also, my mother was a doctor and my father was a rocket expert, and the party did not like highly educated people at that time. During the Cultural Revolution our whole family was sent down from Beijing to Xi'an, where my father was put to work in a factory.

Every family had to post a picture of Chairman Mao in their home back then. Our poster hung in the most prominent spot on our wall, and before each meal we had to say words blessing the chairman with long life. We had no religion then, but we had to pray for Chairman Mao! Everyone, from children to adults, had to read his many books and the works of other great Communist thinkers. We all needed to wear the same gray and dark-blue clothes, and every woman bobbed her hair in the same short style. Everybody the same, that was Communism.

When I was growing up, boys and girls did not really talk in school. If a girl had to share a desk with a boy, she would take an ink brush and make a show of drawing a firm line down the middle of the desk. It implied, "Don't cross this line! My side!" Some girls were very bold and talked to boys, but such brassy behavior was rare. I myself was very shy and could speak only to my girlfriends.

Our family never had enough to eat when I was small. Even though the government forced us to move to Xi'an, they would not reassign our hùkǒu [regional registration document] to our new city. Without a Xi'an hùkǒu, we could not get the ration tickets our family should have received. Sometimes our relatives would try to help us by sending rice or other food though the mail. Even people who had the Xi'an hùkǒu rarely had enough to eat, though, as the country was desperately poor at the time. We were like the North Koreans today.

To this day I carry a vivid memory of Chairman Mao's death in 1976. I was only ten years old, but I remember when the news was announced. People across the country stood crying in the streets. Even though it was raining heavily, we stood outside for hours in a silent vigil. I was wearing a red sweater that day, but we cannot wear red when someone dies, only black or white clothing is acceptable. I struggled to pull a white shirt over my red sweater, even though it didn't quite fit. I don't remember feeling sad about Chairman Mao that day, but I was sad as I watched that red dye bleeding through my crisp white shirt. I couldn't do anything to stop it.

After Mao died everyone got the hùkǒu transferred to their new hometowns, and finally we had enough to eat. Still, my father, the rocket expert, worked as a laborer in that Xi'an factory for more than ten years.

I remember the first boy who liked me. I was fifteen. We didn't have telephones back then, but he would not have dared to call even if we did, because relationships were forbidden. The only way to share your heart was to write a note. One day he passed me a love letter, and though I tried to read it surreptitiously, another student saw and tattled on the boy. I was mortified and could hardly look up as the note bobbed forward and into our teacher's outstretched hand. The boy had to stand while the teacher read the note aloud for all to hear.

Then that clever boy bowed his head and executed a simple defense. "It is not my own work, teacher," he said. "I have copied a note that Karl Marx wrote for his own wife. I wanted only to study the words of the great Karl Marx." The teacher sputtered into an awkward silence. Passing notes was wrong, but how could the boy be punished for emulating the foundational Marxist philosopher?

"Sit down!" the teacher finally bellowed. The boy was not punished. He managed to keep a straight face, but I had to hide my smile.

Despite his laudable methods, I did not reply to that boy's note. Back then parents believed that boys would only be a distraction from studies, and I also thought this way. I wanted to get very good scores and get into a good university, so it was unthinkable for me to write back.

I got my first boyfriend when I was twenty-one. It was the late 1980s, and I was finishing my fourth year of university in Xi'an. One day a boy just arrived and knocked on my door to ask me out. He was a high school classmate of mine. He was also studying at a Xi'an university, some twenty minutes away from mine. This was back when college students were still quite rare. He had a bicycle, he explained, and he wanted to take me to meet up with our high school friends to play volleyball. My first instinct was to keep his visit a secret, since it was forbidden to have a "public" relationship in college, and even secret relationships were very rare. I would suffer great shame if I got caught.

He was a very handsome boy. After that day he came often on his red bicycle, taking me to play basketball or volleyball with our friends. We didn't have any money back then, so we couldn't do things like go to the movies or out for supper, but sometimes we went to read in a bookshop, just the two of us.

For the next four years we stayed together. Much of this relationship was long distance, though, because of a controversial choice of mine: I gave up my "iron rice bowl" job. At that time graduating from college was considered the ticket to a stable life. Employment was still mostly assigned by the government, and university grads always got a good job. The Communist Party created a system in which workers could depend on the government to provide them with a job, food, and support for their entire life. Nobody could be fired from an iron rice bowl job, even if they didn't work very much.

My assigned job was in Xi'an, with a guaranteed salary of ¥150 each month ($40), government-provided housing, and even some food. True, this job was sufficient to meet my family's needs. But I did not want to simply subsist—I had bigger dreams. I wanted to make more money than that, and I didn't want to do it in Xi'an. I wanted to move to Shenzhen.

My boyfriend and my family did not like this idea. They thought Shenzhen was not a good place for a young girl. It was too modern, too fast. My parents just wanted me to stay nearby, so I could be safe and secure and we could share a warm family life. It was also very rare back then to quit these government jobs. But I had visited Shenzhen once a few years earlier, and I just liked it better. People could look for their own job there, pick their own apartment, build their own life.

Despite the objections of those closest to me, I packed a few things and bought a one-way ticket south. The train ride was twenty-nine hours long, and for that interminable time I could only sit. I could not even sleep because the car was too crowded. I could not get up or take a walk or I would forfeit my seat. It was just trees, buildings, sheep, *rumble, rumble*, trees, buildings, cows, *rumble, rumble*, for hours.

When I finally arrived, I brought my resume around to many places looking for work. In other cities, if you wanted to find your own job, it was very difficult. Most shops and companies would just turn you away, unless you had an introduction from a friend or relative. But this was Shenzhen, and job hunting was acceptable.

For three years my boyfriend and I continued our relationship and visited when we could. I loved him very much and thought about marrying him. But we had some personality differences and argued a lot, even from the beginning. Ultimately, he did not want to move to Shenzhen, and I did not want to come home. During one Chinese New Year festival, I finally told him, "I want to stop going out. I just want to stop." At first he did not accept this decision. But soon he met another girl, and they got married within two years.

Meanwhile, I had met somebody in Shenzhen. He was a coworker of mine, not quite as handsome as the first boy, but handsome enough. He frequently helped me at work, and we became good friends. He was from Hangzhou, a beautiful city on the eastern coast, and I admired him because he worked very hard. He also played the piano and the violin. [Smiling, she brushed a few long curls aside and pantomimed his violin-playing, the unseen instrument tucked under her chin.] He was younger than me by a year and a half, but he always encouraged me and gave me good advice. Since our parents lived very far apart and could not meet each other, we skipped the engagement. We just told our parents we wanted to marry, and they supported us. My parents trusted my judgment. Their only request was that I send a picture of the groom.

My husband and I did not consult an astrologer to gauge our compatibility or worry about auspicious dates for a wedding. We just registered our marriage on a day that I had off from work. Afterward we held a private party with friends in Shenzhen to celebrate. The next year we threw a big party for family and hometown friends in Xi'an, and his parents traveled to my parents' home and they finally met.

I think the most important characteristics for a good husband are honesty and trustworthiness. He should also be intelligent and a little handsome, with a good body. Being a little good-looking is important so you can have a pretty baby together. A husband should exercise regularly and have a positive attitude. Money cannot be overlooked either, as it will decide the couple's life level. Especially in the beginning, when we needed to build a new family, money was very important. Now, after so many years, money is not such a high priority.

A good wife should consider her family as her highest priority. She should care for her child, cook good food, and maintain her own beauty. This is partly for herself, so she can feel good, but her husband might also enjoy it. I don't think a wife should let her husband do any housework, but she can hire an āyí [cleaning lady] to help her. It is not important for her to personally wash all the clothes and scrub every corner. My husband likes to cook, and he is very good at it. So I usually prepare and chop everything and do the dishes afterward, while he cooks the family meal.

I learned a few things about marriage from my own parents. For example, my parents always celebrated each other's birthday, which is unusual in China. Even to this day, they prepare a special gift for each other, like a delicious meal or a thoughtful card. They never forget. Most Chinese people only celebrate the bigger birthdays as they grow older, like the fortieth or fiftieth, but the years in between pass like any other day. My parents just made this tradition up on their own, and I think it's very romantic. Because of this, birthdays became a special thing in our family. My sister and I will still travel to see our parents on their birthdays if we can. If we cannot be together, we always remember each other's special day. We never forget.

My parents were introduced by a matchmaker, and while they loved each other, their attitude toward each other was . . . antagonistic. [She crumpled her face as though detecting a bad smell.] They always argued and fought with each other, yelling loudly. They had good intentions. They wanted to improve each other, to push each other to do their very best, but I don't like that style. I do not want to shout. I just want to solve the problem. If I feel angry, then I usually keep silent. Since my husband knows me well, he understands when I am angry!

Some people today like to worry about whether a marriage is happy, but I don't think being happy is such an important factor. It was more important to me that my husband and I were good friends before our wedding, so he could understand me and I him. If I want to make my husband feel very happy, then maybe I will arrange a special thing, like having a gift ready on his birthday. But this idea of being happy in marriage should not be too important. On some days a marriage is not happy. Sometimes even a whole season is not happy. I think it is more important to be comfortable, peaceful, and to just keep moving forward in marriage.

This particular season in life is both happy and sad for me. Our daughter just started at university, so some days I feel sad and a little empty because she is away. But now that she is gone, my husband and I also have time to do things for ourselves.

My husband and I have already worked very hard for many years. Finally, I think we have enough money, and it is time to enjoy life instead. All we have to do is maintain our level. I quit my job, actually, and I have been taking oil-painting classes and classes to improve my English. But don't tell anyone I quit my job! Keep the secret. [She smiled conspiratorially and pressed one vertical finger to her glossy lips.] I like to hike and keep fit, and I want to become a photographer. I have always liked learning new things, tasting different foods, and talking to new people. My mother always said I was a naughty girl! But these things are important for staying young.

I love to travel too. I recently went to India and the Philippines with my girlfriends, and I am planning to visit America soon. [Pulling out her iPhone, she pointed to pictures of herself posing on a palm-lined beach and waving in scuba gear.] My husband did not come with me. He does not agree that we have enough money, so he does not feel this way about enjoying life. He wants to keep earning and saving in case we get sick when we are old.

The Boy with the Baby-Raise-Wife

LIU WUMIN (B. 1966)

Liu Wumin is forty-six years old and was born and raised in Jiangxi province, in China's inland southeast. His parents arranged for him to marry a child bride, but he avoided this fate, marrying a girl from the local brick factory instead. The couple raised three children and recently celebrated the marriage of their oldest daughter. I was curious to hear Liu Wumin's love story and also to know how he felt about his daughter getting married.

Liu Wumin is a cabdriver in Shenzhen, and my husband and I used his services many times. He can't read a map, drives like a calculated maniac, and smokes between trips. Somehow he always got us where we wanted to go, a grin lighting his youthful face.

On the day of our interview, Liu Wumin wore a suit jacket, rather formal attire for him and a cue that he cared about this conversation. We talked over hot stone bowls of rice and meat, and Liu Wumin kept his jacket on the whole time, even though the restaurant was quite warm. At one point I twisted him a little fan from a paper napkin, and he laughed and used it for a moment.

While my mom was still pregnant with me, she took in a baby girl from another village. When I grew up, I was supposed to marry this baby. She was my *tóngyǎngxí*, literally my "baby-raise-wife," a kind of child bride. In those days poor families worried that their first son might not be able to find a wife when it was time. To insure against this problem, they raised a baby girl from another family until she was old enough, and their son married her. They did not need to pay the girl's family, just raise the baby. The other family was always poor too, and overrun with children, so taking one girl away helped them a lot. These birth families often maintain a relationship with their biological daughter as she grows up. Even now my older sister is close to her original family.

There is another kind of early marriage arrangement called *wá wa qīn*, or "baby-managed marriage." Parents often arrange a *wá wa qīn* while both wives are still pregnant. But that wife doesn't grow up in

87

her husband's house. She stays with her own parents and just marries the boy when it is time.

Before I started school, I already knew this *tóngyǎngxí* was not my real sister. Nobody told me directly, but I listened when family and friends talked, so I knew I was supposed to marry her. She actually became a very beautiful girl, but we had no feelings for each other because we grew up together. She just felt like my sister. Other boys in my village also grew up with these *tóngyǎngxí*, including two of my very good school friends. In the end, though, none of us married those baby-raise-wives.

My family was very, very poor when I was young, and we did not have enough to eat. Nobody else did either, because in our village we only got nine months' worth of food tickets every year. We had to plan very carefully, eating a small meal every time, to have food year-round. My family was even poorer than other people in our village, though, because my grandfather died when he was just thirty. My grandmother did not want to marry another man, so she raised her children all by herself, on hardly anything at all. She took in a *tóngyǎngxí* for her oldest son, my father. My mother was his baby-raise-wife.

While I was still in primary school, a brick factory opened nearby. My older sister got hired, and a few years later she married a boy from that factory. My parents accepted her marriage, even though she was supposed to marry me. I wanted to take her place at the factory when she left, but I was too young to work, since I was only fourteen. My uncle had some connections, though, so they decided I was sixteen and gave me the job. The twelve-hour shifts made me very tired, but I liked working at the factory. In our village people thought better of factory workers, because they earned a little bit of money. So I had a higher status.

For the first two years, since I was still in school, I couldn't go to the factory every day. It was hard to make much money that way. My mother saved all the money from my first year and bought me a watch. Then she saved all the money from my second year and bought me a bicycle. The next year I told her I didn't like school anymore. Instead of starting ninth grade, I went to work full-time.

When I was sixteen, I met a pretty girl at the factory and I felt *yǐjiànzhōngqíng*, or "love at first sight." We could talk very easily and naturally with each other. Actually, in the beginning, we didn't know what love was. We just knew it felt nice to be together. We were too shy to say "I love you" or "You're so beautiful." But there was no need to speak these things out loud, because we already understood each other.

After about a year, we had sex, and then I felt free to speak my heart to this girl. I didn't tell my family or friends about this, because we were not supposed to be having sex. But soon her belly started to stick out. We were afraid to tell our parents, but it just kept getting bigger, so eventually we had no choice.

Her parents were very angry. They did not want to accept me. "You never talk about this boyfriend, and then he just shows up and you want to get married!" But her belly would not stop, so they had to accept me. My own parents were actually a little bit happy. In the villages we hope our sons will marry early.

Two months after our wedding, the baby came out. We were both nineteen years old. For many years we lived in our hometown and kept making bricks at the same factory. We were very poor, but happy, and we always wanted to be close to each other. My wife got pregnant again, and we had a second baby, a daughter. Then we had a third baby, this time a son. Our local leader, the party cadre, came by our house after that. The One Child Policy had started, and we were supposed to pay a fine for having too many children. When he asked me to pay, I leaned on the door and folded my arms.

"Look inside my house. You can see that we are so poor we can barely survive. If you want to demand the fine, go ahead, but then very soon I think your position will be damaged."

The leader left quickly and he didn't bother me about the money again. He was afraid because I was part of the hēishèhuì, a kind of gang called a "black society." I am a social person. I like to make friends, so I had all kinds of friends. These hēishèhuì friends all came from the brick factory, and we had a reputation for fighting and doing bad things. There are many of these black societies in China. Some gangs are very organized, like the Mafia. Our society was not like that, but still, this local leader knew we could beat him up or do something unpredictable.

Eight or nine years ago, I left our hometown for an opportunity in Shenzhen. My wife stayed in our hometown to take care of my mother and our children. Of course, during our separation, we missed each other. We called every day and usually talked for one or two hours. I could visit her only twice a year, though, so after a few years, I worried she might get bored. Maybe she would find another man.

"If you feel bored, go and play cards with your friends," I told her. But maybe this was not such good advice, because she started to gamble, and she enjoyed gambling very much. Then she started to lose some money. Five years ago, she lost a lot of money, and we had a big fight about this. We almost got a divorce, but because of our three children, we didn't go through with it.

[At this point Linda asked Wumin if either of them had ever had an outside relationship. He started up in his chair, rapidly jiggled one knee, grinned wildly, and shook his head. "No!" he denied cheerfully. Then he calmed down, took a breath, and told us his story.] During our separation, I felt very lonely, and once these marriage problems started, I also felt very sad. I found a nǚ péngyǒu, or "girlfriend," here in Shenzhen. She was a very young girl, just one year younger than my oldest daughter. We lived together for three or four years. Eventually I realized she really loved me very much, so I pushed her to find a boyfriend, to make a real life for herself. I could not have married her. I thought we were not suitable, because she was so young. [He spoke quietly, his face immobile. The memory was a burdensome one.]

I think it is better if a husband and wife live together, because we are human beings, so sometimes we need each other. If my wife were here in Shenzhen, living with me, that affair wouldn't have happened. Many workers in Shenzhen are living apart from spouses, and in the blue-collar world online dating sites are very popular. These are common men—they do not need to have a high salary—and anyone can register and date some girls. The men lie, saying they are single or divorced. They go to dinner a few times and then go to bed together. Not only men use these sites. Women use them too, and they also lie.

I spoke openly with my close friends about this girlfriend, but it isn't something I would talk about with everyone. Maybe half of my close friends here have had a girlfriend, and all were living apart from their wives when it happened. I think almost every man who lives separately finds a woman. It is a common situation. A man feels lonely, and also a girlfriend feels exciting. An affair is not necessarily related to the quality of the marriage, it might just be a thrill. But other times it is about love.

It is difficult to say whether these affairs are ever a good thing. If you have a happy marriage and you have an affair, maybe you'll go home and treat your wife better out of guilt. But if your marriage is not happy, maybe your new experience will intensify your dislike for your wife.

Wives may have this problem too when their husband lives separately. If either side knows the other is cheating, the couple might divorce. One of my friend's wives discovered his affair, but because of their children, they did not divorce. Instead, she had a revenge affair back in their hometown.

Many couples from my generation have gotten divorced. In the past ten years, divorce has become more common than it ever was before. Remember my two hometown friends who grew up with *tóngyǎngxí*? Well, they are both divorced. One has actually been divorced twice. I don't understand why. Divorce is not a good thing, especially if you have children. Then again, many marriages are kept together only by the children. If married people did not have children, maybe there would be even more divorce in China. Personally, I think our country is too open now. Sex is too casual. Traditionally, couples thought, *We'll live together forever.* But now they think, *If we don't get along, we can divorce and find somebody else.* I would change that attitude if I could.

If my own children ever told me they wanted to divorce, I would probably suggest they stay married. It would depend on whether my daughters wanted the divorce or their husbands wanted it. If my daughter wanted it, I would suggest no. But if her husband wanted to divorce because of another woman, maybe I would support my daughter to divorce. We always say that we are not afraid if a man goes to a hooker, but we are afraid if he develops real feeling for a mistress. We call this *rén zàixīn bùzài*, literally "body is here, but heart is absent." It means even though he comes home, his heart belongs to another.

Just this fall we had a wedding for my oldest daughter. She lives in Shenzhen too, and she works as a secretary for a big international company. When she was in high school, she started dating this boy, but my wife did not allow boyfriends. She wanted our daughter to focus on her studies. I am not so strict like my wife. While I wouldn't have *hoped* my daughter would date so early, I didn't object so strongly. She didn't listen to us anyway, and she kept dating the boy through university. Chinese parents feel you should get married as soon as you become an adult, so at that point my wife started to push her to marry the boy. My daughter said no, she wasn't ready yet. They would wait a few years. When she finally told us she wanted to marry this boy, my wife and I were happy. Chinese parents feel relieved when their children marry, like one of our tasks is finished.

Nowadays most young people mix some Chinese traditions and copy some Western styles when they marry. My daughter and her husband exchanged vows at his family's home and then had a big lunch party. One of their colleagues was the host. We also had a wedding party in my hometown, and her husband's family gave me ¥28,000 ($4,334) for the celebration, because normally the man's side gives money to the woman's family. Her husband is a nice man, a suitable man for my daughter. Even though she is married, she still takes care of us. She very often sends us clothes and gifts.

This past year my wife joined me in Shenzhen, after we had lived apart for seven years. Married life is okay now. We feel happy because we can see each other again and can take care of each other. I feel that I really love my wife. She is very considerate, and she can work very well, very hard, in the house and in our fields. (We have a house and farmland in our hometown, where my mother still lives.) When we got married, we shared àiqíng, or romantic love. We always wanted to be close when we were young. Now, at my age, we don't have this passion anymore. We just want to be in each other's company. So now this yǒuqíng, or friendship love, comes first in our marriage, and qīnqíng, the family kind of love, is second.

I think all three kinds of love matter in marriage. In my grandparents' generation, their parents arranged the matches and couples met at the wedding. My own parents got to see each other beforehand, since they grew up in the same house, but they could not object or choose a different partner. My generation is better off than the ones before it, because we can follow our hearts to find our wives.

My Reasons for Hating My Father

WEN "AYI" (B. 1967)

Wen Ayi is forty-four years old and grew up in Sichuan, a large province in south-western China known for spicy dishes and beautiful women. Wen Ayi comes from a poor village family, and after completing the fifth grade, she worked full-time to help them. Her back is stooped and her skin dark from a lifetime of manual labor, but Wen Ayi wears a constant smile, and her face is surprisingly youthful. ("Ayi" is a friendly term for a domestic worker, so her name is equivalent to "Auntie Wen.")

She and her husband have two daughters. The couple moved to Shenzhen just last year to live with their eldest after her university graduation. Wen Ayi's boss, an American machine shop owner, introduced us. He remembered when a relative of Mrs. Wen's suggested he hire her to keep the shop clean. Hesitating, the relative had warned that her left eye "looked wrong," making it difficult for her to find work. A milky film does swim over her dark left pupil, but the unconcerned shop owner hired her, and he recently promoted her too.

I hate my father for two reasons. The first is because of this eye, and the second is because of my marriage.

For three generations my family has had trouble. When my father was a very small boy, only a year old, his father was pressed into service with the Nationalist Army. He was sent to Taiwan, and our family never saw him again. Even to this day, we don't know if my grandfather died or if he just never came back. Maybe he found a new family.

After he left, my grandmother raised their six children alone, without any money. Because of the family's extreme poverty, my father never attended a day of school. He has always held this against my grandmother, blaming her for leaving him uneducated, for not giving him more. I myself finished just five years of school before joining my family in the fields. My three brothers and two sisters helped too, and we worked together to raise wheat, corn, rice, and sweet potatoes.

My father was a very poor man, but he married a wealthy woman from the dìzhǔ, or landlord class. She lost all her wealth after the liberation, and under Chairman Mao this landlord classification created a very bad situation for my father and our family. There was a lot of pressure. At that time, before you could do anything, like marry, receive a work assignment, or travel, the government needed to check your political status and family background. Landlord people couldn't find a good job. My father had a lot of difficulties because of my landlord mother.

While I was growing up, our difficulties did not improve. My father blamed my mother for the family's political problems and would often hit her and beat her up. My father's mother lived with our family, and she also treated my mother very badly. My mother was angry with her mother-in-law for this and angry with my father for not defending her. He protected my grandmother instead of his wife, because that was his own mother. It was a complex circle and the three of them fought quite a bit. [She quietly wiped away tears during this part.] This kind of fighting was common in our village; it was just normal life. I think at least 40 percent of husbands hit their wives.

This eye [she gestured toward her left eye, veiled in a white film], well, I can barely see out of it. Why do you think this is? When I was a child, I was playing in the fields and I hurt my eye. My father didn't care that I was hurt. He didn't like girl children, so he did not take me to the hospital. After more than thirty hours, some neighbors saw me. "Your daughter's eye is like this? Why didn't you go to the hospital?" they demanded. My mother could not help me either, because my father is a very bossy and traditional man, so we had to do what he said. Because of him, I received no medical attention or care for my injury.

When I was eighteen, some company struck oil in Sichuan, quite close to my hometown village. Overnight, the oil rigs and bosses arrived, and they gave out a lot of jobs. One of our neighbors went to these oil fields for work, and he met a single man there who needed a wife. This man had traveled almost one hundred kilometers from his own village for this oil work. He was twenty-eight, ten years older than me, and very old to be single. This neighbor approached my father and offered to introduce me. I had never been introduced to anyone, and I did not want to marry. But my father said yes, so they arranged a meeting.

A few evenings later this man and I met each other at the match-maker's house. We did not say anything; we just looked at each other. I could tell in one glance that I did not like this man. He was too old and too short. His head was scarcely above mine, and in the villages we think this situation is not very good. We want a tall man, some-one broad and strong who can work hard in the fields. This man was also very poor, even poorer than my own family, and his father was ill. In China we believe it will be very hard for a poor couple to get along well. We have a saying: *Pínjiàn fūqī bǎishì āi*, which means, "A very poor couple will have countless miseries."

After a minute of looking, the man said he would marry me, and my father agreed. My marriage was arranged that very same evening, without any input from me. I could not refuse the match. I could only say "okay." In those days, parents arranged the marriages and chil-dren had to agree. Maybe some children could object, but not in my family.

"Because of your eye, I want to find a weaker man than you," my father said to me. "Maybe he will take care of you then and not abuse you. A big, strong man might beat you, after all." I told you that my father very often hit my own mother, but this was his reasoning.

My father did not care about daughter weddings, so he told this man that he didn't expect much of a bridal gift. In turn, he made it known that he wouldn't be paying much for the wedding. This man gave my father just ¥60 ($17), which was the beginning and the end of wedding gifts from my future husband's family.

During our engagement year, my father was true to his word. I needed to do many things during that time, like travel to visit my fian-cé's family, buy the gifts that must be given, prepare my own cloth-ing, and arrange food for the wedding meal. On all of this, my father spent almost nothing, only ¥1,010 ($292). We presented our match-maker with pork, flour, and two bags of candy, while a rich family might have given twenty, fifty, or even one hundred yuan.

In our village, wedding celebrations are supposed to be a big party with many guests and lots of food. Because of my father's stinginess, though, my wedding was very simple. We did not invite any neigh-bors, only family, and not all of them either. I spent ¥100 ($29) on two pairs of trousers and tops for my wedding clothes, and we cooked very simple food for the meal.

In traditional Chinese ceremonies, we do not exchange vows or make any promises to each other. At my wedding no one said any formal words at all. My husbands' parents did not even attend, as his father's illness and the family's poverty would have made this nearly impossible. But in truth, they also did not care anything about the wedding. Afterward we went directly to my new home, my husband's apartment in the nearby town. My husband's uncle also lived there, and he cooked us some food that night to celebrate our marriage.

I don't know what the meaning of marriage is. In China we have a saying, *Jià jī suí jī, jià gǒu suí gǒu.* It means, "If you are married to a chicken, obey the chicken; if you are married to a dog, obey the dog." It is the way people try to persuade a wife to accept her fate rather than struggle against it. Wives must bear their husband's lot and station in life as their own. They must not hope for change.

By the time we married my husband had left the oil company for a job in building construction. The morning after our wedding I went with him to the construction site, where I would be working along-side him. It was very difficult work. I got ¥1.9 per hour (55 cents), while my husband earned ¥3 because men can carry more. Three months after our wedding, I found out I was pregnant with our first daughter. I stopped working at the construction site for a time to deliver and care for her. The Family Planning Policy was already in effect, but in our village, you could try again for a boy if your first child was a girl. I got pregnant again, but out came another girl. "You should just give her away to other people," my father told me. He disliked girls and didn't want another one in the family. But I ignored him.

Those early years were very difficult for us. My husband waited until after our wedding to tell me he had accumulated some debts. Actually, it turned out that he owed more than ¥ 600 ($174) to various people. Between these debts and having two daughters within three years, we were under constant financial strain. We paid off those debts before our second daughter was walking, but we were cash-strapped and struggling for years to come.

Then, in 1996, my oldest sister had an idea. "Why don't you and your

THE 1960S GENERATION

husband move to Wuhan? It's a bigger city with better-paying jobs."
We could make a better living there, it was true, but what about our
girls? We would get to see them only once a year. My father initially
refused to care for his granddaughters, but my grandmother went
over his head to say she would watch our second daughter, who was
not yet in school. My older sister helped to convince my father, who
begrudgingly relented. She also took in our older daughter, who was
already in the second grade.

Life got a lot better for us after the move to Wuhan. We could earn
enough to support our daughters' education, to give them a better life.
I didn't want them to have to live the kind of life I lived. [She cried
silently again, wiping tears away.] I wanted to support them to go to
university, so they could make a better life for themselves. They are
such good girls. They both studied very hard and did very well, earning their place at university.

When they were young, my husband and I traveled back to the village
each year for the Chinese New Year celebration. Before we returned
to Wuhan, we gave them all the money they would need to pay for
school and other things over the following year. They would manage
the money themselves until we saw them again. [More tears dribbled
down her cheeks as she talked about leaving her children behind each
year.] When they started middle school, I returned to our hometown
to cook for them. Once they got to high school, though, they boarded
at the school and I returned to join my husband.

I don't know what a good wife and a good husband should be
like. I didn't have this situation so I can't say. I hope a good husband
would be responsible and capable so his wife would not have to work
so hard. I was always the more capable one between us. When we
moved to Wuhan, I earned the same amount as my husband, while
most wives earn less. I am not a good wife because I am not satisfied
with my husband or married life. My husband treats me so-so. We
don't hate each other, but we argue a lot about money. To be honest,
I don't care very much about him. I care much more for our daughters. Ideally a wife would care more, and if my husband were a better man, I would. I often wish my husband had looked better, been a
taller man, stronger, more capable, someone who could have earned

more money. I am a little happier with our life these days, though, because of my two daughters' success.

A good husband must be loyal, that I know. He cannot go out with other women. My second sister actually divorced because of this problem. She married a man from the city, and she had a strong character and wanted to control him. He met a younger woman from the village and got her pregnant. My sister didn't find out about this second wife until the other woman was already seven months along. Then she had a huge fight with her husband and they divorced. My own husband has not ever had an affair, and he has never really been interested in other women. He doesn't know how to explain his feelings or how to talk to me, but I feel that my husband really loves me. I don't know why he feels this way. He loves me more than I love him, and even though I have not been very satisfied with him, this part does make me glad. In his heart, he thinks I am the very best. [She could not suppress a wide smile at this point.]

Last year we came to Shenzhen to live with our older daughter. She invited us to live with her after she started her job. Since my husband is already in his fifties, it has been hard for him to find a job. These days he just cooks food for the family and cleans the house.

My dad respects me a little more now, because both my daughters went to university while only one or two of my sisters' children passed the entrance exam. My dad knows that in my heart, I am still angry with him for making me marry my husband.

"You should be thankful now," he says to me. "You have two good daughters." But I will retort that he should not justify his choice for me just because it turned out all right in the end. Before a woman marries, who knows what she'll get? So he shouldn't say this!

My own daughters may marry soon. I think the most important thing is for them to find a man who is really good to them, who really cares about them. The inside is more important than the outside, of course. Their future husbands don't need to be very rich, because these days in China a hard-working person can always survive. People don't have to endure such deep poverty anymore, so it is less important to marry for money.

A Good Fortune-Teller and Three Tips for Concealing Your Outside Woman

MR. ZHANG (B. 1968) AND MR. WU (B. 1977)

Forty-three-year-old Mr. Zhang grew up in a small village in Shandong province, along China's eastern seaboard. Mr. Zhang was the first open member of the Communist Party who interviewed with us. Linda whispered to me that he was a "typical Chinese government person," serious and traditional, a little bit fat from beer, and always trying to follow the rules. Mr. Zhang told us that you don't have to join the party to work in government, but most people do.

Mr. Zhang, like so many Chinese men of his generation, is a part-time husband. While he is officially based in the small Shandong city where his wife lives, he works from the Shenzhen office for six months each year. Mr. Zhang brought a friend along to the interview. Mr. Wu is thirty-five, good-looking, and very funny, but his joking was colder and his face harder than Mr. Zhang's. Mr. Wu is from the same village as Mr. Zhang but now lives in Shenzhen with his wife and daughter. Linda told me that he achieved a high position in his Shandong company, so they sent him to Shenzhen to open a branch office. "He drives a BMW," she confided, eyebrow raised. I got the impression that Mr. Wu doesn't like to go home. Linda told me that even though they live a half hour apart, Mr. Wu will often drive to Mr. Zhang's house to eat with him and stay overnight.

This interview unfolded partially in a Q and A style, with both men answering certain questions. There was much laughter and talk about our topics, and each man likely emphasized certain points for the benefit of his friend while leaving other things out. As such, their answers give a glimpse into both marriage and the culture of male friendships in China.

Mr. Zhang: My wife and I did not meet through a matchmaker. We just met on our own, which was a very rare event for our generation. Before I joined the government, we both worked for the same company. We loved each other, and she really wanted to marry me, but we had a problem: I was a village boy, and she was a town girl.

In those days village families were always poor, it could just be assumed. Town families, on the other hand, could earn a decent income by working in the factories. People thought it was very important to marry someone from the same social level, or perhaps from one level higher. In the eyes of my girlfriend's parents, you can imagine that I was a significant step backward. They fiercely objected to her marrying me or anybody like me.

But I would not give up so easily. They didn't want me to marry their daughter, but I wanted her for my wife. This was a competition, and I wanted to win! [He grinned.] I kept trying to see her. In response, her parents locked her inside their house for days.

Her parents were very concerned about this trouble with their daughter, and they couldn't bear to keep her locked away for very long. They needed help. One day they went to consult one of the family uncles who lived in a nearby village. This uncle listened closely to their domestic dilemma and offered a suggestion. "By luck, a traveling fortune-teller arrived in our village just this morning. Let us go to see him." Her parents agreed and the three went at once to seek an audience with the visiting sage.

"When will our daughter find a husband to marry?" her parents asked the fortune-teller. "What kind of man will he be?" They phrased their question strategically, but the fortune-teller pondered only a moment.

"Your daughter has already found her husband," came the reply. "You shouldn't worry too much or control things more. If you do too much, bad things will happen."

Instantly, surprise and fear clutched at her parents. Was it true? What about their reputation? My girlfriend's parents strongly opposed our relationship, but they knew their daughter wished very much to marry me. It was also a bother to keep her locked up at home. Slowly they changed their attitude. Within a month, they relented and approved our marriage. So that fortune-teller really brought good fortune to us!

Mr. Wu: I did not find a wife on my own. My parents just used a matchmaker. When I was a single man, I lived with them in our hometown village. I was twenty-seven, which is already a bit old for a country bachelor. When you get close to thirty, Chinese parents start to get concerned and excitable. "It's time to get married," they pushed.

Since I hadn't found the right person, my parents arranged a match for me. Our marriage was not from the heart, and I did not feel any natural care for my wife. I just married her because I needed to marry, to relieve the pressure. It didn't really work, though, and this summer is our seventh anniversary. So I want to ask you, if you make it past the seven-year itch, does it keep itching? [Mr. Wu and Mr. Zhang laughed heartily over this question, and Mr. Wu repeated it several more times.]

Q: How would you define marital happiness? How can you make a marriage more happy?

Mr. Wu: Happiness in marriage? [He considered this question for a long time.] Maybe if I wasn't under any pressure to make money, then I could be happy. My happiest time so far was the birth of my daughter.

Mr. Zhang: [After his own lengthy pause.] You know, I have never thought about how to manage my marriage. Marriages do not need to be managed, they are just natural! [Mr. Wu nodded enthusiastic support of this assessment.]

Q: Maybe you have not tried to manage your marriage before. But do you think couples *could* do anything to increase marital happiness? [Again they considered the question at length.]

Mr. Wu: I suppose the man could take care of the finances. Then the wife could stay home and would not need to work outside. But she would need to cook food and take care of the children and make sure her husband did not lose face in public.

Mr. Zhang: I agree with these things. I think the couple also needs to take care of each other and be considerate of each other. Also, we must take care of our parents.

Mr. Wu: Recently I had a very strange conversation on QQ about this very question. [QQ is a ubiquitous Chinese social media site, as prominent as Facebook in the West.] A woman friend of mine was chatting with our group of classmates, telling us the story of a couple she knows. The husband is German, he works for the airlines, his wife is Chinese, and they will soon celebrate twenty-five years of marriage.

He invited all of their good friends to fly to Germany to have a big party, but it was a surprise, and nobody could tell the wife. My friend wrote, "Oh, this is very romantic!" But I was shocked.

"How much money will he need to throw this party? So much money!" I wrote back. "Think of how much food you could buy with that money! Why does he need to pay for such a party?"

"Because they are still romantic, even though they are already in their sixties!" my friend gushed. "What gift would you buy for your wife if you were him?" she asked the group.

"We are already an old couple, so why do I need to buy any gift?" I replied.

"Because the marriage needs romance, right?" she prodded.

But that is all foolishness. I have no time to be romantic. Every day I have to think about how to make money, and there is so much pressure. I have no time to hug and kiss my wife when I come home! I am too exhausted to do anything like that.

Q: What about second wives and mistresses? What is your opinion? [They both laughed aloud and were eager to expound on the topic.]

Mr. Wu: Well, if the man's heart belongs at home, and he still gives his money to his wife, then I think the outside person is only for play. If you have an outside woman, there are three steps to follow. First: never tell. You must do anything and everything to protect your secret from your wife. But, if your wife somehow finds out and confronts you, then you must move to the second step: don't admit it. But what if your wife has definite proof? Then you move to the third step: be silent. [Both men chuckled as Mr. Wu outlined this roadmap.]

Q: And if your wife had an outside man, what would you do?

Both simultaneously: "We would throw her out! Fire her!"

Mr. Zhang: These many years later, my wife is still a good-quality woman. She treats me very well.

Mr. Wu: Mr. Zhang's wife is very good. Every time he goes away, she makes dumplings for him!

Mr. Zhang: In our hometown these dumplings carry a special meaning to a person who is about to make a trip. We think that the people who love you, who want to wish you luck for safe travels, they will make you dumplings. It is a tradition. No matter what time of day or night I need to leave for Shenzhen, my wife always cooks this dish for me. Even though we have been married for many years, she still does this, and I appreciate it very much.

You Know Your Boyfriend Is Married If...

"BIG CAROL" (B. 1968)

Big Carol is forty-four years old and grew up in the icy northern province of Ningxia, a small dab of a place tucked under the expanse of Inner Mongolia. Her parents were university professors, and Big Carol also graduated from college. She was one of the tallest Chinese women I had met, and she explained that her friends call her "Big Carol" because she is taller and a bit broader than the other Carol in her group of girlfriends. Her ready smile was bright and sparkling beneath a coat of peach-colored lipstick. This cosmetic choice surprised me because most women her age wear no makeup at all.

We met at 3:00 p.m. in a tea shop, and Big Carol ordered a beer. Without thinking, I ordered jasmine tea, but I should have called for a second Tsingtao to make her more comfortable. She was the first Chinese woman I had met who openly ordered a beer for herself. Given this and the lipstick, I prepared myself for a nontraditional story.

Against the wishes of her family, Big Carol had never married. Because she is educated, financially independent, and unmarried, she is called shèngnǚ, literally a "leftover woman," a special category of Chinese social pariah. The All-China Women's Federation, a government body charged with attending to women's welfare and issues, recently invented this term for women who remained unmarried past age twenty-seven. The label, which caught on quickly, is meant to deter young women from being "too picky" about their marriage partner. I wanted to talk to one of these leftover women, to hear what life was like outside the boundaries of married society.

Big Carol was clearly an intelligent woman and an independent thinker. In her youth she had observed little about marriage to attract her and much to dissuade. By the time she felt ready for a husband, most of her male peers were taken. Instead, she became their "deep-heart friend," providing the listening ear and the "fresh feelings" so stereotypically required by China's henpecked, over-pressured husbands.

I was born during the Cultural Revolution, and my whole family, both my grandfather and my father, supported Mao's Communist Party. We were happy about the revolution. Actually, my Chinese name means "honoring the revolution."

When I was in school, parents and teachers were anxious to prevent any socializing between boys and girls. We weren't supposed to talk to each other, but since we were also all very shy, this rule was not hard to follow. Girls could have girlfriends, and boys could be friends with each other, but if I talked to a boy, oh! So bad! Girlfriends could hold hands, and boys could put their arms around each other, but if a boy brushed a girl, it was too much. Adults thought very bad things would happen if you had the early love, like having a baby, so it was forbidden.

Parents and teachers didn't care about your heart, they didn't care about your feelings. My parents never spoke to me about emotions at all. They talked only about jobs, about my future. I don't think anybody's parents ever thought about their feelings. Probably they didn't think children had them! If you cried, they thought you would learn something from the situation. They never thought your crying was a problem. They just wanted you to study and not talk to boys so they wouldn't lose face.

Our parents didn't know any differently, because they didn't have much experience with love themselves. Maybe they had an arranged marriage or were forced to marry someone because it was time. "It is time to join the ordinary life," their parents would have said. "It is time to marry."

After I entered university, my parents thought it was okay for me to have a boyfriend. Everyone knew college boys were smart and from a good, equal social class. But even though relationships were suddenly allowed, our cultural training still prevented anyone from expressing his or her feelings directly. If you expressed your feelings openly, we thought you would lose face, lose your reputation, and ruin your future. Instead, women had to appear picky, careful, withholding.

For example, if a young man and woman were alone, and they liked each other, and he tried to hold her hand, she was supposed to bat him away, pretending she was very picky, she was so special. Of course she liked him too! But she was not supposed to express it. People didn't talk openly. Then the girl might ask the boy, "Do you love me?" But he would just hunch his shoulders, retorting, "What do you think!" He could never say "I love you" directly to her. Our parents never said "I love you" to their children or to each other, and we inherited their reserve.

My parents were university professors, so I went to their university, which was quite close to our home. But I didn't find a boyfriend. When I was twenty-five, my parents started pressuring me to marry, always making comparisons with my same-age peers. "Look at your friend, married, so successful!" They introduced me to some boys, but they were all so short! I hated them all. [Big Carol scrunched her face as though eating a sour grape, then laughed at the memory.] "Feelings don't matter," my parents advised. "Marriage matters." My parents are impatient people, and they gave up after making three introductions for me.

What I didn't tell them was that I already liked someone. He was a business partner of mine, ten years older than me. He had been married once but had already gotten a divorce. I dated that man for seven years, but at that time I hated the idea of marriage. I thought it demanded too much responsibility for too little happiness. Many of my married friends, coworkers, and relatives were not happy. About 70 percent were unhappy, I think. And they all found their spouses on their own and married only for love!

At that time, if I had a single friend who desperately wanted to marry, I would comfort her. "If you want to get married so badly, just look at the marriages around you," I would say. "So many are unhappy, and there is too much responsibility and pressure! Is it really worth it?"

Of course, my parents worried that my social life would be dismal and lonely if I didn't marry. Chinese society maintains a very bad opinion of women who are twenty-seven or twenty-eight and unmarried. We call them shèngnǚ, "leftover women." We use the same word for unused parts and pieces at the factory. I have no shame about this term. They can call us leftovers. We *are* leftovers!

It is true that single women face a lot of challenges. If you need help, money, or comfort, no one is there to give you these things. Your social circle is limited, because people are afraid to get too close. Your existing friendships become complicated. Think about it. If you have a friend with the same education, same status, same level, same hometown, same everything, but she gets a husband and you don't, then you won't really be able to continue as friends. Who will talk to her husband when you come to visit? The husband doesn't have anywhere to go. He comes home because his wife wants him to be home. We Chinese are not so independent as you are in America, we don't have so many hobbies or options for our leisure time. So his wife cannot invite you to come over, now can she?

When I turned thirty-five, I started thinking seriously about marriage. *I am getting older. I am less nervous to face the future,* I told myself. I changed my mind from the inside. Since then, I have always had boyfriends. Some last for a short time, some for longer, and I love each one of them. One man I dated for years, but of course, he was married.

I am single, so I am free. Usually these men come to me. Ninety-nine percent of married men will occasionally want to have free sex, fun sex, with no responsibility attached. After all, if there was some shop where you could get everything for free, don't you think everyone would want to go? These men come to talk with me at a bar, and always, after they are drunk, they feel close to me. They want to have a date. "I have a wife," some admit, "but I don't have a good relationship with her." Others don't mention a wife, and I used to be too shy to ask. Others are more direct, asking, "Are you single?" By now I am savvy. I have had so many relationships. If they don't ask about my status, then I know they are married.

Married men always talk about marrying me, but I don't want to push this. If they ask me directly, then I say I don't exactly want to marry them. They are cute, but they wouldn't make a good husband. I am always the one who ends the relationship, but I never quite have to break up with these men. "Let's still go out for a drink now and then," I say. "We can listen to music, but no more sex, no more private time."

If I think the man is not suitable, then I don't feel sad about the end. Less crying is better. One time I felt sad for a few days after calling things off, but I have never suffered emotionally. No one has left me. No one has done something to really hurt my heart.

Now that I am in my forties, I would like to be married. I have enjoyed having fewer responsibilities as a single woman, since I don't need to take care of kids or a husband. I think I would be an understanding and reasonable wife, not so demanding as the others, because of my experiences. Sex is less important to me now that I am older. I just want a single man who can treat our relationship seriously.

Q: Many people tell me a man's looks are not very important. Do you agree?

A: Well, I think they are keeping something from you! [She laughed.] This is just the result of our cultural training. When I was young, I thought a handsome man was very important. I was stupid, driven by hormones. I thought that if the man was good-looking, maybe the sex would be better. Now I think the outside of a man hardly matters. I have fewer hormones, so I can make a better decision. I just want a man who is average in everything. He doesn't have to be so unique, so special. He just needs to treat me well.

My advice to all young people would be, marry young, marry early, as quickly as possible! Don't let yourself get old like I did.

Q: Based on this advice, would you go back and accept one of those three men your parents tried to introduce you to?

A: No. No! Marry those short guys? [She laughed out loud at this horrible thought.] No, I still hate all of them! Maybe you can find the last man I dated, an American. You can interview him and ask him why he didn't divorce his wife and marry me!

PART THREE

The 1970s Generation

Sex and Love . . . or Marriage?

What I saw in my parents' relationship is that marriage
is rough and tough and lasts forever. But I didn't
want my parents' version of marriage.

—Sally, b. 1976

The 1970s generation truly straddles two Chinas. Born in the midst of the Cultural Revolution but coming of age in the era of "reform and opening up," this is both a Mao and a post-Mao generation. Their early life was steeped in philosophies of self-sacrifice and radical collectivism, but Mao soon died, and their world slowly changed. They are the last generation that grew up in big families, only to be restricted to one or two babies themselves. While the party retains the power to meddle in people's lives, this generation watched it steadily loosen its grip on private life and on love and marriage decisions.

The 1970s generation watched as Deng Xiaoping, the nation's influential post-Mao leader, zapped China's flagging state-owned behemoth with the equivalent of a social and economic Taser gun. Starting in the late 1970s, Deng ended the country's decades-long isolation, loosened censorship, reopened the universities, and unleashed the breathtaking economic growth that would change his country, and the world, over the next thirty years. While this generation's parents smarted over the loss of familiar entitlements, like free education and medical care, the children of the 1970s largely embraced their new opportunities. They opened businesses or took work in the factories, shops, and companies of the rapidly spreading private sector. While government jobs and nosy work units remain a reality of adult life for some in this generation, many have never worked inside the government system.

This generation grew up with the notion that young people should have a say in who they married. Parents still wielded a great deal of authority, but this generation watched older cousins and friends play an active role in selecting their own marriage partners. Still, customs changed only to a point. This generation did not question the injunction for young people to "keep love in the heart" rather than express it with words or affection.

The 1970s generation was the first of the groups in this book to enjoy an education uninterrupted by revolution. They did not, however, live and die for scholastic success, as would later generations. Twenty-nine percent of them graduated from a vocational or college preparatory high school, while 13 percent finished university.

Parents, teachers, and friends still did not talk to this generation about love, sex, or the purpose of marriage. But they had access to foreign books, music, and movies, media that had not been available since the 1940s. Centralized censorship exists to this day, but after the start of "reform and opening up," the media could explore previously taboo topics like romantic love and sex. New ideas traveled slowly from urban to rural regions, but by the time this generation hit their twenties, China was in the midst of a sexual revolution. Premarital sex, still a reportable offense in the 1980s, had become socially permissible for engaged couples by the 1990s. Adultery, a crime punishable with prison time until 1980 and subject to work unit censure and fines until the 1990s, slowly dwindled to a private problem and grounds for divorce.

Members of this generation describe themselves as a bit more open-minded about love. As young people, some had sex with people they did not go on to marry. Dating in high school or university was still highly unusual, but as the children of the 1970s hit their twenties, dating became a socially acceptable first step toward courtship and marriage. Their parents were far more likely to ask, "Do you have a boyfriend" than to arrange the introductions themselves. Most 1970s folk consider it acceptable for a couple to meet each other independently and, unlike their forebears, many found partners on the Internet. They are also most likely to think divorce is acceptable if a couple is unhappy.

By the time this generation began marrying in the 1990s, the husband-wife relationship carried almost as much weight as the parent-son relationship. While a man's wife still did not trump his mother, Chinese family life had settled into a hybrid model that made room for the needs of both. In the late 1990s Yunxiang Yan, a Harvard-trained anthropologist, observed that rural couples "were actually allowed to be happy about their wedding and to show [that happiness] openly." A groom could finish a drink for his bride. She could adjust his jacket before the ceremony. Such gestures would barely raise an eyebrow in the West, but Yan described them as a revolution in displays of public affection among husband and wife. He also noted that rural families commonly built separate bedrooms for married couples and older parents, a level of privacy unheard of in earlier decades.

This generation married by the rules of the Second Marriage Law, a set of revisions introduced in 1980. These updates lowered the marriageable age to twenty for women and twenty-two for men, established the infamous One Child Policy, liberalized divorce, allowed interracial unions and marriage with foreigners, and increased protections for wives and children following divorce.

This generation was the first to feel the tremors of the coming era of missing brides and single men. As of 2010, 97 percent of 1970s-born women had married, while only 90 percent of their male peers had found a spouse. In the same year, less than 2 percent of women and 2.5 percent of men from this generation were currently divorced, though many had divorced and remarried.

Today the 1970s generation numbers 215 million people. They are China's "sandwich generation," as almost all are married, almost all support their parents financially, and almost all are working or raising children or both. Almost all of them want love and intimacy to be part of marriage, but they have struggled to achieve this vision.

My Lover's Name Is Sam

FANGFEI (B. 1972)

Fangfei is a slim, attractive, forty-year-old woman who grew up in a small village in Hunan province with her parents and twin brothers. Well educated and well spoken, she is now an instructor in a popular Chinese self-help program that combines psychology, yoga, and self-care. She credits this program with changing her life.

While most storytellers came to me randomly, through various friends and colleagues, I sought out Fangfei. I wanted to hear from a married woman with a lover, as thus far only husbands had admitted such relationships to me. Reaching my goal was a tall order, as "outside people," as lovers are called, are far less acceptable among wives than husbands in China. Linda and I put out feelers with nearly everyone we knew, and while many women admitted to knowing such a wife, they doubted their friend would willingly share her story. Fangfei, however, accepted readily. Her husband already knew about her lover, so there was little secret left to keep.

We met in Shenzhen's OCT neighborhood, where Linda, Fangfei, the mutual friend who introduced us, a third friend of Fangfei's, and I all crowded into a single booth in the back corner of a Western coffee shop. Thus intimately settled, Fangfei said, "Since you are a friend of my friend's, now we are also friends and can speak our real minds to each other." She told her intriguing story with confidence and poise, surrounded by yellow walls, candle sconces, and mirrors framed in wood carving.

Partway through the interview, Fangfei got a text message. She read it quickly, smiled, and said, "So, do you want to meet Sam?" Linda and I turned to each other, wide-eyed. "Um, well, yes. Yes we do!" I said. After the interview we met the infamous Sam, a kind, shy, gangly boy in his late twenties, and shared a meal of shrimp congee, vegetables, and tea.

I think that in China, a woman's traditional place in the family arose in the context of poverty. When I was small, food was still very scarce, and we did not always have enough. My mother gave the biggest portions to me and my brothers, and then my father ate what he wanted.

My mother ate only the leftovers. She gave me the same food as my brothers, because she thought a girl was weaker physically and emotionally, so I needed as much as she could give me. I am like every other Chinese woman older than forty. We have all lived through a time of famine, and our parents had to focus on survival and finding food. Traditional parents could not spend much time with their children, so we lacked their love and quality time.

I grew up in a small village in Hunan, with my parents and my younger twin brothers. After 1976, when I was four years old, our family had enough food, but my parents still spent the bulk of their time working. My parents loved each other deeply but never spoke of it out loud. They just always took care of each other.

My dad was well respected by the other villagers because he was a business man from a well-educated family, so I got this respect too. Everyone liked me—my teachers, classmates, and friends—so I had strong self-esteem. Many Chinese women grew up without food, respect, or love, but I had food and respect and even a little pocket money to buy a snack. But I lacked my parents' attention and love. In all of my childhood memories, I almost cannot remember one with my parents looking at me, spending time with me. My father especially had no time for me, and I don't remember ever being alone with him. For the past twenty years, I didn't consider food and money to be very important. What I have been looking for is love and attention from men.

When I was nineteen years old, I met my first husband through the friend of a classmate. He was seven years older than me, and ten days after we met, he invited me to his home. He had a karaoke machine, and he said if I came over, he would teach me to sing and dance. He did show me how to sing, and it was my first time singing like that. He showed me how to dance too, and then how to kiss, and then how to have sex. So my first singing, first dancing, first kiss, and first sex experiences came all in one night. I had never seen even a photo of a naked man before, so I didn't know what a penis looked like. I thought maybe he had brought a weapon.

I cried the whole next day. I was scared and thought I was very bad. In China we think sex before marriage is dirty. But if you do have sex, then we believe you belong to each other. So three years later, after I graduated from university, I married this man.

My husband was a handsome man, but he was poor and had only a middle school education. His parents were uneducated workers and they did not have a good relationship. They were at war with each other. When he was little, his father was very angry and abusive. One time his father kicked him so hard that he flew over two meters away. Before we married, I knew these stories, and I knew that we were very different people. But I was young and we loved each other and I did not understand psychology. I think I did not even want to marry him in my deep heart. But I lacked my parents' attention, and here was a handsome man who wanted to look at me, so I married him.

My parents were strongly against our marriage. My mother thought he was very rude. Still, when we married, my parents gave us a lot of money to invest in business and stocks, over ¥7,000,000 ($1,000,000). My husband had no money of his own, and he could not earn my mother's heartfelt respect. She was polite, but he was disappointed and depressed. He could not balance his spirit. He loved me, but when we got closer, something changed in him. He wanted to do everything for me, to treat me like a young girl. Sometimes he became very rude, and he could not control his anger or rude language. When I encountered this side of him, I didn't know how to react. He would apologize and feel sorry after he lost his temper. He knew he was wrong, but he could not help it.

One time he wanted to buy me a mobile phone. I told him I didn't need one, but he insisted. He went to the shop with me and we considered many options.

"This one is good," he said.

"Okay, let's buy it," I said.

"You fool!" he shouted. "Why would you buy a phone in this store!?" I was shocked, silent, and ashamed. He had shouted at me in public and in front of our two year-old daughter. When we went home I spoke quietly, "I want to divorce. I cannot endure this treatment any longer."

I moved out soon after that. My husband had never expected this, and he lost fifteen kilograms (thirty-three pounds) that month. He had paid all his love to me, and he assumed we would be together forever. Later he explained that he had intended to buy the phone in a cheaper shop. But how was I to know what he was thinking?

Within twelve months, we were divorced. I felt almost no sadness, because I had already been sad for so many years during our marriage. We had nothing in common and it had always been hard to be on the same channel. So the divorce was more like a relief, a breath of fresh air. We had one daughter together, and she is fourteen years old now. She is a beautiful girl, very strong and human in her spirit. It was she who suffered the broken heart when we divorced.

To this day, my first husband feels I was an angel to him, and his heart is still with me. He remarried, but just for practical reasons, not with his deep heart. I still have dinner with him and his wife once every year or two, and his wife even consulted me a few times when they were having problems.

During my first marriage, I had no male friends. After we separated, I felt very free. I was twenty-nine, single, and a single mother, and I wanted a new husband. Some friends introduced me to a new man. He was good and we got along well, but my daughter didn't like him. One time when she was four years old, she answered his phone call.

"Don't call my mother anymore," she said. "She doesn't love you." So I broke up with that man. I thought I should find a man my daughter liked.

Around that time the Internet arrived in China. I wanted to build a website for my company, so I found a web developer. His name was Sam. After our first business meeting, Sam fell in love with me. He was twenty-four years old, six years younger than me, and it was his first love. He invited me to go to a bar later at night, but I had never set foot in such a place! According to my education, a bar was a very bad place. Plus I thought he was too young, too poor. So I refused him. But he called again and again. He didn't care if he lost face, and he felt no shame at my refusal. I even remember saying, "I hate you!" but still he didn't give up.

After a while, I accepted, and we went out to the bar. I found myself feeling attracted to him and enjoying his company, so I wanted to have sex. That night we went to a hotel and slept together. After a month I got nervous about the future, and I told him I wanted to stop. He did not agree, and he begged to see me again. At that time he hadn't yet told me why he loved me.

"You are very bad," I said. "You don't have the ability to search for another girlfriend, so you just pick me. If you want to see me again, then first prove that you can change your circumstances. Find another girlfriend. Then we can meet."

After that I went to Europe by myself for a month, and he went to Beijing to study law. He still called me often and asked to see me, but I held firm to my offer. Five months later he told me that he was dating a model and he wanted me to come meet her. We went out for drinks. She was a nice, beautiful girl, and she played the piano. I was jealous.

Sam still kept calling me after that, so I changed my mobile phone number and disappeared. Eight years would pass before he found me again.

Within a year I met my second husband on QQ. We chatted for ten days, and then he began calling and asking for a date. He was thirty-one years old and already deputy CEO for a big company. I thought the problems in my first marriage had come from choosing a handsome, uneducated man, so I changed these things the second time around. This man was not handsome, nor was he rich. He had no house, no car, and no savings. But he was very knowledgeable and smart, and he had a masters' degree and a good job.

When he met me, he liked me very much. He thought I had the air of one who came from a well-educated family, like his. I had a very good feeling about him too but decided to wait for sex. I still thought I had failed in my first marriage because we had sex before developing a strong heart for each other. After our first date, this man asked me to be his girlfriend. On our second date, I brought my daughter along to test him. We went shopping and my daughter liked him a lot, right from the start. They both liked each other. Afterward I put my daughter to bed in his home. Once she was asleep, we slept together. I trusted him already, so I gave 100 percent. Six months later we got married, and my family gave us money and a car.

I thought I understood what went wrong in my first marriage. But now I see that in both relationships, I was really looking for a father, not a lover, and my second marriage was very similar to the first, almost 90 percent the same. My new husband was also rude, but less often, maybe only once a month. He had no deep sense of safety in the world. He was insecure, so he wanted to control me and take care of everything for me. But I didn't want him to do this.

One time we were out shopping, and we felt tired and wanted to look for a restaurant. He suggested one place, but I said no, I wanted another place. I could see that he felt very upset and uncomfortable because I refused his suggestion, so I backtracked.

"Any place is fine for me," I said.

"Forget it, we'll go to the place you said," he muttered. He wanted to make all of our choices, and he thought his ideas were better than mine. But he could not communicate his feelings. For many days after that, he felt uncomfortable in his heart and sank lower and lower until he exploded. Even still he is like this. I got a message from him just two days ago, blaming me that our daughter's Chinese characters are very bad. Why do I spend time supporting other people's lives, he accused, while my own daughter is slipping behind? He told me I am not a good mother and that I have mental problems.

My second husband blames his super-controlling mother for his lack of happiness in life. In some ways my husband is a great man, an ideal man, because his mother controlled him. Always she perched over him, saying, "You can't do this or that" or "You must do this and that," and he treats me the same way. He is aware of this, and he doesn't want to be so controlling like his mother, but he can't help himself. There is a conflict in his mind. I know many men like him in China: they love their family, but they don't really know *how* to love them. They know they have a problem, but they can't change. My husband refuses to study psychology and he cannot stop or change.

About a year into our marriage, my husband wanted to help his younger brother have a good life. He asked me to arrange a job for him at my company, and his brother moved in with us. This brother was a very stupid person, though, and he did something bad at work. He left the job after one month and he showed us a very cold and angry face after that. My husband and I fought over this problem, and my husband felt a lot of pressure.

Soon after that, when I was three months pregnant with our daughter, I passed a room where my husband was sitting. I heard him say, "I'm at home." Just those three words, but I had a feeling in my heart that he was talking with a woman and that he loved her.

My husband is not handsome, so I had never thought to doubt his fidelity. I knew his phone password and his bank card password but had never checked for signs of a *xiǎosān*. This is one word for "lover," it means "little three," because your marriage suddenly has a third person.

Immediately I confronted him, and he admitted the affair. He met her through work and they had been together for one month. This woman had the same values as he did, so she supported his idea about his younger brother, agreeing that even if your family member does poor work, you should let him keep the job because you should always help your family. My husband promised to stop this relationship.

This is a very painful story to tell. After I found out, I cried for three days and three nights without sleeping or eating anything. We were supposed to be having a baby, but how could we go on? I strongly considered aborting the baby. I consulted my mother about this situation, but all she said was, "Your husband is an okay man."

At my own request, I met with this other woman alone. We talked for eight hours. She was the same age as me, very beautiful, highly educated, and wealthy, a very good woman. She promised to stop their relationship and even told us she was leaving China. This was just a lie to make everything easier. She actually stayed in China, changed her mobile number, and disappeared.

In the end, I chose forbearance. I endured his affair and we kept the baby. But still I think our married life has been very bad and very painful over the past ten years. Two years ago, when my husband took work in another city, I felt it was time. I decided to look for Sam.

Initially I just wanted to know how he was. Did he have a good life? So I contacted his friend, but the friend had lost touch with him too. "He's never on QQ anymore," he told me. But I looked him up anyway, and eventually we got in touch. He hadn't changed his QQ picture in nine years, not since he first met me.

Our first date was in this restaurant, in this very same booth. [She smiled knowingly as we all reacted with surprise.] When he arrived, he just looked at me many times, silently. We met a second time, three weeks later, and this time he pushed a thick, tattered book across the table. It was his diary of the past eight years, a record of his love for me. For three hours, he watched me as I read it and cried. After I switched my number and he couldn't find me, he sank into a bleak panic. He drank heavily and grieved for a long time. He failed his English classes and didn't get the lawyer license in Beijing. Working odd jobs, he was only able to earn money under the table. He also lost a lot in the stock market. For six years he waited for me. He had no girlfriends, no sex with anyone. Many girls loved him and tried to chase him, but he ignored them all. Finally he felt maybe he needed a family and a baby, so he found a girlfriend.

His diary also spoke of his tragic childhood. His background is truly even sadder than my two husbands'. Sam was a secret baby. It was 1982, just after the start of the One Child Policy, and his mother was not supposed to have a second child. Sam needed to be hidden, so his mother sent him to the north of China, to Shaanxi province, to be raised by his grandmother. His older brother stayed in the south, cared for by his paternal grandmother.

Sometimes Sam would come back to visit his parents, but his grandmother and great-aunt did not welcome him. They treated him very unfairly. Sam remembers that if the family ate some sweet food before bed, his grandma would only give some to his older brother, not to him. The older brother did not know how to take care of his little brother, so Sam just watched as he ate the sweets. This is just one small story.

When he was seven years old, Sam started to run away from home. His parents found him many times, and always he would be with the hēishèhuì, the local "black society." This group was really like the Chinese Mafia. When he was little, he was in charge of collecting the protection fee from local stores. Sam didn't go to school.

After a few years of this running away, his parents sent him to a government school for bad children. Theoretically, they meant to reform him, but in practice he just studied every bad activity from all the other bad kids. By the time he was twelve, he had racked up so many offenses that he was not allowed to leave the school grounds for an entire year. One day he tried to kill himself by swallowing a metal screw. They took him to the hospital, and then the school sent him home.

When he was thirteen, he ran away from home again, and this time he didn't return for four years. He was always very brave, so the Mafia made him a little leader. Sam was a bad man, and he has many scars from those years. One time a man beat him with a chair in a restaurant fight. His head is mottled with faded red marks, and his wrists are striped from when he cut himself.

When he was seventeen, he was in a big fight with more than one hundred people. Someone cut his leader's arm off, and his group carried the dripping limb to the hospital along with their leader. Sam felt deeply shaken after that experience. It was too cruel. He was afraid these bad men would find him again, and he was right. When they did, they hurt his arm very badly too.

After that attack Sam went back to his mother's house. She hid him in south China and decided to retire, focusing entirely on his care. During his long recovery, he studied computing and web design. I met him the year after that, when he was only nineteen. He lied when we met, saying he was twenty-four! His eyes already had the cold glint of adulthood, so I believed him.

After I read his diary, Sam kept meeting with me, but he didn't break up with his girlfriend. I pitied him. He hadn't told me his real age yet, so I thought he was already thirty-three, without a wife, a career, or any savings. I told my husband that I was taking on a legal consultant for my business, and I hired Sam.

"This will be strictly business, not sex," I cautioned him. Several weeks later Sam admitted his lie and told me he was actually ten years younger than me. This meant he was only twenty-seven, and it was completely normal for him not to have any money or a wife. For a moment, I didn't want to help him with business anymore. But I continued.

During that first year, I taught Sam everything I knew. I still refused to sleep with him, but he would hug and kiss me, and I loved that feeling. He quickly pulled away from his girlfriend. They slept together only one or two times that year, whereas before maybe it was a few times a week. After about a year, he and I made love. Soon after, his girlfriend felt there wasn't any more love left between them, and she broke up with him.

Several months later, I encouraged Sam to resolve this matter of cheating, to take care of his ex-girlfriend's feelings. So he got in touch with her and told her our whole story. She listened to all of it.

"This is really love, Sam," she said. "I am glad to find such a story in real life, because usually I can only read about it in books. I wish you the best."

These past two years, Sam and I have had unbelievable chemistry. We can talk about everything. Because we share this deep-heart love, we both feel a very strong sexual attraction for each other, and making love with Sam is amazing. He had closed his heart for so many years, but now he opens it for me. Early on we had a fight because he thought our relationship would turn sour like everything else in his life. But I think we have what it takes to build our future. I sold him my trading company, actually, so now he is the president and I am his consultant. My only worry is that he might want his own baby one day. The One Child Policy prevents us from having any children together, so maybe he will leave me and meet a new woman.

Now, with 99 percent of my energy, I want to divorce my husband. Only 1 percent of me wants to go forward. This choice is very painful. Since I found myself through my study of psychology, my life has been powered by a different energy. We study theory, but primarily we practice action. We take yoga, and we make time for group discussion and healing. I am changed now, a different person from when we married. I want to balance my mind, heart, and spirit. I want to care for them all. My husband, on the other hand, is a very unhappy person. He thinks the only good thing in life is our daughter. If I stay with him, I would need to endure his unhappiness each day. I would need to be patient every day of our life together.

My husband and I have not touched each other or had sex in eighteen months. For him, sex was never from his deep heart, like it was for me. He is not happy inside himself, and I want my lover to be capable of feeling this deep happiness. He loves me in his way, but he makes himself like a metal box, with the spirit hidden far inside. So it is hard for me to receive his love. My husband does everything for family, but he also blames everything on family. He refuses to study how to be happy. He refuses to try to change his life.

I told my husband that I want a divorce. I told him that I have a lover. My husband was very pained by this news, since he does love me very much. This fall we are sending our daughter to Canada for high school, so we agreed to wait until she goes to decide our future. We still discuss everything about our family and our finances together.

Just recently Sam finally told me why he first fell in love with me eleven years ago. It will sound like such a small thing. I drove him home, but he wanted to stay with me for a longer time. I put my hand on his arm. "We can see each other again," I said. My touch felt very warm to him, and he was moved deep inside his heart. The feeling was so wonderful that he loved me right then and remembered me for a long time. He wanted us to spend our lives together, so he could not give up until he found me.

For One Tree, Do Not Sacrifice the Forest

MING-MING (B. 1972)

Ming-Ming is thirty-eight years old and grew up in a small city in Anhui, an inland province due west of Shanghai. She has lived in Shenzhen for fifteen years and met her husband on the Internet. They opted for a *luŏhūn*, or "naked marriage," just six months after their first date. Such a marriage is controversial, as the union is sealed without the exchange of cash, an apartment, or cars or any elaborate wedding celebration. Parents and friends may worry about a girl who enters marriage with "nothing to show for it," but true love, or advancing age, may entice her to go the naked way.

Linda introduced Ming-Ming and me, and we met in a Beijing-style noodle house. She shared her story over a lunch of rice, tea, and the fried green beans that would become my favorite Chinese dish. Ming-Ming is chubby by Chinese standards, and short curls frame her round face. Though she burst into occasional laughter as we spoke, Ming-Ming did not smile often, and her eyes were flecked with layers of old and new sadness. She brought along a set of handwritten letters she and her husband had exchanged before their divorce.

I grew up in a small city, where my father worked for the government highway office. He focused very hard on his job to earn money for our family. My mother stayed home to raise my older brother and me, and she took in some tailoring on the side.

My mother was very strict with us, and in truth, my childhood was not so happy. [Ming-Ming frowned, sucked in her cheeks, and blew the air out.] My favorite times were when I could climb the local mountain with classmates to pick wild fruit. I could not tell my mother about this climbing, because she would not let me go. She did not like us to go out, because she was afraid we would be injured and she would have to pay money to the doctor. Really, when I was young my strongest hope was just to grow up faster, so I could get out of her control.

My mother did not allow boyfriends, but I didn't like anyone in primary or middle school anyway. In high school, though, I loved one boy very much. He was an older boy, my brother's friend. My mother treated this boy like a second son, and he was often in our home. I don't know why I liked him. Actually, he didn't look so good, but still something attracted me. I guess I thought he was funny. He had a good sense of humor, and he was easygoing.

I did not share my heart, but this boy understood my feelings. He was studying calligraphy and often practiced his characters at our house. One day, while I lingered nearby, pretending not to watch him practice, he drew his brush slowly and thoughtfully, making these characters in the ink: "I regard you as a little sister." He did not look at me. He just painted the strokes, but I understood that he wrote them to me.

I was very sad. I tried not to show it, but the boy saw that I was hurt, and soon after, he wrote a letter to me. It was very long, more than three pages. I don't remember much of it. He told me I was a good girl and things like that, but one thing I do remember. *Wèile yī kē shù fàngqìle yīpiàn sēnlín*, he wrote. It means, "For one tree, do not sacrifice the whole forest." I knew he was trying to give me courage, to build up my heart so I could move on.

But I could not. For seven years, I continued to love that boy quietly. Other boys liked me and tried to chase me, but I could not love again until I forgot him. It was my *shāngxīn* season—a sad thing, something that hurts the heart. It wasn't until I moved to Shenzhen, at age twenty-four, that I began to forget my first love. Even then, nearly nine years would pass before I fell in love again, this time with my ex-husband.

My real love life started on a Chinese matchmaking website. My second match was a man who worked in a factory in Shenzhen. We chatted online and talked on the phone for about a month before deciding to meet. I lived in the Sea World neighborhood at the time, and he had to ride a bus over two hours for our first date. I was already waiting for him when he called to say he had arrived. I had posted my picture online, but he hadn't, and there were a few guys milling about. So I didn't know which one was him! [She laughed.]

I called back, and he answered and walked toward me. His skin was dark, and he wore glasses and a pink shirt in the village style. His clothes were not nice. *He looks like a farmer*, I thought. He also had a bit of a belly. I wasn't happy and was hesitating about whether to even continue.

"Maybe I should just buy an ice cream and go back home," he said, teasing himself. This joke made me feel a bit better. He also called me *yātou*, which technically means "little girl," but it's a cute nickname for good friends or close relatives. This made me feel more comfortable too, so to be polite, I went to lunch like we had planned. Since we had already talked a good deal on the phone, we chatted comfortably while we ate.

After lunch I took him to my office, because all of my colleagues care about me and were curious to see this boy from the matchmaking site. They wanted to protect me, I suppose. He stayed about one hour, and after he left, none of them were satisfied. "He is not suitable for you!" they all declared.

He kept trying to call after our date, but I ignored him, smarting from my friends' critique. I needed time to think. After a few days, I decided to continue anyway, because the boy seemed honest and considerate and I felt I could trust him. Also, I was already thirty-three years old. This boy was clearly dating to find a wife, and I liked his seriousness. I didn't like the other men online, the ones who just wanted to play. So we dated, but all of my friends persisted in disliking him. They didn't explain their objections, but I guessed they didn't like his "villager" appearance.

Eventually we moved in together, because otherwise he could visit me only once a week. This boy had some money saved, but he told me that if we married, he would give it all to his parents and start from zero with me. I felt a little uncomfortable about his plan, but I reminded myself that he cared for his parents, so he was a good man. I shared my concern with one of my friends, and she was very angry when she heard what he said. In China we are very open with our friends. We tell them all the bad and good things, and they are very open about their opinions in turn. This friend tried for an entire afternoon to persuade me not to marry this boy. She thought he didn't trust me and that his "gift" to his parents was really a defensive maneuver against me spending all of his money. "If you don't listen, you'll regret it," she warned me.

But I didn't listen. *He has a job, and I have a job too, so we can work up little by little,* I thought. "How can he outmaneuver or defend against me? I am more sophisticated," I told her, brushing away her concern.

"I can tell from his face that he isn't lucky," she retorted, a final barb. We Chinese believe in luck, and we think you can see someone's luck in their hands or face.

In truth, everything about this boy was not up to my standards. I like big, tall men and large eyes with a double fold. [I asked what a "double fold" was, and Ming-Ming described an extra fold of skin that a minority of people have on the upper eyelid. This fold is thought to make the eye look larger and consequently to make the face more beautiful.] He had none of these characteristics. Also, I like a gentleman, somebody classy, but he worked in a factory and was rough and unpolished. We did have similar educational backgrounds, as we both went to university. But he was still from the village, whereas I came from a small city.

My parents also didn't like him, and neither did my brother. They all worried because he couldn't buy a house. "Oh my god, if you marry but don't have money, then you'll have to live in the air!" they warned.

I am very stubborn, though. I ignored all these criticisms. *My family and friends don't know him that well. They are just going on their first impression,* I told myself.

I was still a virgin and my first time was with this man. Before we met, I knew that I had a problem with my body. My periods had not been regular for many years, and sometimes they were heavy, or light, or not on time. I had consulted doctors about this problem, but since I was a virgin, they were hesitant to use certain tools in their evaluation. I knew this man wanted children very much, so after our first time together, I went for another evaluation. This time the doctor confirmed that I had a problem in my ovaries.

Men in China care very much about babies and having children. After my appointment I went back home and told him what the doctor had said. "Maybe we are finished," I sighed.

"No," he said. "We will marry and try to cure it." I felt very appreciative of this gesture, thinking it showed that he really loved me. So I said, "Okay, let's do it."

A week before the 2008 Chinese New Year festival, and just six months after our first date, we got married in his hometown. He is from a village in Jiangxi, and there was a lot of snow. His family is poor, so I didn't ask for the traditional money the bride should get for an engagement. I didn't care very much about money. We stayed in his hometown for several weeks, and I remember feeling happy that winter. Our life together was not yet difficult.

When we got back to Shenzhen in early spring, he told me he had quit his job before our wedding. Later I found out the truth: he had been fired. Since I was working as a manager in my brother's small real estate agency and my new husband didn't have a job or savings, I had to pay for everything. We rented a small apartment near Sea World, and I also owed monthly mortgage payments on an investment property. That year the financial crisis pummeled the real estate market and my salary dried up. For months I used my own money to pay our employees, until my brother was forced to close the office. I was under constant financial pressure that year.

For six months my husband searched unsuccessfully for a job. Finally he asked his parents to send us ¥25,000 ($3,600). They did, but we spent that pretty quickly. I pushed him to ask them for more, and he did. His mom claimed to have forgotten the password on their bank account. Clearly this was an excuse. The relationship between my husband and I was still good then, but I was stressed and my health was deteriorating.

At the beginning of 2009 we had to move to Bao'an, since neither of us had a job. Bao'an is an industrial, factory-dotted district just outside Shenzhen's special economic zone, and a friend offered us cheap rent in an apartment she had purchased there. It was the best we could afford, but this location was a big step down in the world for me. Six months later, and a full eighteen months after our wedding, my husband found a job. I felt very exhausted by then and needed to rest. Once his paychecks began to arrive, I went to the hospital, and the doctors found another problem. This time it was in my uterus and required an operation.

On the day of the operation, my mother and brother came to the hospital. They were both very worried. My husband came too, because it was a weekend. When I was released from surgery, my mother and brother rushed to my bedside immediately, while my husband dozed in a chair. This inattention made me feel low and miserable, but I forgave him because maybe he was tired from his work at the factory.

During the time that we lived together, my husband's character was not so good. He was very sensitive, and he always thought others were targeting him, even in casual conversation. He also did not understand the cost of daily life, since he had lived in factory dorms for years, where food and rent are "free." He kept talking about a baby, but we had no money. "Don't be naïve," I told him. "Look at our condition."

Nevertheless, after my uterine surgery, I started infertility treatments. I had to go to the hospital once every two days, which was expensive and exhausting. This treatment was very precise, so they always needed to check my temperature. After three months, I ran a fever and they had to stop the treatments.

Then my husband lost his job again, and I still didn't have one. One month later he got hired at a new factory, but he had to board at their dorm and could come home only on weekends. He held this job for one month before losing it. Then I introduced him to a friend and he got a third job with a better situation. This employer was more like a company, not a factory, so he could come home each night. But he was not happy there. He didn't know how to communicate with people, so he struggled to get along with his colleagues, including my friend who had arranged the job for him.

After two or three months, he quit and found work with yet another new company. He made a better salary there and was more satisfied, but after a year he lost that job too. My health deteriorated steadily during this stressful time, and of course his intermittent employment also derailed our fertility efforts. Every time he got fired, I had to quit the treatments, and they are most effective if they continue uninterrupted.

Throughout our marriage, our sex life was never good. My husband didn't really think sex was important. If we had it, it was okay, but if we didn't, that was also okay. This man was my first sex partner. After our first year, I always bled during sex because of my medical problems. Also, the infertility treatments changed my hormones and I began to break out in pimples.

Two years into our marriage, all of my friends said I had changed a lot for the worse. My appearance was not so good. I had gained weight.

My husband gave me a bank card, but whenever I spent money for anything, I had to record it. He also didn't care very much about my disease. He wasn't very supportive and didn't take care of me. He cared only about the result: whether or not we could have a baby.

We had a big fight on our third wedding anniversary. My husband forgot the day, but he had invited me to visit his factory, where he was still boarding at that time. There was a nice park for walking, and I was expecting a gift, or a nice dinner, or for him to at least say something nice. When none of this appeared forthcoming, I reminded him that it was our anniversary. I felt very unhappy.

"Why do you care so much about things like an anniversary date, or a birth date?" he said. I was very disappointed. Our sex life also came up that night. My husband told me that, for him, sex is only for making a baby. "If we knew that we couldn't have a baby, I could go my whole life without sex," he said.

A few days later, our arguing continued. He accused me, saying that I hadn't told him about my health problems before our marriage. I was so angry! I showed him my hospital record, proving that I had seen the doctor before our wedding date. But my husband maintained that I had concealed my disease until after we married. He also said that he thought it was disgusting that there was blood every time we had sex. I boiled over that day. I was so enraged. I accused him of caring less about me than I cared about him. "When we go out, I always buy clothes for you, never for myself!" I shouted, throwing our marriage certificate in the trash. *I'll give this one year, to see if it gets better,* I vowed to myself.

A few months later I went to the hospital again and they found more problems. I needed another operation, one that required me to stay in the hospital for many days. At the same time, my husband's brother had a car accident in their hometown. Just two days after my operation, my husband returned to his hometown because his brother needed money. This made me feel disappointed. Anyway, I was still the wife, and I was recovering from a serious operation. I deserved more from him.

A few months after that my husband lost his last job and did not get another one. He returned home, and I was very unhappy. For a woman, her husband must have a job. I felt that my husband was not responsible, because when he lost that job, we had to stop the treatments for my disease as well as for infertility. I felt completely let down and insecure. And he only wanted sex for a baby! I had decided: I wanted a divorce.

We lived together for several months after that, but we barely spoke. Every day my husband just sat in front of the computer. I remember the day, last July, when I stopped calling him lǎogōng [an affectionate word, like "hubby"]. I was still taking some medicine every day then, and that morning I also had a particularly heavy period. When I got out of bed, my body felt very weak and blood dripped onto the floor. But still, I went into the kitchen, and I cooked two eggs with brown sugar for myself and another egg with salt for my husband. He took a few bites and put down his chopsticks. "In the future, don't cook an egg for me. I don't like them."

I thought this was very cold. "Look, I have my period," I growled, "and I feel so uncomfortable, but you won't cook anything. I forced myself to cook this for you, and you only have bad words for me. You could still eat, you know, you don't have to say such things to me."

"Every woman has her period every month," he shrugged. "It's normal."

This comment infuriated me and also made me feel sad and heartbroken. After that I never called him lǎogōng again, and on the rare occasions that he would ask for sex, I refused him. Five months later, just before our fourth anniversary, I wrote him a long letter asking for a divorce. "Once I decide something, I won't change my mind," I wrote at the end. "Now that I have decided to divorce, I must do it."

He replied to my letter. "Ahh, now that I don't have a job, and I don't have any money, that's why you want a divorce." He reminded me that for a few years I hadn't had a job either, which had put a lot of pressure on him. He also talked more about his sexual views. "If sex is not for making a baby, then I believe it is like rape. If not for the desire to have a child, I could live my whole life without it." Ultimately, though, he agreed to the divorce. We are still living in the same apartment, in separate rooms. But very soon I will move out and try to move on.

Shenzhen Marriage Park
Want Ads of Last Resort

JASON (B. 1974)

In Shenzhen's Lianhuashan Park, seven huge notice boards stand huddled inside a pleasant grove of fat Chinese palms. This public space is dedicated to matchmaking, and parents and grandparents of all types gather in the shade of the palms to read ads, meet each other, and match up their overripe children. Unmarried men and women in their thirties and forties drop by as well, perusing the signs and discretely punching numbers into their phones.

One drizzly Saturday afternoon I met thirty-seven-year-old Jason in this curious glade. Despite a light rain, the place was jam-packed with matrimonial hopefuls. Jason generously agreed to an on-the-spot interview, speaking frankly of his efforts to meet a girlfriend through the marriage boards. Our interview was fated to be quite short, though, as someone reported that "research was being conducted" and Linda and I were summarily thrown out of the park by three uniformed policemen. Our unconventional adventure that day is a story in itself, so I will share our story along with Jason's.

Hundreds of typed and hand-scrawled advertisements crammed the margins of Lianhuashan Park's public notice boards, each one a little missive of hope. Most of the heads that craned to read the ads were gray, and most of the shoulders were sloped beneath the matrimonial needs of the younger generation. And yet they were *there*, willing to try, not yet ready to give up their dream.

Parents Looking for Marriage Partner for Daughter

1985 Hubei Province

    160 cm, very open-minded

      2 bachelor's degrees   First major: Information Engineering

                                Second major: Business Administration

Working at foreign company, saleswoman. Came to Shenzhen in 2008. If your interest is sincere, please call me. If you are not interested in marriage, then don't disturb.

                      Father's telephone: 555–5555–5555

Another one, professionally printed on a pink, floral placard, sought remarriage:

Looking for Marriage Partner

Basic details: Ms. Liu, b. 1979, 163 cm, divorced in 2008, has 1 son, 5 years old. Hometown: Anhui. Has Shenzhen hùkǒu [regional registration document]. Master's degree, government employee with stable job, healthy, open-minded. Has apartment, no car. No bad hobbies.

Requirement details: Man, Shenzhen hùkǒu, under 45, education at least bachelor's, with stable job, financial situation is okay, takes care of his parents, would like to take care of children, healthy, easygoing, has a big heart, and no bad hobbies.

Tel: 555–5555–5555

P.S. Welcome all suitable men who meet these requirements and are serious about marriage to contact me. If you are not really interested, please don't disturb.

A third ad offered a rather unusual arrangement:

Looking for Heir

A man, university graduate, high-level government employee, divorced for many years, in Shenzhen, owns a home, lives by himself. Very easygoing. Now looking for marriage or a friend. (Which one? It depends on fate.) When I die, the woman can be my heir. Will discuss the details face-to-face.

Require: Single woman, less than 50 yrs. old, must have education, must be nice, kind, and not lazy. No children who live with her.

Tel: 555–5555–5555

On and on the ads went, threading across the message boards, divulging the age, educational status, height, employment, residency status, and partner requirements of Shenzhen's hopeful singles. Each board was fitted with rows of green clipboards on which to hang the ads, but many more ads were pinned to the sides, slung from palm trees, or clipped to out-of-the-way places.

Several months earlier, I had stumbled across this section of the park completely by accident, during a hike with my husband and in-laws, who were visiting us from America. The place's mishmash of traditional matchmaking and urban modernity captivated me. Linda and I had intended to go back ever since.

As soon as we entered the thick stand of palms, several pairs of eyes glanced in our direction. I am a tall, blonde American woman, so I often attracted attention in China, but that day I was also the only foreign person in the matchmaking area. I didn't think much of the stares and reached for my camera, desiring to take a few shots of the marriage boards. Linda waved me back, suggesting that might not be such a good idea. She was already on guard, instinctively understanding that our curiosity might rankle the older generation. Instead, we shuffled forward a few feet, smiling at kindly ladies who peeped at us from under their lace-trimmed sun hats and umbrellas. Some were dressed casually, in loose pants and floral-print shirts, but others were decked out in dresses, high heels, even a daub of lipstick.

The friendly ladies were quickly obscured by five smiling older men who descended upon us. "Is she looking for a Chinese boyfriend?" they asked Linda. Still a bit oblivious to the social tempo of the place, I suggested she tell them that we were working on a book about love and marriage and were curious to understand the story behind these marriage boards. Linda poked up one eyebrow at me but dutifully translated this proclamation. She had barely gotten past the word "book" before the men shrank back as though she had said "anthrax." All five eyed me at once, stiff with suspicion. I am an optimistic person, given to wrongly assuming others will understand the purity of my motives and share my excitement over social mysteries. Clearly this was one of those instances, and I would need to step more lightly and attempt to win trust more gently. Swallowing, I moved on.

"Okay," Linda coached, "from now on we don't tell anybody about the book because they will be scared. We will just blend in, talk in a friendly way." She beamed at me with her "closing the deal" smile, and while I didn't quite understand why my presence and purposes were so upsetting, I agreed that her strategy sounded wise.

Approaching one of the boards, we chatted for a while with a sweet older lady fitted up in a blue dress and close-clinging brown curls. She told us she was looking for a husband for her thirty-six-year-old daughter. "Have you found any promising ads today?" I asked.

"Not today," she said, waving her hand as though nothing could be expected from this pitiful place. Two other ladies joined us, and they affirmed her with enthusiastic grunts, sun hats bobbing in agreement. I was surprised. Not a single person in this veritable deluge of marital hopefuls was any good? The first lady explained that while every man sounds good on paper, once you call him, he invariably specifies a heap of additional, impossible criteria for his future wife. "It is very, very difficult to make a match," she sighed. The other ladies nodded and said they too had called some of these numbers but had never found a suitable match either. One woman said she didn't really trust the paper ads in the first place. Instead, she came to the park primarily to meet and chat with the other parents.

"If the parents seem nice and good, then I might exchange information with them and put their son in touch with my daughter," she explained. Then, motioning toward my head, she added that her own daughter was also very tall—1.73 meters (5 foot 7 inches)!—and stubbornly insisted on a boyfriend taller than herself. I offered her my commiseration. Apparently tall ladies around the world have it tough in the dating department.

As Linda and I ventured farther into this section of the park, it dawned on me that my understanding of the matchmaking operation was all wrong. I had assumed people darted into the park in the early morning, furtively hung an ad, and darted away, prepared to await any replies at home. I imagined the boards as a sort of analog dating service, a process prizing distance, screening, and privacy. At the very least, I assumed people left their ads unattended for weeks at a time.

Quite the contrary, most parents came to hang their ad and make a day of it, sitting nearby to chaperone their marital memos. Nylon bags of water and snacks hung from the hardened fronds of the Chinese palms, and older folks lounged on every bench, nibbling lunches, fanning themselves, and talking animatedly. Despite the urgency of their mission, most of the people in this matchmaking park looked like they were enjoying themselves.

While most ads had been printed at home, on China's standard A4 paper, several were professionally produced and others were scrawled by hand on cardboard. Linda told me that the bulk of the ads were for single women seeking husbands. In addition to the normal divulgation of age, height, degrees earned, employment, assets, and hùkǒu locale, a few ads tacked on personality descriptors. Women were touted as tender and charming or open-minded. The proffered men were easygoing and responsible.

In the whole place, I saw only three ads with a photo. I noticed one small picture that was actually a business card, so I peered in to examine it more closely. Along the bottom ran a row of eight tiny women seated on a floor, their bare legs propped suggestively on traditional Chinese instruments. No woman was circled, so it wasn't clear which microscopic young female was on offer. I found this all a bit amusing and had started to unsheathe my camera when a wizened, dark-skinned old man in a loose linen shirt jumped up, clearly upset. Deep wrinkles ran around his mouth and eyes, and he waved me away with flapping arms. "Don't take pictures! You shouldn't take pictures!" he barked in Chinese. Startled, I tried to make conciliatory gestures while I backed away. I had just presumed these ads were public, since they were so, well . . . *public*. "I think it was his daughter's ad," Linda muttered, guiding me away with pursed lips.

By this point I felt like some kind of social elephant, trundling unawares over one tripwire after another. In retrospect, I realize that day was one of my first experiences in a crowd of strangers from the older generation. The older people I had met thus far had always treated me kindly, but they also knew me through friends or family members. The average strangers I met were usually younger people who treated me with friendly curiosity. The older people in the matchmaking park, however, did not know me, and while many were welcoming, some reacted with suspicion and mistrust. Not only was I a foreigner, but I was also intruding into a vulnerable corner of their lives—their children's marriages.

Anxious to connect with a friendly person, I suggested we visit with the one woman who appeared to be stationed in the marriage park for business reasons. "Linda, let's find the suitcase lady." I had noticed her on our way in. She was a hefty woman, dressed in a billowy black blouse and seated on a low stool. From the stool, she presided over a large plastic suitcase, open on the ground at her feet. It held a jumble of notecard-sized plastic booklets fastened together with binder clips. All smiles, she welcomed us to peruse her wares. She explained that she made her living by copying down the park's marriage ads, since each one might be on display for only half a day or less, while the parents were physically present. For a fee of ¥50 ($7.87), we could buy a one-year all-access membership to her suitcase. If we were willing to part with ¥100 ($15.75), she confided, we would become members for life. Considering that one can easily spend that much procuring a few noodle dishes and a bottle of Tsingtao beer in Shenzhen, her pricing scheme sounded quite reasonable.

Partway through her pitch, an older Chinese man tried to sneak a peek at the booklets from the sidelines. Swatting at him as at a naughty child, the woman shot him a dark look and protectively pulled her suitcase shut until he shuffled away. Composing herself, she turned her attention back to us and rummaged around in her booklets to find a particular photograph. It was a dimly lit photo of an attractive Chinese woman smiling into the camera at sunset. "This beautiful woman wants to meet a foreign boyfriend," she told Linda. "Ask your friend if she knows any foreigner I could introduce her to?"

We chatted with this lady and looked through her suitcase with interest for several minutes. Rather coyly, I asked her if she herself was married. "I am sixty!" she scoffed. "Of course I am married!" After we made friends, Linda told her we were quite curious about how she got started in this business of suitcase-based matchmaking and asked if we could come back to interview her. She agreed, producing a pink, floral business card for each of us. "I will tell people about your product," I promised her.

I was curious about the suitcase woman because Linda had come across a notice on the park's website announcing that formal dating services could not use the matchmaking notice boards. Park visitors had complained that too many dating agencies were taking up space with ads for their astronomically expensive services or with large, professional notices for their single clients. The park had agreed to preserve the boards for common use, so the entrepreneurs were out. "She must have bribed the park guards," Linda confided.

We spoke to many other parents about their single children, asking if any had found success through park-prompted matches. One man in his sixties told us he had introduced his daughter to someone from the message boards and the couple met in person, but they elected not to continue their acquaintance. "It is very hard to find a good match, a suitable match," he sighed. Since he seemed a bit chatty, I nudged Linda to ask if he'd be interested in telling us his story. Linda clearly didn't want to, but I asked her to please try, so she spoke to the man. "I already talked to you for a while," he said, averting his gaze. "You can put that part in your book. There is no need to say more." Thanking him for his time, we left him to enjoy his bench.

By now I had the distinct impression that my presence was distressing to some people. And that didn't feel good. Everywhere I walked, people stared. Some came within one or two feet of my face, without blinking or speaking. Taken aback, I tried to smile and say, "Nǐ hǎo," which means "Hello." They said nothing in return, acting as though I had not spoken. I felt like a new bug at the entomology lab. Several men and women asked Linda if I was looking for a husband. One chubby younger guy, afflicted with bad skin and square glasses, kept popping up in the groups of older people who stopped to talk with us. When he finally caught Linda alone, he told her in serious tones that he was looking for a wife, not a girlfriend. "We are both married!" she sighed in exasperation.

Others asked Linda if I was Russian or what I was doing there. Linda kept saying we were just passing by, just curious. One woman, memorable for her extremely swollen eyes, grew quite insistent about introducing me to some Chinese man in her acquaintance. She pressed on even after Linda had explained many times that I had a husband. In the end, Linda rolled her eyes and pushed past the lady, gesturing for me to follow. Creepiness aside, I appreciated this woman's desperation. I was starting to understand that the people who made use of this park came often and spent a lot of time only to reap a paltry reward. Perhaps many of her days had been spent in this very park, taking numbers, meeting other parents, all for nothing.

After about forty-five minutes in that palm grove, I was ready to leave. I asked Linda if she could take a few pictures of the ads close up, so we could leave and translate them later. She told me she was too nervous to do it, so I quickly snapped pictures of five or six ads at one end of the park. We then strode promptly to the other end. I thought we were making our exit, but Linda paused by the suitcase lady. "Let's talk to some of the younger people, the ones who are here for themselves," she suggested. I had noticed a few people under forty milling about in the crowds, and her suggestion was intriguing.

I pointed out one younger man who seemed to already have a membership to the matchmaker's suitcase. He was a shorter guy, maybe 5′5″, and wore a white athletic shirt that showed off a wiry, muscular frame. His teeth were yellow and wandered in irregular directions, but his smile was nice, and he seemed relaxed and friendly. He chatted with Linda for a few minutes and even spoke a bit of English with me, then agreed to be interviewed. He suggested we go to a different section of the park to find a seat and talk.

As we left the bustling marriage boards, this man introduced himself as Jason. He told us he had studied English at a university in Hubei, his home province, and that his job in Shenzhen involved "integrated cellular circuits." I asked if he was an athlete, since he seemed muscular and strong. He beamed and said that yes, he was a runner and also lifted weights. Unable to find an unoccupied bench, we settled on standing in a field while Jason told us his story.

"Several years ago I heard about these marriage message boards. I have lived in Shenzhen for thirteen years and often come to this park, but I had never visited the boards before last year. Most young people come here as a last resort, when they can't find a boyfriend or girlfriend any other way. Maybe other young people like to go to bars, and now many meet on the Internet, but I am a traditional man, so I think this place is better.

"The first time I visited, I felt very shy. The first few times, actually, I could only bring myself to look around, not to write down any phone numbers. After that I thought I should take the next step. I remember the first woman I called. We exchanged numbers and sometimes sent messages, but we never met and she eventually stopped returning my calls.

"The first time I met a woman in person was nothing special. She didn't have any feelings for me, so we didn't continue. Many of the women I call agree to meet me right here, at the message boards. Some are very beautiful, very fashionable, but they always have too many requirements. If I don't meet even one, they want to stop right away. And when they refuse me, they always tell me why. 'You are too old, too short, too skinny,' whatever it is. Come on, I own a house! I don't have a car but this is not a problem in Shenzhen. But these women want more than that. They want love at first sight. They want a good-looking and handsome man. They want to have feelings the first time we talk." Miserably, he shook his head.

I was truly surprised to hear of Jason's troubles. It was true that he was short and his skin was darker than Chinese preference demanded, but I didn't think he looked unattractive. His smile came easily, and he exuded a warm, comfortable sort of energy. He seemed relaxed and straightforward. I felt badly that no one would marry him.

"There is another problem too. If I don't tell a woman about my financial situation in the beginning, she will assume it is bad. But if I lay it out directly, she will think I am showing off. So I am confused! What do they want?"

We had spent only about ten minutes with Jason when, out of the corner of my eye, I saw three blue-shirted men with red armbands firmly approaching our spot in the field. They were park officials, and their expression was grim. Once they had us encircled, one yelled, "Kick you out! You get out!"

They were as upset as I was astounded. I wanted to laugh out loud at the absurdity of it all, but before I had time to react, Linda bristled and shot back. "Why!? Why are you throwing us out?" She narrowed her eyes and folded her arms across her chest.

Jason, by contrast, smiled affably at them. "No problem." He attempted to usher us toward the gate, but Linda would not be moved.

She shouted again, "Why can we not talk with this boy in the park?"

"Someone said you are doing some . . . some . . . research!" the guard bellowed, becoming quite red in the face.

"So!?" Linda sputtered. "Why can't we do this research? We are talk-ing to people about love and marriage in a public park!" Linda, who is pushing eighty pounds on a good day, looked hardly more threatening than a burning match in front of an igloo, but she was furious and punctuated her shouts with fierce gesticulations.

At this point Jason good-naturedly but firmly grasped Linda by the shoulders, urged her into an about-face, and marched her away from the fight, toward the gate. To my surprise, Linda didn't struggle but kept leaping up and shouting over her shoulder at the guards. Resolutely, Jason propelled her forward.

When we were a safe distance away, he tried gallantly to calm her down. "There's no need to be so angry at people who have no education." He seemed genuinely unruffled, whereas my own heart was pounding thickly. I was impressed with this Jason from Hubei.

As the three of us walked toward the gate, he told us a bit more about himself. "Before I came to the park to look for a girlfriend, I had one girlfriend in Shenzhen. But our personality was not a match, so we broke up. I really just want a wife. I don't have any special requirements. I want to be able to talk easily, communicate well, and understand each other. I am more mature, not like these young women who only care about a good appearance, only care about feelings."

At that point we arrived at the path Linda and I needed to take to leave the park. Jason bid us farewell and headed north, jogging back into the park for a run.

Linda and I climbed into the first available taxi, both quite worked up, but for different reasons. As a moderately well-behaved academic type, I had never been thrown out of anywhere. For goodness' sake, I'm the sort of person who would collect love and marriage stories for the sheer pleasure of curiosity satisfied and testimonies made. I found the incident disturbing but a bit exciting too. I knew Linda was upset by the guards, but I thought she was just getting into a fight, giving the authorities a good kick in the pants.

"That was so crazy!" I cried, in a neighborly sort of way. "What even happened? Who do you think reported us?"

It took me a moment to realize my friend was practically shaking with fear. "It was the old people," she said quietly. "You were everywhere, shining, a foreigner, and too many people noticed us. The old people became very worried, so they complained to the security guards."

"What were they worried about, though?" I was trying to understand the root of their concerns. "Let's say that we were journalists, planning to write some secret article about the park. The only outcome I can foresee is that the park might get more popular, and then more people would come to read their ads, right?" I could understand their mistrust, but not their outrage.

Linda's theory was that the parents felt those message boards were a private thing, even though they are publicly displayed. "Their instinct is to protect their children," she supposed, though she couldn't say from what. I couldn't guess either, but after considering this curious day from all sides, I doubt that rational fear of a particular event prompted whoever reported us. I think we just ran into a knee-jerk reaction toward foreigners, particularly Americans, and their snooping.

Linda was silent for a moment but then began to worry aloud that "they" would find her, maybe by using footage from park cameras or piecing together details from someone who would rat us out. "Who are 'they'? Who will find you? What do you mean?" I was confused and alarmed. Had I foolishly put my friend in harm's way?

"Our government is very powerful," she said. "We had better do what they say."

"But our work isn't illegal, is it?" I asked, bewildered.

"They don't care what you say, what your reasons are. In China, they can just put you in jail if they want to." I was quiet for a moment. Clearly, illegality was not the issue.

"Do you know many people who have had a problem like this?" I was trying to understand if she was speaking from fear or experience.

"Yes, of course! Many!" she cried. "Well, at least some." She mentioned authors who had been sent to prison for years for writing about China, a genuine problem of which I was certainly aware. "Our books, movies, and TV shows, of course, all are still censored. But even in your book for America, maybe you shouldn't say anything about politics. Maybe we should not publish any of the stories from the 1950s or 1960s generation. And don't use my name! We need to be very, very careful to conceal our storytellers' identities." She was so rattled. I had never seen her this way.

"Gosh, okay. Don't worry, please, we'll make sure our storytellers and you are as safe as possible. The book won't hit the shelves for two years at best, so we have plenty of time. The last thing I want is to get you into trouble." I don't think she heard a thing I said. She labored through a sort of fog.

"If our government really wants to do something, really wants to do it, then they can do it immediately. They can put you in jail the same day."

I shrank, recalling my cheery, open attitude in the park. I felt foolish and naïve. Why hadn't I foreseen that an American writer would raise suspicion with the older generation? After all, several of my own interviewees remembered a time when America was Enemy No. 1. They had grown up hearing the news from a single media source and had lived early lives free of the cross-dialogue of meddlesome bloggers, warring domestic outlets, and foreign newspapers. I had been too comfortable. I had not considered the risks.

Even so, I was unprepared for the urgency of Linda's response. We had known each other for many months, and she had never given any indication of discontent with her nation's government. To the contrary, she usually took the position of defending the Communist Party, saying that of course there is some corruption and some bad people, but on the whole, they have done a good job. China is an infinitely better place to live now, she would say. The economy is stronger, people aren't starving, and many people can go to college. One time when she was recounting a heated discussion about North Korea with her European-born husband, she said, "We see the North Koreans on TV, and they are happy! They are fine! Nobody looks hungry!" And yet this brief and innocent incident in a public park, when she had broken no laws, had reduced her to quaking.

As our taxi sped away from the marriage park, I couldn't help but think I had learned more about marriage, and about my borrowed homeland, than I had bargained for that day.

The Ultimate Perfect Happiness as a Stay-at-Home Mom

SALLY (B. 1976)

Sally is thirty-six years old and was born in the big city of Xi'an, during the final year of the Cultural Revolution. Xi'an is the capital of Shaanxi province, an interior region of eastern China known for wonderful dumplings and the recent discovery of the terra-cotta warriors. Sally is a pretty, confident woman whose laugh comes in a burst, as though she is pleased and slightly scandalized by what you've just said. After college she dumped her "iron rice bowl" job, rejecting her parents' idea of a safe and stable life for something of her own making. She moved to Beijing, got a job in media, dated lots of men, married a foreigner, and then got a divorce. Shortly after that she opened her own thriving business in Shenzhen. Sally is a spiritually attuned person who believes in knowing oneself well and pursuing change and healing. In almost every way, she has carved a life path for herself that would have been simply unthinkable in earlier generations.

Eleven years ago my first boyfriend broke up with me. The next day I moved to Beijing with a suitcase, a purse, and a big stuffed pink teddy bear. That was it. He was a taxi driver, so every place in our factory town was a memory. I had to get out of there.

Up until that moment, I had spent almost my entire life in that town. It was actually a huge complex for airplane-engine factory workers and their families, some sixty thousand people in total. We had hospitals, six elementary schools, and even our own radio and TV stations. My parents did not work in the local factory, but three of my grandmother's other children did. It was normal in those kinds of towns for all three generations to live and work together.

Out of the forty or fifty families in our neighborhood, I was the only "only child." The family next door to us had six kids! It was very obvious to me that boys had more privileges than girls. If a family didn't have enough money to pay school tuition for all of their children, for example, they would send only the boys. Schools charged tuition back then; they weren't free until the early 1990s.

My dad was the director of a small bus station and my mom worked in a bus-parts factory until the close of the Cultural Revolution. Then she joined the first generation of self-improvers, going to college on the weekends so she could get a better job and improve our social status. Eventually she approached the principal of a middle school and talked her way into a job. That was very abnormal at the time, especially since this school was outside of our compound-town, but somehow she made it happen.

On our street, all the husbands were transport system workers. They all drank a lot, and almost all of them beat their wives and children. It was perfectly normal and very well accepted. My dad beat me too, as did my mom. My parents would say "I love you" to each other, but in a sideways way. "You're my wife," my dad would say. "Who else could I love?"

"You're my husband," my mom would reply. "Who else could I love?"

When they were angry they wielded love as well, shouting, "I don't love you at all!"

My mom was a particularly tough cookie with a very bad temper. She once got into a physical fight with a male coworker at the middle school. She chased him all over the campus, and nobody dared to stop her! I was so embarrassed. When she was angry or upset with my father, she didn't show any respect to him. It didn't matter whether they were at home or out on the street, she said whatever she felt. Witnessing this hurt me a lot, and I felt sympathy for my dad for many years. As a teenager, I often had nightmares about my mom. I would wake up crying after dreams in which she beat me, scolded me, or yelled at me. When I was seventeen, I asked my dad, "Why don't you just divorce Mom?" It took a lot of time and spiritual work in my thirties before I learned to treat people with respect and to respect myself.

What I saw in my parents' relationship was that marriage is rough and tough and lasts forever. But I didn't want my parents' version of marriage. I daydreamed about a different kind of love, a romantic relationship like the ones I read about in Chiung Yao's novels. She was a hugely popular Taiwanese romance novelist, and she wrote about pure romance and love between girls and boys. At the time, every teen girl read her books, and I had personally devoured all thirty-two of them. Some of her stories were tragedies, but most were sweet and their lovers ended up happily married.

When I was thirteen years old, I had a huge crush on another girl's boyfriend, and I felt like I was in one of those romance stories. He didn't like me at all, but I couldn't stop myself from staring at him. He was the best-looking boy in the class. I would think, *Maybe he'll like me one day.* Back then everyone had a notebook with stickers, and I would fill mine with love poems about that boy.

I'm waiting,
waiting for him,
waiting for him everyday.

I didn't think these feelings were bad, but I didn't tell anyone about my crush either. I wasn't girly like that. I didn't really have girlfriends, and actually I looked down on the girls. I thought they were too silly, too fake, and I preferred guy friends. The rigid gender divide of earlier generations had crumbled by then, at least in my city.

Starting in sixth grade, the last year of primary school, boys and girls began to notice each other. One girl in particular stirred up some controversy. In public, kids started to say of a particular boy, "Oh, he's her boyfriend!" They would run their finger from their cheek to their chin, meaning "For shame!" They were parroting what their parents undoubtedly said about this girl. But in private, people were admiring, excited, and curious about this girl with a boyfriend.

A few years later, these kinds of public social judgments deepened. When I was fourteen, people started to whisper about some of the girls. "She's not pure anymore!" They meant she wasn't a virgin, a huge transgression and the trigger for big shame. It's hard to say if their gossip was always accurate; maybe it was right half of the time. No one ever spoke this way about the boys who were involved with the girls, though. They were boys, so they could do whatever they wanted. They could live with impunity.

It was the early 1990s, and the influence of the "reform and opening up" policy had finally reached the interior of China, arriving in Xi'an. Movies from America, like *Break Dance*, which showed black people break-dancing in the street with big, gold necklaces, big hair, and tight tank tops, were very popular. Everyone was learning to dance the "moonwalk" and the "wave," and we had new ideas about relationships. There was a popular saying in high school: *Nánrén bù huài nǔrén bù ài*, which meant, "If a man is not bad, no girl will love him."

I continued on to university, studying English. At that time only certain majors in university were free, like education. Many rural kids studied education, which is why, at least initially, our teachers were so bad in China. After college I was assigned to a job within the bus transit system. This job was in a remote, mountainous area and it had nothing to do with English. I arrived for a week of training along with ten other college graduates. For breakfast, lunch, and dinner, we all ate together in the cafeteria, which served the same three dishes every day. I could see how my life would unfold for the next twenty years, sputtering along in the same dreary way that it had for my dad and uncles before me. I didn't want that life. So I quit.

I returned home and told my parents I was not taking that job. They were shocked and enraged and we had a huge fight. My dad, a shy person, actually beat me. To my dad and mom, that job was the "iron rice bowl." It meant stability. It meant I would always have food and never be fired. My dad wrote me a thirteen-page letter to convince me to take the job. "I can't fall asleep every night," it began. "I feel like there are one hundred cats scratching my heart." That first sentence was enough. I folded the letter and didn't read another word. My parents' love felt too burdensome.

I managed to study English for one more year, and after my parents reconciled themselves to the idea that I was truly not going back to that railway job, they got me a position as a translator in our local airplane engine factory. This factory had joint ventures with foreign companies like Pratt and Whitney and Rolls Royce and kept a staff of twenty translators for international communications. Translation was high-status work, and translators got to hang out with foreigners and go the best restaurants. It was a cool job.

Then, one day, I climbed into a taxicab in my hometown. It was a very nice day, and the driver was playing a Cantonese tape and singing along. He seemed happy and he had a great sense of humor. It is rare for Chinese people to be witty, and he made a very good first impression. When we arrived at my destination, I asked for his number. I told him I wanted to learn how to drive.

We met for these "driving lessons" and I found him very funny, sweet, and intelligent. I felt very comfortable with him, and after our third date, we slept together. We were together for more than two years, and it was the first time I really fell in love. This boy was from a lower-status family and he introduced me to the "other side" of our little town. We ate lots of street food, and he knew about karaoke bars that sold beer for ¥3 (36 cents) and charged only ¥1 per song (12 cents). At the places I frequented, beer was five times that price! His whole way of life felt very fun and free to me.

Of course, these dates were initially a secret from my parents. In our little transit system world, social class concepts were very rigid. By default, my entire family looked down on his entire family. My family members all had work that gave them a status above normal laborers. Even though this boyfriend's taxi was his own entrepreneurial venture, it was still considered a very low-status job. Despite our class difference, after more than six months I decided to tell my parents about this boy. They were furious and we had another huge fight. "Well, then, I won't live with you any longer!" I finally yelled, and I moved in with my boyfriend. He was living with his parents and his niece, and they all liked me a lot.

I lived with his family for more than a year before I realized we had a problem in our relationship. He was cheating on me with a girl who was from an even lower class than he was. He liked gambling and often went to the poker and mahjong houses that dotted our community. This girl hadn't even graduated from middle school and had no job, so she played mahjong. While I was working, he was hanging out with that girl.

The way I handled this problem was to blame and pressure him. I remember crying and saying things like, "You need to leave her right now!" "Call her right now and say you don't like her at all!" "Delete her number from your phone!" I forced him to choose between us, and he chose her.

I am controlling, or I used to be, and I hold people to very high standards without realizing it. I think if such a problem happened at this point in my life, I would listen to my partner, I would tell him how I was feeling, and then I would think rationally for a while before making a decision. I would not force him to choose between me or the other woman. Instead, I would decide for myself whether to stay or go.

Two days later I landed in Beijing with my pink teddy bear, ¥700 ($85), and the address of a friend's work dormitory. Within a few weeks I got a temp job translating World Cup news from the foreign media. My English was good and I worked very quickly, so I published more stories than anyone else. After the World Cup was over, the paper offered me a full-time job.

I dated casually for the next several years before I met my first foreign boyfriend. He was a freelance photographer from the States, and after dating for four or five months, we moved in together with a third flatmate, also from America. I loved him, and we were together for more than two years. I was emotionally dependent and controlling, and when he broke up with me, it felt very sudden. It really hurt me. Now that I look back, though, the breakup doesn't seem very surprising. Almost immediately after our relationship ended, he had a casual girlfriend. He was a big loner at heart, and to this day, he has never married.

After this second painful breakup, I launched into a year and a half of extremely casual dating. Bars, men, sex, it was all very easy in some ways. One friend started referring to all of these men as "Mr. Calendar," since there was someone new every month and she tired of keeping up with the teeming threads of my love life.

None of these relationships ever ended well. I got hurt, or I hurt other people. I had a few friends that I spent almost every weekend with, but we did not share a deep connection. I got tired of it all and I pulled back for a few months.

It was during this break that Shawn came into my life. We met through a mutual American friend, and he offered to walk me home, even though I lived over thirty minutes away. We had an immediate soul mate connection, and I told him about my confusion over real friendship. Shawn said real friends need to be on the same level mentally and spiritually. He really opened up to me, and I felt he understood me. Later on, when I met his family, his sister told me that he fell in love with me at first sight. He is a very spiritual person, and I called him my mentor for a long time.

We began dating right away, and four months later, I was offered a very prestigious opportunity to work with the Associated Press, a top-tier foreign media outlet. I wouldn't be a full-fledged journalist, as it is illegal for mainland Chinese to work as journalists for foreign media outlets, but they were hiring news assistant and researchers. The Associated Press organized a trial trip, and we journeyed to four different places in China to cover environmental protection stories. It was during that trip that I got some shocking news: I was pregnant.

I called Shawn early in the morning to tell him. He was twenty-three years old at the time and living in a foreign country. "Oh my god, that's *awesome!*" he said excitedly.

When I got home later that week, he told me he wanted to marry me and be the baby's father. I, on the other hand, strongly considered abortion. I couldn't take a job with the Associated Press and then ask for six months of maternity leave almost right away. In the end, I made my decision: I would say no to the AP's offer and yes to motherhood. When I told Shawn, he was moved to tears because I was keeping the baby. He bent down, rubbed my belly, and said, "Did you hear that? Mommy wants you too!"

We got married, and I continued working in media until I was eight months pregnant. Shawn was an instructor at a small Chinese technical company, and a few months after we had the baby, he was reassigned to Inner Mongolia. Then we moved to Beijing six months after that, and then finally to Shenzhen. It was during this season of new motherhood and new cities that I started blogging about our lives. I talked about love and work and life, and my stories were touching and honest. My readership grew and grew. One of my stories was recommended on the front page of China's largest website, and my blog got over one hundred thousand hits that day. My husband was handsome, my baby boy had mixed blood, and I was a stay-at-home mom. This whole package was intriguing to people. One newspaper gushed that I was enjoying "the ultimate perfect happiness as a full-time mom."

Fame is a double-edged sword. After we moved to Shenzhen, people began to recognize us on the street. One reader, a sixteen-year-old girl with mental health problems, even created a fake blog that looked like mine and wrote an entry saying that our baby had died. She sent me a lot of angry, mumbo-jumbo messages, but I never responded to her. Another time, two girls were waiting for us when we left my son's preschool. They lived nearby and recognized the building from a photo I posted. They were harmless fans, they were just excited to meet us, but Shawn worried a lot after that. He thought I was too loose with our pictures and information and he blamed me for putting our son at risk.

Shawn was not good at understanding that I thought he was overprotective and too worried, and I was not good at understanding his complaints about me. Now I see that he felt I was selfish and too careless. We both tried to express ourselves, but we didn't listen to each other. We did not shout, our arguments looked calm and respectful on the surface, but really they weren't. I felt unappreciated, and he felt I didn't respect him.

Our problems piled up slowly for almost one year, and the distance between us deepened. Meanwhile, the blog's popularity continued to soar, and publishers started calling, asking if I wanted to turn the blog into a book. I was leading two lives: one as my "ultimate perfect happy" online self and the other as a miserable, unappreciated wife at home.

In his own way, Shawn put a lot of effort into making our relationship stronger. He suggested we make time for a two-hour date every Saturday afternoon. He didn't really consider what I needed, though. He wanted to take me out for a "hot date," but that made me feel like I had to be happy and pleasant, while really I was confused and struggling. I complied with these dates in body, but my mind was not present. What I really needed was a few days alone in the mountains, a chance to be quiet, to rest and meditate. I needed a break, not one more thing on my calendar, but I didn't see this clearly at the time, so I didn't insist.

These dates went on for three or four months with little result. It seemed like the more Shawn wanted to be close to me, the more I lost interest in him. By the end of that year, our problems reached a breaking point. It was a very small catalyst in the end. We got into a fight about something unimportant over the phone while he was on a business trip. "Get out of my home. I don't want to see you when I get back," he commanded. I took this statement very seriously, and by the time his business trip was over, I had moved into a new apartment. I have some regrets about this decision. I think he was more upset and hurt that I actually moved out instead of just getting out for a while. After that he started texting and calling to say even more hurtful things. He told me I was a bad wife and a bad mother.

Around that time I joined an online group counseling site. My therapist told me that one real, happy, strong parent is much better than two screwed-up ones who stay together. That bit of advice has saved my life and my son's life. I think Shawn heard similar things from his own support networks, and because of that we are both able to put our negative feelings aside when we spend time with our son. I got really great help from this counseling group, right when I needed it. After a while I didn't feel crazy anymore. I felt peaceful, stronger, and more confident.

We also started seeing a counselor at our son's preschool, to ensure our problems would affect him as little as possible. We worked out some better plans with this counselor. For example, we had been doing two days with Mom, two days with Dad, but the counselor thought this constant shuttling back and forth might be too stressful for our son. She suggested we rotate every four days, and later we increased it to every week. It was also during these sessions that Shawn brought up divorce. He had already made up his mind, but I told him I would not make any final decisions for at least nine months. He got pushy after that.

"If we are not getting divorced, then I want an official separation agreement," he demanded. I refused. I told him I didn't want to agree to a separation because it was the same as a divorce in my mind. He countered by threatening to withhold the ¥3,000 ($432) he gave me each month for our son.

"Fine," I said. "Don't give me the money. I'm not signing it. Don't try to control me!"

We were separated for nine months, and during that time I didn't have any romantic relationships or any connection with men at all. I thought I had a big crush on another American guy in my building, and I remember telling a mutual foreign friend about it. She narrowed her eyes.

"Well, what do you want to happen with Nick?" she asked.

"I just want him to come inside the door of my apartment, then I want us to have sex, and then I want him to leave. I don't even want him to come all the way into the living room!"

She sighed with relief. "Well, that's not a crush at all! That's just attraction and sexual energy."

Toward the end of our marriage I felt less interested in my husband, but the high sexual drive I always had was still there. Remarkably, I felt this instinct calm down over the months I spent in my online group counseling. I felt centered and productive. Within five months of our separation, I finished a Chinese translation of a foreign friend's book, completed my own book of collected blog entries, and got certified to facilitate online blogging courses. "You look so much younger!" my friends told me.

During those first several months of our separation, I still held out hope that Shawn and I would get back together. My therapy group encouraged me to loosen my grip on that desire, to turn my life over to a higher power. One night I wrote, "We will get back together" on a piece of paper and burned it in the sink. I said to my god, "I turn this wheel over to you. I let it go. You decide." I felt much calmer after that.

That October, eight months into our separation, a friend told me he saw Shawn and another girl holding hands in Hong Kong. I felt sad to hear it but also truly happy for Shawn and okay with it. Knowing Shawn was having sex was a trigger for me. At least I hadn't been the one to make the first mistake. If he could date before he was officially divorced, then so could I. I felt released to find a new partner myself, and I quickly found a fuck buddy. To be honest, I didn't even like him very much. It was just sex. I didn't have to worry about pleasing him, I didn't even worry about whether he was pleasing me! I would just call and say, "Are you home?"

"Yep," he would say.

"Okay, I'm coming over." After we said hi, I'd usually say, "All right, let's take our clothes off."

That fall, when our son turned four, I told Shawn I agreed to the divorce. I felt I was not the one leading my life path, it was my god, and I was just following.

It wasn't until my divorce that I realized how different each family is. Families are not just "bad" or "good," and it is nearly impossible to judge accurately from the outside. It wasn't until my divorce that I also saw that the best marriages are those in which both partners feel free to be themselves and to let the other be him- or herself.

My life is freer and better now. I feel stronger and more peaceful. I am the only parenting decision maker now, so there's less conflict. My personal growth has affected my parenting too. I can give my son more and more freedom and respect. I think giving unconditional love and trust is the most important thing I can give my son, more important than information or education.

I didn't have any complicated moral feelings about my divorce. As my first foreign boyfriend used to say, "Ending a wrong relationship is right." If I could give my younger self any advice, I would just say to take good care of myself first—mentally, emotionally, spiritually—and to be a self-nutritious person. Otherwise, I don't regret any part of my life and I wouldn't give myself any other advice, just that.

A Man Who Could Speak His Own Name

CHOU XIAO (B. 1978)

Chou Xiao is thirty-three years old and grew up in Shandong province, along China's northeastern coast. After graduating from university he moved to Shenzhen to work in the software industry. Chou Xiao is a tall, good-looking man with a strong face and an easy smile. A few years ago he married a woman who loves him very much, and they have a baby son. He sees his new family only a few times a year, during public holidays, as his wife still lives and works as a teacher in Shandong. Chou Xiao's tales of the heart did not center on his wife but on misguided efforts to chase his high school crush and on three passed-over opportunities to have an extramarital affair.

I still remember the day my life changed, late in the second year of high school. It was a weekday morning, and I wanted to go to the park to play badminton. But I didn't own a racket. I tried to borrow one from a few friends, but nobody wanted to lend his racket to me, and this made me feel very bad. On my way to class my face was dark and stern, until I ran into a certain girl.

This girl was not an ordinary person. Her name was Sunming, and she was famous in our school for her beauty, top-notch family background, and excellent scores in all her subjects. She and I were in the same grade but not in the same class. Tentatively, and fully expecting a fresh rejection, I spoke to her. "Sunming, I saw you playing badminton the other day, and I really want to play too. Could I borrow your racket?"

She cocked her head, making a joke face. "Well, that racket wasn't mine," she said, "but I can do something better for you. I can help you to ask." When she spoke, I felt like bright sunshine broke over my day. Surely this famous and beautiful girl would have more influence than I. She could borrow a racket from anyone!

True to her word, Sunming arranged for me to borrow this racket within a few hours. She asked me to meet her after the last class and smiled sweetly as she handed it over. I was very appreciative of this beautiful woman, and from that moment on I studied very hard. I thought that if she could be so good and study so hard, then I must achieve the same level as her.

I wanted very much to chase Sunming, so I thought of a clever idea. At that time I was lucky enough to be on mail duty for my entire grade. Each morning it was my responsibility to collect our letters from the general mail pile and distribute them to the head of each class. It would be the easiest thing in the world for me to slip a letter for Sunming into her classroom pile. I began to write anonymous letters to her almost every day, often taking up many pages. She didn't know who was sending the letters, but sometimes she sent a reply. Her reply was never more than half a page long, and she never talked about love, only about her studies.

Several months into this mail campaign, our teachers rearranged the classes within our grade. Classes usually had fifty to sixty students, grouped together based on some characteristic. The same class stayed together all day, while teachers rotated in and out of their room. I was placed into the class for students whose overall scores were high but who usually did poorly in one or two subjects. Sunming, of course, was in the class for students who did well in every subject. In this new classroom, somehow it happened that her old desk mate sat right in front of me.

Later that week I thoughtlessly placed one of Sunming's reply letters on my desk, and this friend turned around and saw it. "Oh! Who wrote this letter?" she asked coyly. "I think I know this handwriting very well!"

"I . . . I don't know," I sputtered, flustered.

This girl was very clever. When lunchtime came, she invited Sunming to come and sit with us. She wanted to push me to admit that I was this secret admirer. But I pretended that eating lunch with this famous girl was nothing special, and so my classmate did not get the proof.

Soon we progressed to our third and last year of high school, and still I continued to write letters to Sunming every day. Even though we were always in a different class, we shared one teacher in common: our physics instructor. After a test teachers would always pick one student to copy down all the scores on a list, which would be posted in a public place. Since my penmanship was good, I was often chosen for this task. One day this physics teacher asked me to write down the scores for both my class and Sunming's, as we both took exams that day. Wanting to show off, I made a special effort to write each character even more beautifully than usual. I had not, however, considered my plan very carefully. I posted these grades in both classrooms and Sunming recognized my handwriting at once. Finally, she knew it was me.

Even still, we pretended that nothing had happened. I did not reveal myself in my letters, and she did not confront me directly. We exchanged letters until the end of high school, going on in the same style. In the end, Sunming and I got the exact same score on our college entrance exam. Finally, I had achieved the same level as this special, beautiful girl.

Even after starting university, I sent many letters each week to Sunming, sometimes as many as twenty or thirty. I loved her very much, and she always occupied my thoughts. I could freely share my heart with her in those letters, but I could not reveal my name. I don't know why I had such fear.

Then, one day, Sunming wrote to me. "I am in love," she said. She had met someone else. A man who could speak his own name.

Slowly I stopped writing her those letters.

This is my character. I can't do things directly because I always overthink them. When I was in high school, I really wanted to taste love. I wanted to have someone to date. But I always thought too much, worried too much. Until this very day, I have never done what I truly wanted to do for love without hesitating. Only when I have no feelings, it seems, can I act decisively. When I was a senior in university, for example, I had a one-night stand. So far in my life, I think this may be the greatest thing I've ever done. This girl was a schoolmate of mine, a sophomore, and we started chatting on QQ one evening. I only had to use fourteen sentences before she agreed to go to bed with me. What a triumph! It was raining when I went to her place. I didn't have any feelings for this girl; I just hoped she would feel comfortable while we had sex. At the time I thought she thought things went okay. But now, when I look back, I think it couldn't have been very good for her. After all, it was my first time, so I didn't know how to please a woman.

I met my wife soon after I graduated from university. My first job was close to the school, so I took an apartment nearby. One night, after spending the day with a good friend, I escorted his sister back to the university. My friend had some work to finish and asked me to do this because we didn't think it was safe for a woman to walk back to school by herself in the dark. After we arrived she took me to meet two other friends of hers, and I had dinner with these three girls in the school cafeteria. I started going to the university very often after that, because it was nearby and I could spend time with my new friends. One of these girls I liked very much. The other was to be my future wife.

A little while after this dinner I was on a business trip when I got paged from a number at the university. At that time nobody had a cell phone, but I had a pager. College girls were always impressed with my pager, which we called a "BP," because they didn't have any money for themselves. I returned the call, hoping it would be the girl I liked, but it wasn't. It was the other girl, asking me to come join them for some fun event. It was quite a surprise to get a call from this girl! At that time, if a girl called a man first, it made him feel very special. Before she did that, we had always gone out in a group with many people. But her call really gave me a lot of courage. After that we began to go out very often, just the two of us.

Back then a man would never say, "Do you want to be my girlfriend?" It was just assumed, so there was no need to ask. After a couple went out a few times and all their friends knew, everyone understood that they were girlfriend and boyfriend. A girl could safely assume that an unmarried man was not seeing anyone else. Eventually my girlfriend and I moved in together. I could tell that she loved me very much, even more than I loved her. Students are very poor, and they never leave campus, so my girlfriend did not know anything outside of her books and exams. She was impressed by me because I was older and more experienced. I knew many things, I had seen more of the world, and I had money. I knew how to talk so people would listen. All of those university girls thought I was very unique, like a hero.

My wife is nothing special. She is not the best woman; she is just a very normal woman. She doesn't have any special points, other than that she is very good to me. I married her because she was the most suitable for me, the one who fit me the best. She treats me very well, and she always looks up to me, which makes me feel I am a real man. She is also understanding, good to my parents, and easy to communicate with. A good wife makes her family harmonious. I think a good wife should be rational, not stupid, and interested in learning. Her physical appearance is not very important. I like to be around beautiful women in general, but a wife does not need to be attractive.

If I could live my life over again, I would still marry my wife. I think she is a good mother and a very good relative. I have the relative feelings toward her. We call this qīnqíng, or "family members' love." In China we talk about three kinds of feelings between a husband and wife: qīnqíng, or the feelings that make you want to take care of each other; yǒuqíng, the feelings of ease between friends; and àiqíng, the romance and passion between lovers. Probably all couples in China, especially from the older generations, shared qīnqíng, and maybe also yǒuqíng, but very few ever had àiqíng.

Between husband and wife, I don't think romantic love is very important. My wife does not have a very high sex drive, so she does not want much sex. This situation is okay for me. Having sex is okay, but not having sex is okay too. I do qìgōng, a powerful self-healing practice that allows me to cultivate and control my body's life force. Using this practice, I can calm my body and control my sex drive when I am apart from my wife. Qìgōng helps me to balance my energies (qi), to balance the yin and the yang. Some qìgōng practitioners control their body so completely that they can make themselves very light, light enough to walk over eggs and balloons without breaking them. I think the mind is more powerful than the body.

Nowadays a man and woman can have sex together but they don't have to be a couple. Their minds and hearts do not need to belong to each other. We have a saying about this: tóng chuáng yī mèng; it means "same bed, different dreams." It means that your bodies can be close while your minds are far apart, thinking of other people. If I did have an affair, my heart would still belong to my wife, because I can separate the psychological from the physiological. For me, I think having sex is nothing different from shaking hands.

I haven't had an affair yet, but I wouldn't refuse this thing if it came to me. Every person plays a different role in society—a wife, a husband, a friend, a lover. A man cannot tell everything to his friend, nor everything to his wife. He needs to find the right person to share all of his thoughts with, and the perfect listener is somebody who can take care of him without bringing him any trouble. Who can do this? Only a mistress. Her role is to be the person who really understands the man. She is the one who can sit back-to-back with him when he is exhausted. For me, this psychological support is more important than sex. I want a woman with whom I can fully unburden my mind.

Recently I went out alone with a female friend, and we discussed this very topic. My friend said she believes a reasonable mistress can make a marriage and family even *more* harmonious, because the man will share all of his problems with her. I agree, but I believe the man must also be reasonable. What do you call a man with a mistress? Perhaps a mister? "I could be your reasonable mister," I suggested to her.

"Why you?" she asked, surprised.

"Because I won't give you any trouble," I explained. "I won't fall in love with you and you won't fall in love with me. If you try it with some other man, maybe he will fall for you and you for him. But in the long run, that love will damage both of your families." She refused my suggestion. She told me she didn't want to have an affair.

I myself have had three chances to have an affair, but I did not act on any of them. Maybe I gave up on a particular girl who was interested. Maybe I got close with another but lost my resolve. Maybe a third woman was very drunk and could not decide properly, so I didn't want to take advantage of her.

A few years ago, before the New Year, I was at our company holiday party. I drank quite a lot and hugged many women and took many pictures, but I hugged one woman in particular more than others. The next morning I thought that perhaps I had sent the wrong message. Maybe she was confused. So I invited her to have dinner and apologized for my behavior. Afterward I drove her home. But when we arrived, she paused, holding the door handle and looking away.

"You can come upstairs for a drink if you want." I hesitated, and then she confided that her boyfriend was abusive and often hit her. "I am afraid to sleep by myself," she said quietly. We talked for a while longer.

"I really should go," I insisted.

"Don't go. Please stay. You can sleep outside my bedroom if you insist." She was so earnest that I relented and went upstairs with her. I slept in the hallway, keeping the light on the whole night.

The next day she sent me a message. *Last night I didn't sleep at all. The whole night I only watched the ceiling.*

Another time a woman friend called me in the middle of the night. "Are you sleeping?" Her voice swung sluggishly uphill. "I had a big fight with my boyfriend. I am at Window of the World [a theme park in Shenzhen]. Please come here immediately." Right away, I left to meet her, and I took her to a hotel. She didn't have any money, and she had drunk far too much red wine. Maybe nobody would believe that I didn't do anything, but I didn't. I arranged the hotel for her, and then I left her to sleep.

My third chance happened soon after my marriage. After a night out with friends, I called one of my schoolmates, a girl from a very rich family. As she answered the phone, I heard a bottle smash on her side. "I am drinking," she explained indifferently. I was worried about her, so I took a taxi over to her apartment. She lived by herself in Qingdao, in a fifth-floor apartment. When I arrived, she opened the door, and her floor was a glittering expanse of glass shards. She was drunk and naked, standing there without even shoes or socks. I pushed the door shut, picked her up, and carried her into the bedroom so she wouldn't cut her feet. Here another strange scene awaited me: her bed was stacked high with foreign cash. In all my life, I've never seen so much money. I laid her down among snowdrifts of dollars and euros and pounds and yen. I left her there while I swept up the glass, coming back several minutes later.

"What happened?" I asked.

"Go and buy more liquor for me," she demanded listlessly. "If you don't go, I will scream." If she screamed, surely all the neighbors would come to see, and how would this look? Not well for me, surely. So I went downstairs and waited for a while. Then I came back up.

"All the shops are closed," I lied. "So I think we cannot buy anything more tonight." She had calmed down a little bit and just nodded at this announcement. Some of the money had been pushed off the bed, but she still hadn't put anything on.

"Well, then, whatever you want to do to me, you can do it now," she purred, twisting some hair around her finger. She was like a drunk mermaid in a money sea.

"You think about what I could do," I said softly. What I *could* do, I reasoned, was not hurt her and consider carefully what she needed. I could feel that she trusted me, so I just pulled a blanket over myself and slept on her sofa. I was tired, as I had done my own share of drinking with friends before I went to her place. But I also wanted to be sure she would be okay during the night.

A few days later she invited me to dinner. "I am leaving Qingdao," she announced. When we were saying goodbye, she said, "Among all my friends, you are the only one who does not belong. But, only when you are beside me, then can I sleep soundly." In that moment, I intensely regretted not taking my chance with her when I had it.

"I would rather kill one thousand in error than miss one," I replied. This is a Chinese saying—*nìngkě cuò shā yīqiān, bùkě cuòguò yīgè*—that means I regretted my caution. It means that in the future I would not miss such an opportunity.

Except that of course I will miss them all, because that is my nature. As I said, I have never done what I truly wanted to do for love without hesitating. I always think too much, worry too much. I could accept an indiscretion afterward, if only I could overcome my own inhibition in the first place. But I could never accept it if my wife had a lover. I believe she will never do this. I am confident, because she loves me very much.

PART FOUR

The 1980s Generation
Reform and Opening Up of the Heart

> In the old days, Chinese people didn't care about sex.
> Our parents and grandparents just cared about survival.
> Nowadays, though, people expect more.
> My generation wants more out of love.
> —Pan Shanshan, b. 1984

The bālínghòu, as the 1980s generation are commonly called, were born into a rapidly changing world. The economy was booming, the practice of arranged marriages had all but disappeared, factories and cities seemed to leap up overnight, and romantic love clamored to become part of courtship. At the same time, education levels and women's earning potential were increasing, the guarantees of the "iron rice bowl" were crumbling, and foreign products were pouring into the country. Members of this generation were influenced by discussions of love in foreign and domestic books, movies, and television, all of which sprang up in the 1980s. Media from Hong Kong, Taiwan, and Korea were especially influential.

Change can be dizzying, even nauseating, and as this generation reached adulthood, many suspected they had gotten a raw deal. A friend of mine shared this telling and comedic rant about the plight of the bālínghòu, taken from a popular Chinese website:

Before we could be hired, jobs were arranged by the government. But by the time we came of age, we had to worry about our own job. Only after we worked so hard that our head was broken and our blood flowed out, only then could we get a job reluctantly, and that job could barely sustain our life. When we were not able to earn money, houses were arranged by the government. By the time we could earn money, houses could not be bought, because they were so expensive. Before

163

we could enter the stock market, fools were earning money. When we were finally old enough to play, we found out that we were, in fact, the foolish ones. Before we were looking for work, elementary graduates could be our leaders. By the time we needed a job, a university student was suitable only to wash the bathroom. When we could not yet have children, other people could have a hoard of babies. When we came of age, no one was allowed to have more than one.

As people gained more control over their personal lives, China underwent a kind of sexual revolution. Describing the fashion and attitudes of 1981, a 1991 *Los Angeles Times* article attested, "Chinese women still wore baggy clothes designed to hide their figures. Romantic love was viewed as almost counter-revolutionary. And a kiss came close to being a marriage proposal." But by 1991, the *Times* explained, attitudes had changed dramatically. While the children of the 1980s were playing in the schoolyard and taking exams, dating and premarital sex rocketed from nonexistent to commonplace in the society around them. Prostitution soared and the number of extramarital affairs exploded. Sexual satisfaction started to matter to married couples, and many wives were no longer willing to tolerate their husband's girlfriends. For better or worse, it appeared that Mao Zedong had been blocking the revolution his people really wanted: the sexual one.

The collision of changing mores, medical advances, and the One Child Policy meant that the 1980s generation also grew up in a world of skyrocketing abortion rates. As knowledge of contraception was very poor, many abortions were simply the solution to an accidental or illegal pregnancy. Others were sex-selected, though, carried out by married couples who no longer had room for a daughter. The spike in this kind of abortions quickly pushed China to outlaw prenatal gender testing, though some 20 percent of pregnant women still find a way to get such screenings today.

Along with everything else, divorce was also changing in the 1980s. The Second Marriage Law of 1980, which established the notorious One Child Policy, also decriminalized adultery, instead making it grounds for divorce. The updated law also specified that partners could divorce because of domestic violence or drug and gambling addictions. Notably, one spouse could now seek a divorce on his or her own. The powers of the work unit had not diminished, though, and couples still had to obtain work unit approval before filing for divorce.

As this generation was growing up, many were consumed with their education. Test taking was a big deal, as a student's life and opportunities were powerfully affected by the exams that determined their middle school, high school, and university placements. Parents and teachers still universally forbade romantic love in the 1980s and 1990s, warning that such feelings inevitably led to low scores and a bad future. This generation's scholastic experience hinged on test-oriented memorization and regurgitation. Nobody remembered things like sports, dances, or group work happening in school. Many told me that their high school teachers cared only about the best students, as teachers actually earned a hefty bonus for every student accepted into a top university. School might not have been much fun, but this group is the country's best-educated generation by a mile. A full 43 percent completed some form of high school and 24 percent have a university degree: a noteworthy turnaround for a nation that had scorned its scholars and shut down its universities just a few decades earlier.

Not everyone born in the 1980s had the luxury of being swept into the new school craze. Millions dropped out before or after middle school, and millions more completed vocational high school or didn't make it into college. These young people joined the mass migration of low-skilled workers streaming from China's villages to its cities. Working far from home, they tasted personal freedom years before their college-bound peers. For the first time in history, they could easily date, or even live with a lover, without their parents' knowledge. And millions did.

This generation may have new attitudes about the dating experience, but they have not yet dramatically reformed their vision of marriage. In contrast with older generations, 1980s-born people often assume sex after engagement is acceptable. Many are tolerate of sex before then as well, now that dating in one's twenties is considered normal. While this generation expects romantic love to characterize the boyfriend-girlfriend relationship, however, most presume such feelings will quickly fade after the wedding. Romantic love has not really made its way into this generation's story of their own road to marriage. Rather than marry when they meet someone they love, members of this generation still emphasize marrying "because it is time." They care primarily about parental approval, financial stability, and getting along with their partner and in-laws. Born in times of exploding prosperity, this generation's brides now often expect a large cash payment upon engagement and an apartment or car, or both, before the wedding.

Many in this generation are married, but millions more will never find their way into the institution, at least not with a Chinese spouse. According to UN statistics, while 79 percent of women age twenty-five to twenty-nine had married, in 2010 only 64 percent of their male peers had. For both sexes, these numbers are very low and will only get lower. Thanks to the calamitous consequences of the One Child Policy, today's marriageable generations are facing a massive bridal shortage. In total, the 1970s, 1980s, and 1990s generations have twenty-three million fewer women than men. They are playing a stacked game of musical chairs, and everyone can see what's coming: millions of prized sons who will never find a wife.

Today the 1980s generation is 228 million people strong. Often referred to as their parents' "only hope," these young people will shoulder a difficult burden as the much larger, older generations age above them. Their budding households must find a way to support not only the needs of one or two children but also the needs of two sets of parents, and possibly grandparents too.

Girls

BEN WANG (B. 1980)

Ben Wang is a broad-chested man whose satisfied belly and slick hair make him look older than his thirty-one years. He grew up on a farm in Shandong province, where his parents hoped to raise enough wheat, corn, green vegetables, and chickens to feed the family, profiting from any surplus. In this northern region, people usually prefer wheat over rice, making a kind of bun called *mántou* each day. Ben has worked in a number of cities as an engineer but recently joined an architectural firm in Shenzhen so that he and his wife could live together.

The couple married three years ago but worked and lived apart for their first two years, visiting only twice annually. Such separations are common enough, but I was startled to learn that for one of those years Ben had lived in Guang-zhou, a mere two hours north of Shenzhen by car, bus, or train. Even their far-thest separation, Hangzhou to Shenzhen, is only two hours by plane and less than a day by train. Nonetheless, the couple reserved their visits for holiday times, a common enough decision, but one I could not understand.

When we were fourteen, it began: *girls*. At our middle school, six to eight boys slept in each dormitory, and at least in my dorm, girls were the most important topic. Of course, we didn't talk to the girls, just about them, but that was excitement enough. If one boy loved a girl, we would crowd round his bed to help write the note. A good note filled up half a page, or even a full page if the boy's feelings were strong.

Many boys passed notes to girls in class, but seldom did anyone receive a reply. I remember the first note I passed, maybe I was fifteen. "You are charming and attractive," I wrote. It was nothing as dear as "I love you," but still this girl was extremely angry with me. She marched over to me, her face as red as an apple.

"We are too young," she fumed. From that day until this one, she never talked to me again. Even now, when we are in our thirties! If I had written her this note in high school, I think she wouldn't have been so angry. She would have refused me, but just by saying, "We should study hard."

I wrote other notes after this one but never received any note in return. Perhaps you will feel very sorry for me. [He hung his head in mock sheepishness.] But in truth, we boys were not very sad about this lack of response. Maybe we felt a little sadness, a little self-pity, but our love was not mature. Maybe I liked one special girl in high school, but I did not tell her, I just held the love in my heart. We call this *àn liàn*, like your saying "to carry a torch for someone."

When I had a little bit of confidence to talk to some beautiful girl, my greatest hope was just to sit near her at dinner and talk for a few minutes. That was all I expected. Nobody ever snuck outside of school to meet in secret. My generation was not as open as young people are today. Maybe one or two couples loved each other in high school, but it did not last.

Of course, parents and teachers actively discouraged such relationships. They offered only one wise path: "Study hard, get a good job, leave the poor village, and live in the big city. Knowledge changes life." My classmates and I accepted this dream. We studied very hard. We obeyed our parents. Then, one strange week in middle school, twenty or thirty of my classmates just stopped their studies. They did not come to school anymore after that. I didn't understand at the time why I didn't see those friends anymore, but probably their parents wanted them to learn a skill. Maybe they sent them to a restaurant to study under a chef, or to learn how to fix cars with a mechanic. But I worried about them. How would they change their life without knowledge?

The situation with girls barely improved in university. I majored in mechanical engineering and we had only four girls in my department. I never managed to approach any of them! I was very shy. I don't know why I felt that way.

I had a little bit of luck, though, because my university had a modeling department, and those beautiful girls shared our section of campus. We engineers could not talk to any of them, of course. They were too tall, too lovely! But nothing could stop us from watching them. Every day, these modeling girls had to study walking. And every day, can you guess where we were? A huddle of mechanical engineers could invariably be found studying nearby. In some ways, nothing had changed since middle school.

But we did have one new tool for the love life: binoculars. My dorm was across the street from the girls' dorm, and some of the boys had these binoculars. [Here he paused, a bit embarrassed, but Linda and I burst out laughing and encouraged him to go on.] Well, I will tell you one story about binoculars. I don't know if this is true, it is a friend's story. He went to a different school, and he remembered that at the start of classes one year, the university opened new dorms. They had not finished decorating them before the year started, so none of the windows had curtains. Unable to believe their good luck, he hurried out with some friends to buy binoculars at a local shop. But a surprise awaited them. Upon hearing their request, the shopkeeper shook his head sadly. "Not a single pair is left," he said. "The girls already came and bought them all!"

After I graduated from college, it was time to think about marriage. In my village, the majority of people use a matchmaker to meet a wife, and I knew one who was practically a professional. She has successfully introduced over three hundred couples! [He shook his head, marveling at this feat, and I asked if matching was lucrative work.] This woman has another job too, so her matchmaking is just part-time work. According to custom, matchmakers do not charge a fee. Rather, if the matched couple gets married, they give her a gift, like a leg of pork. And she is always invited to enjoy their wedding for free. She does not need to bring a gift.

Eight years ago this famous matchmaker introduced me to a very beautiful girl. I was moved that she thought of me for this woman. We saw each other a few times over the course of several months, but I didn't have a good feeling about dating her. I felt nervous when I was with her, and I didn't have much money to spend on her. After a while she called me directly and said, "Not suitable." I felt very low and dejected when she discarded me. I was working in Qingdao by then, a big city, and I felt lonely. I didn't know many people, and certainly very few women.

Before this unsuccessful introduction, I had chased another woman too. I met her in the elevator at work, and we ran into each other very often. After three months of polite greetings, I started to talk with her more purposefully. I found out we were from the same hometown and had even gone to the same university, but we had never met! Now, we both worked on the same floor of the same building in the same city. I was lonely and didn't have a girlfriend, so I tried to chase her.

"I love you," I announced one day.

"Let me think it over," she said. This was in 2003, but she withheld her answer until the following spring! She waited until I left our office and moved to Qingdao. On April 1, 2004, she sent me a message: "Yes, we can try." But, because it was the Fool's Day, I didn't know if she was serious or not! She was very clever.

After that, if I went home, I would invite her to dinner or to go out somewhere. But we broke up after six months, because of the distance. In China women want to live in the same city as their boyfriend, so it's very unusual to date long-distance. We did not say anything direct like, "Let's break up," we just stopped talking for more than a year. It was not a very deep love at that point.

During that year I moved to Beijing, where I felt more isolated than ever. One evening, as I was looking through my phonebook, I noticed her number. We hadn't talked in a long time, but she answered my call. "I miss you so much," I said, without planning it. She recognized my voice from only those few words.

"I didn't think you would call," she said.

"So much time has passed, but I didn't forget you."

A few years later she told me something amazing about this phone call. She had already moved to Shenzhen when I called and had bought a new cell phone with a new number. She was no longer using the phone I called her on, hadn't used it in weeks. The night I called, she had turned it on for three minutes, just to download a song. Had I not called at the exact moment I did, we might never have gotten back in touch. [He leaned back, in awe over this fortunate event.] Many people I tell this story to think it is astonishing. A miracle. We call this kind of thing *yuánfèn*, the destiny that brings a couple together at the right moment.

After we reconnected, she and I spoke very often, because now we had cell phones. Several months later, though, she suddenly announced she was breaking up with me. I didn't know what I had done, but I felt a great urgency to undo it. For two weeks I could hardly sleep, and I lost two kilograms (4.5 pounds). I knew I didn't want to lose her, but I didn't know what to do. I called a friend for help. "Call her every day, every night," he said. "And tell her only happy things." I can assure you, this message was very useful. I called her every day and every night, just like he said. Two weeks later I bought a train ticket to Shenzhen.

I knew where she lived, so I didn't tell her I was coming. It was Sunday morning when I arrived. I just knocked, and she opened the door, quite startled to find me in her hallway. "Please forgive me," I pleaded, getting down on one knee. She didn't say anything, but she let me kiss her. I gave her eleven roses, which has a special meaning in China. Since eleven is the union of one and one, we call it yīxīnyīyì, or "one heart, one soul." It means I will be loyal, because my heart and soul are only yours.

After this greeting I felt very tired, as my ticket was standing-only and the train trip had taken many hours. She let me come in and sleep. The next day she told me she forgave me and we could continue. [Forgive our prying, but after we heard his romantic story, Linda blurted, "So, after this apology, then you had very good sex?" Ben looked surprised and a bit bashful. "No, no sex. Just a kiss. I was very tired from the train."]

I stayed for two days, and before I left, I gave her ¥30,000 ($3,947). She accepted it. In China, usually a man doesn't ask, "Will you marry me?" If a boy and girl have loved each other for a while already, he doesn't have to ask. We call this yīqiè shùn qí zìrán, it means that everything is going as it should go, according to its natural tendency.

Soon after I returned home, I developed a serious medical problem and had to have surgery. I did not tell my parents or my fiancée about it because I didn't want them to worry. Nobody helped me, except for my colleagues. This was a very difficult time for me. I had just given my fiancée three-quarters of my savings, and by the time I recovered, I had nothing left. For an entire month I survived on ¥20 ($2.63). During that same time, my sister was almost killed in a serious car accident.

After all of those bad things that year, I needed a good thing. "Let's get married this fall," I said to my fiancée.

"First," she replied, "we need a house."

This was her condition for our marriage, and it is a common one. Home ownership is an extremely important consideration for a single woman. If a man wants to marry, he must own a house. If he already has a house, then his wife will feel stable and relaxed. Even if the couple cannot live in the home, the wife will still insist, thinking of that house as her safety net. Also, if the couple divorces later on, perhaps she will get a portion of the value. A new law changed this part in 2010, though. Wives no longer have any claim to property purchased before the wedding. We call this "the law that makes men laugh and women cry"!

My girlfriend knew I could not afford anything in Shenzhen, so she did not insist on that. In reality, I didn't have enough money to buy anything, not even in our hometown. But she didn't know this. Also, it wasn't a suitable time, as the market was at its peak. I wanted to marry that year, though, and to do that I needed to buy a house. So I bought one.

My parents gave me some money, and I paid almost ¥100,000 ($13,157) for the down payment. Still, I had to borrow ¥200,000 ($26,315) from the bank. To this day, that loan is a secret from my wife. She would not approve, because Chinese people usually don't take out a mortgage. We have not lived in the house yet, since we still work in Shenzhen.

We got married at the start of the Midautumn Festival that year, just four months after our engagement. The day before our wedding, I cried the whole day. My wife and I come from different traditional cultures, and we had to prepare many unexpected things and give many gifts to many people. With these expenditures added to the purchase of the house, the engagement gift, and my surgery, I had nothing left. Again. I remember my fiancée and I were walking through the mall that day and she saw a beautiful necklace. She knew I didn't have much money, but she didn't know the extent of my poverty. "If you like it, you can buy it," I managed weakly. But she shook her head.

"No, it's okay, I don't want it."

I cried on the spot.

I hadn't told her about the surgery or the mortgage, because I was afraid she would break up with me. In China, usually a man doesn't tell his wife the truth. If he has some good news, he will share it. But, if he has some bad news, he will keep quiet.

Now that we are married, my wife treats me very well. I almost don't have to do any housework. [He flashed a big smile.] When we got married we weren't living in the same city, and even during the first two years of marriage we lived apart. I moved to two closer cities before I finally found work in Shenzhen, just this year. Meanwhile we had a baby son and kept in touch by telephone. Because of our limited vacation time, we could visit each other only one or two times each year, during the long holidays.

Honestly, sometimes I really missed my wife and felt very lonely, but most of the time I didn't miss her. I believe she must have missed me, though. Every time our holiday ended, my wife would go into the bathroom after helping me pack my bags, and I would leave alone. One time, when I went back to collect something I left at the apartment, I found her in tears. So then I understood why she stayed in the bathroom each time I left Shenzhen.

I think it is very hard for a couple to live far away from each other. I know a number of couples or lovers who have divorced or broken up because they were unable to live together. After I finally moved to Shenzhen, my wife told me seriously that she will never again accept any plan for us to live apart. I think most women share her opinion about life. They prefer to live stably with their family. While it is normal for couples to work and live in different cities—maybe 25 percent or more live apart like this—I think it is not good for marriage. These separated couples can't enjoy their family life, and their children have only a single parent. A couple in this situation is more likely to feel lonely and that causes affairs and unstable marriages.

But if they have the chance to have an affair, I think a majority of Chinese husbands will take it. After we have been married a long time, we lose interest in our wives, and it is normal to think another man's wife is better. I would guess that more than half of husbands have had a prostitute or a lover. Many of these men still love their wives and enjoy a good sex life with them too. They might feel a little bit of guilt over these affairs, but just for a short time. Later on they will forget. I'd say two-thirds of them just explore other women for fun, for sex, not for love. They want to occupy another woman. This is a natural instinct.

For example, I recently had a three-day meeting in Dongguan, a city famous for prostitutes. Lots of my married colleagues visited these women. They had the chance to have an affair, so they took it. Among men, we can speak openly about these things, knowing full well that no one would ever tell our wives. Also, me, I have this instinct. I can't hide it. [He spread his hands and shrugged.] Yet I still love my wife very much. [He then hurriedly put up his palms in a "whoa" motion.] But I have not had an affair myself since I have been married!

We husbands often say, "At home, we treat our wives very well. Outside, we treat other women very well." [He chuckled.] For me, treating other women well is just for fun, but my wife will still be a little bit angry if I have a late dinner alone with a girl. If nothing special happens, then I will tell my wife the truth. But if there is something special, then I won't tell my wife who it was.

Just this week my wife prepared dinner for me, but I went out for a late supper with a woman friend. Finally, my wife called. "When are you coming home? I made dinner for you." I told her where I was, but when I got home, she wasn't there. I called her, but she didn't answer her phone. She was angry, but after a day or two, she will forget. She is not really angry. My wife and I do argue about things, usually about our son or about giving money to our parents. If my wife seems very angry, then usually I don't say anything. I just listen.

If a wife finds out her husband is having an affair, usually she will be truly angry. Maybe half will divorce, half will forgive. If a wife has her own affair, maybe some men can accept it. But for me, I could never accept the lǜ màozi, which means "the green hat." We have a story about a man whose wife gives him a green hat to wear when he travels for business. He thinks it is a sweet gesture, but it turns out she is using the hat to signal her lover that it is safe to visit. So, in China, we say a man "is wearing the green hat" if his wife is cheating. It is a great loss of face. If my wife ever cheated, I would divorce her. [I pointed out the discrepancy I had heard again and again all over China: a man's affairs were okay, but his wife's affairs were unacceptable. I then explained the American concept of a double standard.

Once Ben understood the phrase, he nodded enthusiastically and said, without guile, "Yes, this is a good way of putting it!"]

All in all, I believe that the majority of Chinese couples will share the family love and will stay together forever. But, in recent years, weighed down by the pressures of life, more couples have divorced than ever before.

Six Times Love

PAN SHANSHAN (B. 1984)

Pan Shanshan was born in Fujian, a southeastern coastal province that faces Taiwan across the East China Sea. Her childhood was spent even farther south, in Shenzhen, but after primary school she moved many times for educational and familial reasons. She recently returned to Shenzhen to do office management and recruitment for a foreign import/export company focused on Zambian copper mines. Shanshan is tall, slim, and attractive, with bright eyes, dimpled cheeks, and a vivacious spark behind her warm smile. She talked easily, laughed often, and brushed her bangs out of her face while she spoke.

Tomorrow my boyfriend and I will go to the Shenzhen Civil Affairs Office to register for our marriage certificate. Just last month, before the 2012 Chinese New Year, he said, "Let's get married as soon as possible. Then we can make a dragon baby." In the lunar calendar, the dragon birth year is the best one, because it means lucky and clever. Millions of couples will try to have their babies this year, and we will also try.

I grew up here in Shenzhen, where the young people are very open-minded. I remember that some of the boys and girls had already noticed each other when we were nine years old. Fledgling couples talked privately in the corners, gave each other little gifts, ate lunch side by side, and even held hands. There wasn't any kissing in primary school, though.

Before I started middle school my family moved to Hangzhou, another big city. There some rare students would even hug and kiss in the school hallways! It wasn't common, but when it did happen, the teachers would criticize those students and inform their parents. The parents, greatly upset, would always forbid the dating relationship.

When I was fourteen, I noticed a special boy. I did not speak to him, I just watched him closely. He did not notice my vigilance, but that was my intention. I felt I was too young for love. I only wanted to àn lián, to keep my love a secret. *Maybe in high school,* I thought, *maybe then I will tell a boy if I like him.*

Apparently, the boys had similar ideas about timing. In my first year of high school, one of the boys in my new school (we had moved again, to Hunan province) took notice of me and quickly pursued. I loved him for about two months, but then I didn't anymore.

"I want to break up," I told him.

"Why are you leaving me?" he asked, very sad.

"Because I don't like you," I explained.

But I withheld the second, more compelling reason: another boy was pursuing me and I loved him instead. For six months, I dated this second boyfriend in secret. He held my hand and even kissed me, and my parents never knew. At the end of that year, my parents sent me back to Fujian province to finish high school in our hometown. Parting from this second boyfriend was a little sad for me, but we had only kissed and held hands, so it was not such an intense love. I think he was heartbroken, though.

It wasn't long before a new boy started to chase me in Fujian. This boy walked me home from class every day, since I didn't board at the school. My aunt and uncle eventually noticed this routine and told my parents about my brash suitor. They were furious. "Don't date!" they yelled. "Go to a famous college. Don't pay any attention to these love feelings."

"Okay, okay, we are broken up," I promised.

But I lied. My school held study sessions every evening and I kept up the pretense of attending, while really I was meeting my boyfriend for a date instead. Sometimes I would even wake up at 4:00 a.m. to meet him at a twenty-four-hour Internet café. We talked, surfed the web, or watched movies until the sky softened into dawn. Then I snuck home to "wake up for school." This plan worked very smoothly until I got caught.

On morning my aunt got up earlier than usual and was startled to find me coming into the house at 6:15 a.m., fully dressed. "I woke up early," I stammered. "I was hungry, so I went out for an early breakfast. I didn't want to disturb the household." My aunt was appeased, or maybe just too tired to feel suspicious, and I continued to sneak out to see him for two more years.

We often skipped classes together. After coaxing other friends to join us, we rode our bikes, bought warm drinks, or took a nap in the fields. By the time I was seventeen there were many couples in my high school. Usually the boy would suggest a date and pay as well, while parents remained delicately uninformed. We already knew what they would say.

When it came time for me to take the college entrance exam, I realized my love life had caused me some trouble. My teachers barred me from even scheduling the exam. "You are not prepared," they informed me. "You'll need to repeat the twelfth grade." I decided I should break up with that boyfriend.

After that summer I started attending classes regularly and paying attention. I got a new boyfriend, one who encouraged me to study hard so we could both finish high school. At the end of my fourth year I took the college entrance exam and did very well. Well enough to be accepted into a good university in Harbin, a city far up in the icy north.

This boyfriend traveled all that long way to visit me soon after classes started that fall. He was a bit too late, though, as I had met a new boy. I was in love again, and this time with a better boy, a boy I wanted to marry.

After the first year of college, this fifth boyfriend and I moved in together. We lived together for the rest of school, and after graduation we bought a house together in Harbin. It was a tiny house, and this kind of purchase was very cheap. Eventually, though, we moved back to Hangzhou to live with his parents and look for better work. After six months, I found a job in another city, two hours away from him. He still hadn't found a job, so he traveled to visit me once or twice a month.

By then both of our parents were encouraging us to marry. This is a funny thing in China. In middle school and high school, we cannot tell our parents anything about a boyfriend, or they would say to forget our love and focus on our studies. After university, though, they want us to marry right away! Neither my boyfriend nor I felt ready yet, so we did not follow their advice. My mother and father did not follow the traditions when they were young, either. They actually met by themselves and just loved each other. Somehow, my grandparents accepted their marriage, but it was not arranged. That kind of match

THE 1980S GENERATION

was exceedingly rare in those days. My parents both came from very poor Cantonese-speaking families, each with seven children.

In my case, my parents wanted me to marry so I could have a baby as soon as possible. This was a high priority for them, and they offered to buy us a home. "Your body is young now, so you can make a baby easily and raise a baby easily. It is not important to work now. If you do, fine, but if you don't, that's okay. Marry and have your baby or later it will be very hard."

During that season of living and working apart, my boyfriend and I started to develop different friends and different opinions. He eventually got a government job and joined the Communist Party. His business involved drinking with colleagues and even visiting prostitutes together. Meanwhile, I found success at my own company and quickly became a manager. We both changed a lot, and we started to argue more often. We didn't know how to solve our problems, and we felt very angry and very, very, very sad. We had been together for five years and I loved him intensely, but I knew I wanted a different kind of man.

At one point my company sent me to Romania on business for two months. Before I left I tried to break up with him, but my boyfriend did not accept it. Somehow, when I did go, he thought I had left the country forever. He started drinking heavily. During those eight weeks he met a girl who listened to his sadness and took care of him. They spoke their feelings to each other, and before I returned from my trip, they were married. In China this shǎnhūn, or "lightening marriage," is very popular nowadays.

I have had other boyfriends since then, but none as deep as this fifth love. I worked in Hong Kong for a while and met a boyfriend there. He was a virgin. "That's it?" he shrugged after our first time together. "That wasn't so special."

Last year I met my fiancé. He is seven years older than me, and in the beginning, I actually thought he was very ugly. But now I think he is very handsome! It's strange how love can change your perception. He is an honest man and he is mature. He doesn't drink. I can believe in him and I feel very secure in our relationship.

After tomorrow we will be officially married, but we will wait for six months, until this summer, to throw our wedding party. While most people would not use the words "wife" and "husband" until after the party, for me, I will call him "husband" after we have the certificate, because that is the real marriage for me. We are planning three wedding parties, one in Fujian, one in Shenzhen, and one in Hong Kong.

Normally in China, we hire a wedding host to tell our love story from the beginning, how we met and how our lives came together. Even in old China, with arranged marriages, this host introduced the couple, showed old photos, told their stories, and announced the couple's marriage. Our host will walk us through how to say the promises to love each other forever and will prompt us to exchange our rings.

My fiancé already gave me a ring to wear on my middle finger, and when we marry, he will give me one for my fourth finger too. We have a different meaning for a ring on each finger: The thumb means you are his girlfriend. The pointer finger means you love each other or the boyfriend hopes to marry you, like a promise ring. The middle finger means you formally plan to marry, which usually means you have told your families and thrown a big engagement party and the man has given some money to the woman's family. After this formal engagement between the families, couples can have sex. The fourth finger means you are married. Last, the pinky means you are divorced. Not all these rings are required, though the rings for the third and fourth fingers are important.

In China children are the most important thing to parents. So if your parents are rich, they will pay for your wedding and will arrange a house and a car for you. If they are not rich, then parents and children can pay for the wedding together.

After the wedding, I think a good husband should listen carefully to his wife, be responsible, take care of her and the baby, support the family, and get along well with both his own parents and his in-laws. He should be ambitious, someone who wants to make his own life rather than take money from his parents. A good wife should be responsible for the family, taking care of her husband and baby. She should cook meals, do housework, and encourage her husband to talk to her about his pressures at work. She should foster the communication between husband and wife. It is important for a wife to understand her husband: if he makes a mistake, she should forgive him.

"No problem, we'll do it better next time," she can say. A good couple can laugh together and can understand each other's heart and mind.

In the old days, Chinese people didn't care about sex. Our parents and grandparents just cared about survival. Nowadays, though, people expect more. My generation wants more out of love. I think having love feelings, sharing a mind, and having good communication are more important than sex. Sex is second; it is only one part of life, and it might go away one day. I think couples do not always find it easy to communicate about sex. If the sex is not so good, most women won't tell their husbands directly. Maybe they will just complain about other things instead. But if it were me, I would tell my husband directly. [She cracked a wide, confident smile.]

Everyone Knows That a Girl Shouldn't Like a Girl

RILEY (B. 1985)

Riley is a twenty-seven-year-old architect from Sichuan province. She was my very last interviewee, as it proved quite difficult to find anyone in China who was openly gay and willing to share his or her story. Riley was a friend of a friend of a friend of mine, and when I asked if she would tell us her story, she texted back, "I would love to."

She came straight from the office one evening to meet Linda and me at Sher-zher's, the Coastal City Starbucks. Riley is short and perky, and she sported a bowl haircut, a black Angry Birds t-shirt under a checked collared shirt, and Puma sneakers. After we sat down, I noticed the faint hairs of a pubescent mustache lining her upper lip and a masculine watch hanging from her wrist. Her cheeks dimpled when she smiled. When she laughed, her energy was magnetic.

Riley's singularly long love story spans a period of fifteen years and tumbled out over the course of four interviews totaling fourteen hours. She grew up in a world absent of any language about "her kind" of love, mirroring the society-wide love silence described by earlier generations. She came of age slowly, convinced that girls must like boys but feeling the contours of something else in her heart.

Riley explained that the word for lesbian in Chinese is *biàntài*, which means "sexual or psychological perversion." "It means you are abnormal, maybe sick," she explained. "But I don't use this title. I just say, 'I love some people, and those people happen to be girls.' This love is normal, just like the love in other people's hearts."

This interview had an impact on Linda, who had never (knowingly) talked with a lesbian woman before. She was deeply touched by Riley's story. "Before, I thought gay people were kind of sick, that it was all just some weird sex thing," she confessed to me later. "But now I understand that they really do suffer, and I feel in my heart that my opinion is changed."

I came out to my mom during my first year at university. At the time, I just mentioned it a little bit. I told her I liked girls. This year, though, I had to tell my parents everything because another girl's mom burst into their living room, shouting that her daughter was already married and I had ruined her life. Their daughter's name is Ming, and she was my first love. This story is very long, and the ending is not so happy. Are you sure you want to hear it?

When I was eleven years old, I stepped onto our upstairs landing and spotted an unfamiliar girl sitting downstairs with her parents. Immediately I had a strange and special feeling. It was love at first sight, but I was so young that I didn't know what it was. I just knew it felt good, and I sensed that something would happen between us later in life. This girl was ten, one year younger than me, and I didn't know who she was or where to find her after that day.

A few years later she tested into my middle school, and she brushed by me one day, in a cluster of new seventh graders. Oh, I was so excited! I wondered if this was *yuánfèn*—a kind of destined coincidence that brings two people together.

At first Ming rejected my friendship, because she was a good student, while I acted like a boy, always fighting, gambling, ignoring the teachers, even smoking and drinking. Most of my friends were bad kids too. They had boyfriends and girlfriends and even had sex with them, in eighth or ninth grade. Luckily, a bad girl like me usually has an easy time making friends. One by one, I made friends with Ming's classmates, figuring she would become my friend too. It worked.

Ming became my best friend, and I treated her very well. I brought her snacks, walked her to class, and stuck around to talk with her after school. I hadn't thought deeply about my motivations, I just knew being close to her made me happy.

After a while, the other girls noticed that I treated Ming differently. When I was fifteen, a mutual friend pulled me aside.

"Do you like Ming? Like, *like* her?" she demanded.

"You are an idiot! Everybody knows that girls should like boys!"

I was vehement because I had never considered this possibility. I lived in a small city, so I had never heard anything about a girl liking a girl. My friend's question got me thinking, and then I was very confused. I didn't know who to talk to, so I found a Chengdu psychologist listed in a magazine and wrote him a letter. *Dear Mr. Wong, can a girl ever love a girl?* He never replied. So I decided not to think about my special feeling for a while.

Despite my resolution, I was still always thinking in terms of Ming. My mom wanted me to practice our traditional Chinese ink brush painting, so I would do it, languidly writing Ming's name over and over. I filled up many diaries too. *Touched Ming's hand today—so excited!* Eventually, I felt guilty and nervous, so I burned them all. I didn't think of myself as a lesbian, since I'd never heard that word. I wasn't even sure if I loved Ming—what if I just really liked her a lot? Even if I did love her, did I just love Ming, or did I love other girls too? I was confused for a long time.

Ming and I tested into different high schools, and after that I could not see her as often. Around 2001 the Internet arrived in Chengdu, and I finally read about lesbians. It said my feelings were abnormal and wrong, so I pulled back and tried to change. If I ran into Ming, I treated her coldly. But the more distance I tried to create, the more I missed her. I kissed another girl in high school, but I didn't really like her. I liked Ming. Every night I stood at my window, looking over the scattered rooftops toward Ming's home. "Good night, Ming," I would whisper. I found a chat room for lesbians online, and those other women made me feel a little more normal. But my heart still had a broken wing.

I chose Shenzhen University to be very far from Ming and home. I thought I would finally forget her, but I had trouble making friends and I began to get drunk every day. *Maybe I should kill myself,* I often thought as I drank. I promised myself that I would first earn a lot of money for my parents after university. Then I could end my life in peace.

My nineteenth birthday fell that summer, and I invited many high school friends to a restaurant to celebrate. Ming's family also invited many friends to that very same restaurant that day, because she had passed the college entrance exam. *Yuánfèn* [fate] had brought us together again. I joined her party to drink and celebrate, and later that evening Ming spent a long time in the bathroom. Before she left, she pressed a letter into my hand. "Read this when you get home. Don't ignore your friends for my sake." When I opened it later, my heart quickened. She confessed that she was attracted to me, like a boy and a girl are attracted to each other. I was astonished. Could it be true?

It doesn't matter if I lose face, I thought, since I will die soon anyway. I started to write my reply and found that I couldn't stop. I stayed up for an entire night and a day, not sleeping at all, tumbling through eight long years of bottled-up feelings and thoughts. I filled more than twenty pages with the truth from my heart.

When Ming opened her door the next evening, I gave her the letter. "Tonight you will cry!" I teased. I felt nervous for two days after that. Would she be happy or sad or refuse me directly, thinking I was evil and nasty? I finally called to see if she was okay.

"Why didn't you tell me earlier, so I could have shared your pain?" she said immediately. "For years, you did so much for me, but when you were sad, I didn't know, so I couldn't help you. Don't do something so stupid like killing yourself."

I was elated. Now Ming and I could call each other as often as we liked, and we could talk and share about everything. I started my second year of university, and Ming encouraged me not to smoke and to be a good student. Sometimes it felt a little bit like a love relationship. She would ask me strange questions. "Two women, how can they have sex?"

The next summer we could visit again, and we were very happy. We slept over at each other's houses often, but Ming acted differently now. She liked to hug me when we said goodbye and wanted to hold me while we slept. One night she came so close to me that we could have kissed. I could feel her desire. She wanted to hug, to play on the bed, but I held back.

After that night, I didn't pick up her calls, and I returned for my third year of university without seeing her again. To me, Ming was a treasure, and I didn't want to damage her or break this beautiful, pure relationship. I didn't want to kiss her or have sex with her. In China it is not acceptable to be a lesbian, and I didn't want to heap that life of trouble on Ming.

Weeks later Ming called with a penetrating question. "One of my classmates has been working very hard trying to kiss me. What is your opinion?" Ming is a typical Chinese girl, so good, so sweet. Of course many boys were trying to chase her.

"That is good," I encouraged. "You should find a boyfriend, so you should get together with this boy."

"Are you sure?" She sounded surprised.

"Yes," I said. Ming was silent for a long time.

"Well, I hope you don't regret this," she spat. Then the line went dead.

After Ming got a boyfriend, we didn't talk as often. At the time I thought my decision was right, because I wanted Ming to make a good life for herself. It never really occurred to me that she should be together with me. How would that work?

That year I met a girl on the Internet, and she came to my home to have sex. It was my first time. After that I met other girls, sometimes through lesbian friends, sometimes at a lesbian bar. Because this lesbian life is so sensitive in China, we always have our own circle of friends. Plus, whoever introduces you to a possible date needs to know whether you are the male or female role in the relationship. Even though two women will get together, one person is always like the man, and the other is more traditional, like the girlfriend. When we did talk, I told Ming about these little-bit-serious relationships, so she knew.

In 2008 there was a terrible earthquake in Sichuan. Nearly seventy thousand people were killed. Children were buried in their schools. For two or three days, I couldn't get through to my family or to Ming and I was inside-out with fear. In an instant, I saw that my parents and Ming were still the most important people in my life. I was even thankful for Ming's boyfriend, glad she had someone with her to protect her.

Around that time I got involved with a girl named Amy, my first serious girlfriend. During the Chinese New Year, I went back to my hometown and told Ming I was in love. I was so bubbly and excited that I didn't notice how quiet she was. She had planned to tell me how much she still missed me, that despite the years with her boyfriend, she still thought of me in her heart. But when she saw my sparkling eyes, she choked back the words. After that, we rarely spoke.

Months later, Ming called with important news. "Riley, I am married."

"What!" I shrieked. "Why didn't you tell me? I should have been in your wedding!"

"We only got the certificate. We didn't have a party."

I was incensed. Ming deserved a big party, a beautiful wedding!

"I didn't want one," she insisted. "We only married because of the earthquake. The government was compensating each household based on family size, so his mother pushed us to marry so they could get more money." Years later, she confessed she had avoided a big party because she thought if she really married this man, invited her friends, made it public, then she would snuff out her last chance to be with me.

Amy and I were together for two years, but by the second year we were fighting and arguing constantly. In the end, Amy cheated on me—with a boy—and dumped me soon after. I was so sad that I started drinking every day again. Eventually, I called Ming.

Ming listened and felt very worried about me after that. She called often, and I would ask her about married life. She always said her husband treated her well, and I was happy for her. Her father passed away that year, but she didn't tell me for a long time so I wouldn't worry.

After a while, Amy broke up with that boy and tried to come back. Actually, she never moved out, and we still had sex sometimes, despite her boyfriend. I turned her down, though, because of the cheating and our different personalities. I didn't have the heart to kick her out completely, and we often fought, even in street. One time Amy smashed many things in my home, and then I resolved to break it off forever.

I was twenty-five, desperately lonely, and confused. Many friends and colleagues had stable boyfriends, and classmates had started to marry one by one. Had I made the wrong decision by living a lesbian life? Everybody was always pressing, wanting to know why I didn't have a boyfriend. My parents faced constant pressure too. "Why isn't your daughter married?" If things were already this difficult at twenty-five, what would become of me by age thirty?

I mulled over these things carefully and arrived at an important truth: friends and parents could not stay with me forever. Only a life partner could do this, but how could I find one? Many lesbian couples were happy, but their parents pressured them so much that they eventually broke up and found a boyfriend to marry. Should I insist on my way, or follow society and get a boyfriend? I drank a lot because I could not see my future.

One night, during a very bad spell of drinking and crying, I messaged Ming: *I miss you.* The reply came immediately. *Can I call you now?* We made plans to visit during the upcoming holiday for Chinese New Year.

Ming had become a doctor by then, working at the same hospital as her husband. She came to see me on New Year's Day, while I was playing mahjong with friends. At one point she said that maybe she should leave, but I caught her by the wrist. "Don't go," I said. "After this, we need to talk. It has been so many years, we must catch up."

After everyone left, we started to chat on my bed, and I gave her a gift. It was a Tiffany's necklace, and she liked it very much. We talked for one or two hours, until I could barely pay attention because I wanted to kiss her so badly. For so many years, I had been afraid of this moment. I wasn't sure if Ming wanted this too or if she would be angry.

"Can I kiss you?" I blurted. She stopped midword, her chocolate eyes searching mine. Without saying anything, she closed them and sat perfectly still. Did that mean okay? I froze, waiting for a long time. "I want to kiss you on the mouth," I finally specified. Ming did not move. I was very nervous, shaking even, but I leaned forward and pecked her mouth. We were both silent for several minutes.

"Are you afraid?" I whispered finally. "Or do you regret this kiss? Or hate me?" Ming still could not speak. It was her first kiss with a girl.

"It's strange," she finally managed. "I don't feel like I want to refuse you. It's more like I am expecting something . . . something more." This made me very excited, and then we shared a passionate kiss and touched each other.

Afterward we talked for a long time, airing the many years of misunderstandings and confusion. When we had discussed it all, we fell silent.

"So, what happens tomorrow?" Ming asked, taking my hand.

"I don't know," I said.

"I'm sorry. I shouldn't have asked that question."

The next morning Ming sent me a message. *I don't know why those things happened last night. Do you hate me for doing them? As a married woman? With my body and my spirit both, I have cheated on my husband.*

Don't say that, I wrote back.

Do you want to return to our prior friendship?

Okay, if you want to return, then I won't do anything like last night again.

Ming came over that night, but we didn't touch because of our agreement. We felt embarrassed and awkward until I fell asleep watching a movie. I woke up to Ming's kiss.

"Whahh?" I blubbered, confused, grasping for consciousness.

"I was just checking if you were sleeping," she giggled.

"Don't disturb me or you will be responsible for the outcome," I warned her. She leaned forward and kissed me again. Then we had sex. The next night, our third date, we slept together again.

After these three days, we talked and talked over what to do, but we couldn't see any solution. "We should stop," Ming finally decided. "Let's not do this anymore. We can't see each other again." I felt very sad.

"Okay, if this is what you want, then I will accept it. But I will remember these three days forever."

"Me too," promised Ming.

I tried not to message her the next day, but she broke down first. *It's difficult to control, not to miss you. So many years I could contain it, but now I feel I cannot.*

If you can't contain it, what hope is there for me at all? I wrote back.

Maybe we can change our promise not to see each other anymore? We agreed that she would take me to the airport in the morning.

Bring the letter, I requested.

I was feeling reflective because of the New Year, and I had a sudden urge to reread the letter I had written Ming six years earlier. On the bus to the airport, I read it over, my eyes filling with tears. "Don't read anymore!" Ming finally urged. "I want to see you smiling when you leave!"

Swallowing hard and wiping my face, I took her hand. "Now, I will give you a promise. From now on, I will wait for you. It doesn't matter if ten years pass or twenty, whenever you feel it has been enough with your husband, then you can come back to me. It doesn't matter who I am with or where I am, I will return to you immediately."

"Don't wait for me," Ming whispered.

"You have your own choices to make in life and I have mine. This is my promise to give, so you can't stop me from making it."

The day had been bright and fresh until then, but as soon as we said goodbye, the sky burst into rain. "Look outside, such heavy raining,"

I wrote from the plane. "I feel that even God is crying for us. For too many years, my love for you was too young, too immature. But now I will grow up. I will learn to love you as a grownup."

I woke up to a message from Ming. Its four words sank like a stone: *I want a divorce.*

Please don't think about divorce! I felt charged with anxiety. *I really disagree. What about your mom, your husband? It is hard to find a family. Don't throw it away. Come visit me, but don't do this thing. You can come only if you promise not to destroy your own life!*

She agreed. Ming was coming to Shenzhen! I whirled about, very happy, preparing many things. We talked excitedly every night.

Two days before Ming's flight, I picked up a call from a new number. "Do you know who I am?" It was a man's voice, broken with sobs. "I am Ming's husband. Can you keep your promise that you will always take care of her?"

"Yes, I can take care of her always," I stumbled, a bit in shock. "And I need to say sorry to you, for all of this."

"No, you don't need to say sorry, just always take care of her." He hung up, and I felt that he was a very good person. Despite her promise not to ruin her life, Ming had told him about us and showed him the letter. He read it for over an hour and cried, while she held his hand. After they talked, he told her he would accept her idea to divorce.

By the morning of Ming's flight, however, his friends had convinced him not to let Ming go. He tried to stop her, but she insisted. In a fury, he told Ming's mother about the divorce and me. She exploded.

"I don't understand why you want to ruin your life!" she wailed. "Your father is dead, so now I am all alone. Your older brother is already divorced and has no job. He just uses drugs and drinks and runs with the black society. He lives like a dead person. All of my hope is fixed on you. When your brother divorced, I really couldn't take it. You are sending me into my grave!"

In desperation, Ming let her mother read the letter too, hoping she would see our love and understand. Her mother read it in silence. She didn't say anything else, but she kept the letter. Ming got her to agree to the Shenzhen trip, but only for the purpose of ending our relationship forever.

THE 1980S GENERATION

When Ming arrived, I brought her around to so many places—the beach, KTV [karaoke], and dim sum with friends. I shared my special lake at Shenzhen University, showing her the place where I sat for many hours after the earthquake, reflecting on my love for her. As she and I walked around the lake, I gave her a gift. I had bought a matching set of watches, one for her and one for me.

"This watch is a symbol of waiting," I told her, fastening it on. "I want you to know that I will wait for you. I don't want to give you any pressure, and I don't mean for you to do something right now. Even if you still want to stay with your husband, I can wait. This gift just means that I am giving you my time."

A few days after Ming returned to Sichuan, she and her husband visited the Civil Affairs Office to formally end their marriage. The next evening, Ming's mother forced her way into my parents' home. "Look, everything is your daughter's fault! She has destroyed my daughter's life!" She waved the letter in their faces. My cousin called to report from the front lines.

"Oh, now there is big trouble! Ming's mom tore in here and now your mom is crying. She is so angry." I felt sick. In desperation, I called my parents many times, until my dad finally answered.

"Look, your mom is very tearful, very sad, so she does not want to talk to you right now. Up until now, we have not bothered you. We have not demanded anything about your life, because you have always been a good girl. Think to yourself now, how are your parents going to live with no face? We saw your letters. You were good to Ming. You wanted her to have a good life. It's not all your fault. But look at all these problems—Ming is divorced, and her mother and your mother are heartbroken. Don't you think you are being too emotional?"

My dad is old, so he can't understand what happened between Ming and me. He has been a good husband, a good father, but he doesn't know what love is. He doesn't understand our kind of love. My dad divorced his first wife and later married my mom, but they never shared romantic love, just family love. In his generation, people just married because it was time. Even among my own generation, people don't usually marry for love. They marry because they must, so they don't think about the love part as much. I didn't expect my dad to understand, but I had hoped my mom would, because sometimes I take my mind to my mother.

For days I called, and my mom wouldn't talk with me. She only cried. "Mom, this situation hurts you too much. I don't want you to suffer like this, but I can't control it. I love Ming so, so much, and she and I finally have this chance to be together. I can't give up this chance. I hope you can understand me."

After all of this, Ming and I felt happy and sad and so mixed up. When we could talk about our future plans and dreams, then we felt very happy. But the path to that future was littered with the people we hurt in the process, so we often grew quiet and sad. Was our relationship right or wrong? A joyous love or a catastrophe? We didn't know. Were we selfish to think we could really love each other, just because we wanted to?

Ming had it much worse than I did and was often tearful on the phone. She was surrounded by pestering colleagues who didn't understand her divorce. "Why would you do this crazy thing? You can still go back to him!" Nobody understood her, except for one friend who knew the real story. Her mother never relented, either. Ming told her our relationship was finished, of course, but one day her mom called me to say that if I got back together with Ming, she would kill herself in my parents' living room. After that, Ming was afraid to talk to her mom. Her ex-husband still sent her regular messages, too. Sometimes he would write, *I hate you, you screwed up my life, and I can hardly live. I want to die.* Other times his tone was gentle, pleading: *Please come back. I wait only for you.*

Ming started to have trouble falling asleep, and when she did, she lapsed into nightmares and turbulent dreams. I felt so sad and guilty about her sufferings. "When I am talking with you, listening to your voice, those are the only moments I feel happy in the whole day," she whispered to me one night.

Had I destroyed everything? I didn't know how to help her. I just listened to her tears with a broken heart.

A few months later I flew to Sichuan and stayed with Ming for seven days in her new apartment. That week was one of the happiest times I've ever had. When she got out of work, Ming would come home and cook for me. She never wanted me to do any housework, just wait for food and chat with her. I felt so happy. We both dared to hope: Maybe this is our future? We loved every minute we could be together. When I dragged myself back to Shenzhen that time, I couldn't hide my tears from Ming.

Ming came to visit me in Shenzhen a few months later, but otherwise we could only talk over Skype and in phone calls. It was painful not to be together in person, and the distance made it hard to maintain our relationship. Every time I said I would be out late with friends, Ming would chirp, "Okay, no problem," but inside she was unhappy. She would wait up until midnight to talk to me, but I would be too exhausted to say much. This kind of thing made Ming very upset, and we started to argue frequently about this problem, and about Amy, who was still in my life, and about how to solve all of our other problems. We were not as happy as before.

By the end of the summer, Ming wanted to break up. "Ming," I pleaded, "we worked so hard to get here. Why do you want to give up? Don't you know that I plan to move back to Chengdu, to buy us a house and a car? We can even make a baby. Don't you want this life?"

"I do want to keep our relationship!" she insisted. "I have desperately wished I was an orphan, so I wouldn't have this pressure from my mom. I fantasize about running away all the time. But I can't sleep, I'm developing social anxiety, and I've started taking psychiatric medicine because I can't stop the roar of my own thoughts."

I knew it was true, and my heart ached because this suffering was not what I had wanted to give Ming. I hadn't wanted to lose her, and I hadn't wanted to hurt her, but everything had gone terribly wrong. I had hurt her, and I had lost her. I was the one who had brought things to this point, so I should be the one who was strong enough to let go.

"Okay, I understand. I respect your decision," I choked, warm tears flowing down my cheeks.

We lasted two days. *Can't break up. I miss you*, Ming wrote. So we started talking every day again and limped along for another two months, until we started to fight for all the same reasons. In September Ming called things off for good.

Every day after that, I was drunk and crying. I messaged her sometimes. *Are you sure you have considered this carefully?*

Yes, this time I have decided for sure. I had always pushed her to choose a normal life, but now I could not accept it. I couldn't sleep, couldn't go to work, couldn't do anything.

The only thing left to do was fly to Sichuan and try to convince Ming to come back. I bought a ticket quickly, rushing and feeling many things. The next day I showed up at her hospital. "I just want to talk for a minute," I implored, sitting next to her in the cafeteria.

She started but composed herself quickly. "You have come too far. So, what do you have to say?" She was like ice, and I felt flustered.

"I . . . I don't know what I want to say!"

"Okay, so that's it? You have nothing to say?" She crossed her arms.

"Well, when I bought my ticket, I wanted to say, 'Give me another chance.' I took too much time to think, Ming. I never wanted to disturb your life, so I was always tentative. I never insisted, 'Please, stay together with me forever.' I never fought to win you. You had to do everything—get a divorce, change your life—while I did nothing. I came here because I need to do my best this one time. I need to fight to get you, to make sure that I ask you to give me one more chance. If you won't accept me now, then maybe I will quit my job in Shenzhen, come back here, and do nothing except try to win your heart."

Ming rolled her eyes and gave a hollow little chuckle. "You know, I used to think you were kind and mature. But now I see how childish you've always been. You'll do 'nothing but try to win me back,' eh?!" She spat sarcastically. "What kind of life is that? I have to go. I'm very busy."

She stood up to leave me, but I caught her wrist. She wasn't wearing the watch anymore.

"What do you want? Tell me," I pleaded.

"I want you to have a good life, and I do really hope that you'll have one. But I know you, always drinking, smoking, and skipping work, so I know you won't really be able to take care of yourself." I was crying by this point, but her face was a pool of taut indifference. She was like a stranger.

I followed her secretly down a hallway, and when she saw me, she pulled me into an empty office.

"You are so childish!" she hissed. "You are not realistic. Before, we were both too selfish. I just want to go back to my proper life. I hurt the people that I love, and I think that was wrong. I want to be a good daughter, and taking care of my mom is my basic guiding principle in life. Lately I haven't been a good daughter, and I haven't been a good person either. I can't keep grabbing everything I want like before. I am going back to my ordinary life, and I don't want you to come. You can't join me there."

"I understand how you feel, but why do things have to be this way? You and I don't want to hurt anybody. We just want to be together."

"Maybe it's *yǒu yuán wú fèn*," Ming shrugged, using a phrase that means "fate without destiny," for a couple who is fated to meet but not destined to stay together. "I hope I won't see you face-to-face again for a long time. Maybe in a few years we can be friends."

"Impossible!" I shouted hotly. "I will never be your friend! Because I will love you forever, so I can never be your friend!"

That night I couldn't sleep. I just stayed up, drinking and fuming and crying, until eight in the morning. When I banged on Ming's door a half hour later, she answered it. "Why are you here?" she asked as though she didn't care.

Then I did a stupid thing. I pushed Ming back through her doorway and shut the door. She didn't resist, so I flung her onto her bed. Tearing at her clothes, I pulled them off and tried to rape her. Maybe it will be good for her, I told myself. I want her to hate me. I thought she would hate me, slap my face, scream, do something. But Ming didn't do anything. She gave no reaction, made no sound, just lay limp like a dead fish. Finally I stopped my charade.

"You aren't angry? Why?"

"Why do I need to be angry?" she sighed. "You don't need to do this thing. You can't get what you want."

I finally understood that Ming had already given up. Anything I did was going to be wrong. In despair, I fell down on her body, crying desperately.

She hugged me, patting my back. "Everything will be fine. It will pass by."

After several minutes, I stood up, and then I kissed her and took my bag to leave.

She stopped me at the door, catching my arm. "It's raining outside. You'll need an umbrella."

"Just let me go," I said heavily. She didn't drop my arm and didn't say anything either. She looked so small now, like a wet cat. I peeled her fingers off gently. "I hope you will be fine in the future, Ming, and happy. I hope you'll have a good life, a better life than me." Then I slammed the door in her face.

The end of Ming still feels like a dream. It was just a few months ago, but I heard she already moved back in with her husband. I've called her only one time, when I was drunk. "You are so selfish," I slurred. "You didn't even give me a chance. You think I'm poison or what? Now you and your husband are starting over again. How nice for you, just like nothing ever happened between us. I wish I had never met you, Ming Fong!"

And it's true. I loved her for fifteen years just to be together as lovers for fifteen days. It wasn't worth it! But another part of me believes that we still love each other. Fifteen days ago I met a new girl named Emma. She knows everything about Ming, and she thinks we'll get back together one day. "Her mama will have to die one day," she pointed out. "Maybe after that, she will find you again." But I think it's impossible. Ming will have a baby by then, and she will have to make a normal family. She and I will never be normal, so I cannot spend any more hope on our love.

A Wife of Noble Character, Who Can Find?

LIGHTLY CHANCHAN (B. 1985)

Lightly is twenty-six years old and grew up in a town in Hunan, a landlocked southern province. She was not raised in a religious home, but in 2006 she converted to Christianity and got involved in a local church. I was curious about the life experience of religious people, since the Communist Party extends a tenuous hand at best to gatherings of the faithful. Christianity is officially recognized in China, along with Islam, Buddhism, and Taoism, and churches can register and operate somewhat freely. Government control may be exerted at any time, though, and the extent of religious freedom is often dependent on the opinions and inclinations of local leaders. In most places, foreigners and locals must worship separately, to prevent unwelcome missionary work. Foreigners can show a passport in order to get into "international" churches, while Chinese citizens must go to locally approved churches.

Lightly has lived in Shenzhen for a few years now and currently works as a foreign-language teacher. We were introduced by a mutual friend and met up one afternoon at a bus stop near Shenzhen University. Lightly is a short, cute girl with shoulder-length hair and a ready smile. By the time she arrived, she was running quite late.

"I had to cook lunch for my husband," she apologized, slightly out of breath. "He doesn't do any housework." She sighed and brushed her blunt bangs from her eyes. "I prepared bone soup for him, which takes forty minutes, and I probably wasted some time too. I am sorry to be late."

Smiling brightly, Lightly took me to a trendy tea café where we sat in free-hanging swings and sipped milk tea with black tapioca pearls while we talked. She had found a two-for-one deal for the place online, which made me smile because I love a good coupon too. Lightly had married for love and was forthcoming about some of the difficulties in her marriage.

Several months after our interview, the mutual friend who had introduced me to Lightly shared her own concerns about the marriage. "Actually I wanted her to divorce her husband. He may be Christian, but he is not a loving man. He only ever says critical things to her, like, 'Oh, you don't look very nice today.' Never anything positive. I think he just abuses my friend emotionally." I couldn't help sharing some of her sentiment and recalled how I had wished Lightly's husband was a kinder man as I listened to her story.

Two years ago, in front of all of our students, a fellow teacher asked me, "So, what are your requirements for a spouse?"

"Only one," I told her. "He must be a Christian."

After a moment's pause, one student raised his hand. "Hey, I have a friend who is a Christian. He is a college classmate of mine. Maybe you can go for a try?"

In China only one person in one hundred usually knows anything about God, so I was surprised this student had a Christian friend. As it turned out, his friend was from my same hometown! He was a youth pastor and a guitar player in a band. He had returned to our hometown just the month before to pray with a Christian sister who had cancer. I felt he was a very special person.

"To protect you, let's meet downstairs in your apartment building," he suggested before our first date. So we did, and we talked for several hours. Later that same night, we prayed on the phone together, which was quite emotional. We both cried. Almost immediately, we felt we had met the right person.

When I was in high school, teachers didn't allow dating. If they saw any couple holding hands, they would tell their parents immediately. Still, the boys would always pass notes to the pretty girls. Some aggressive girls would even pass notes to the boys! These notes were very direct, like, "Be my boyfriend." These aggressive girls would send text messages to the boys too, inviting them to watch a movie or have dinner. Not dinner at their own house, of course, because such boys must be kept hidden from parents. They would ride their bikes to the date instead.

I was a good student, so I never had a boyfriend in high school. But in my heart, I liked some of the boys, and I wrote all my secrets in a diary. If I had a crush on a boy, I would tell my best friends too. One crush I had was very intense. That boy figured it out eventually, because I blushed every time I saw him. I felt very shy. He was an older boy, and he liked a pretty girl in my class. In my heart, I was very sad and hurt about this boy. I cried a lot over him, and I listened to music and wrote in my diary. I felt broken in my heart.

One time I wanted to talk to my mom about this boy. I reached for words, finding only useless ones. I told her there was a good boy at school, a top student, and that many girls liked him. I couldn't make myself clear. I couldn't tell her I was one of these girls and that I wanted her guidance. My mother knew later on about my love, but she never said a word. I wish she could have talked with me. I wish she could have said, "Move on, Chanchan. Move on."

Dating was a little more open by the time I started university. Some girls dated just for fun in their freshman year, but I was the kind of girl who seldom dated, even as a senior. Some couples lived together, and some Christian couples did too. Our university could accept dating, but they were against pregnancy. Students would be shocked to hear if someone was pregnant, and the university would suggest that woman drop out. A pregnant student on campus was shameful. It meant the teachers did not supervise well.

Abortions were also common. I knew a few girls who had an abortion in college, and it was very sad for them. All Chinese feel abortion is sad, but non-Christians don't think abortion is morally wrong. For a Chinese Christian, though, abortion is always a sin.

I started with my first boyfriend when I was twenty-three. Before I met my husband, I dated several guys who were not so good. They didn't have the same rules to respect, and they didn't follow God's way of loving a woman. After breaking up with those boys, I wanted a Christian man. But after I got one, I could hardly stand my new boyfriend's caution. I was eager to hold hands and to kiss him, but he didn't want to touch me or even feel any attraction. He was fearful for the Lord. "Affection doesn't mean I love you," he said.

He was not alone in his diligence. Another sister's boyfriend would touch her only above the shoulders! She was quite proud of him. Later on I understood that my boyfriend was actually being good to me.

He was never very romantic with me, though. I was always the one asking, "When will you marry me?"

Finally, he encouraged me. "Before we can be married, you should read the Bible five times," he said. So I read it five times. I told him the very day I finished.

"I'm only on Exodus [the second book of sixty-six]," he said. He is such a good boy.

I think the purpose of dating is to look for a husband. Before I became a Christian, I thought the ideal husband should be loving, adorable, good-looking, and nice to his wife. I didn't have any financial requirements, since I wasn't very materialistic. I wanted a man who would care about his children and be responsible for his family. After I became a Christian, though, I also valued a very honest man, one who wouldn't cheat on his wife. In Chinese we call cheating chūguǐ, "going off the correct path." I think most of my peers agree that you shouldn't cheat, even if they don't believe in God.

If there is an affair, some couples might divorce, but it's more common to cheat and stay married. Many men who find a mistress are rich, but others are just under lots of pressure. Maybe their wives berate them for many things, so they seek comfort where they can. This happened to one of my adult students. He was a rich businessman, and his ex-wife was very aggressive. She never said anything gentle, and this made him want other women. He cheated, and after she discovered it, they fought every day. She wouldn't forgive him, so they divorced.

I had another student who cried while introducing herself on her first day of class. She said she was learning English because she wanted to be financially independent. Then she added, her eyes leaking silent tears, "I also need to keep busy and distract myself because I'm getting a divorce. My husband cheated on me and then moved out to live with a younger, prettier woman." That poor woman was very upset.

Divorce is growing more common in China, and it's quite easy to get one. You just go to the same bureau that registers marriages. It's actually done in the same room! There is a queue of happy couples on one side of the room and a queue of sad couples on the other. There are many jokes about this problem. We say people who want a divorce must get up early to beat the lines. If there is a fight over whose turn it is at the end of the day, one couple will shout, "We must divorce today! We cannot wait another minute!" Nowadays many young people don't want to bother with the responsibility of getting married, so they just live together.

"Okay, congratulations, now you will get married," my boyfriend announced one day. His mom had told him to prepare something for our wedding, which meant she accepted me. His family visited my family during the Chinese New Year holiday, and his dad asked my dad's permission for the marriage. My mom knew I loved him, so my parents said yes.

Soon after, one of our friends announced our engagement to the whole church. While I was up front with her, she asked, "So, how did Addison propose?"

"Well, he didn't exactly," I admitted.

So she made him propose then and there in front of everybody. He got down on one knee. "Thank you for your love, for being a fighter for us, for always loving me. Will you marry me?"

Proposals are becoming more common in China. Some boys will ask their girlfriends at Starbucks, or Pizza Hut, or in front of the mall, with a ring and flowers. But my boyfriend was not very romantic. A simple ring is okay for me. I can't have a diamond. I need to do housework! Anyway, you can change your ring every five years.

My husband and I talked a little bit about sex before we got married, but he didn't want to talk very extensively. He didn't want to be tempted, he said. Actually, nobody ever talked to me about sex in my whole life, except for one girlfriend, so I didn't know anything.

We invited six hundred guests to our wedding, and we used the opportunity to introduce the Gospel to our nonbelieving relatives. After the wedding we traveled to Xinjiang province with another couple from our church. Xinjiang is an enormous place in northwest China, along the borders of Pakistan and Afghanistan. It is the homeland of the Chinese Muslims. We traveled to many places, visiting the desert and the snow-peaked mountains and trying delicious new foods. They have wonderful fruit in Xinjiang, excellent watermelons, apricots, mulberries, and figs. I loved them all.

We went to this region to buy a house, actually. My husband has a call to preach to the Chinese Muslims, and our new home is quite close to the border of Pakistan. I feel okay about moving there. We are moving with the couple who joined our trip, because they feel the same call. This is very dangerous work, since the Chinese Muslims will kill the Christians as infidels. Many have already died, at least fifty, but the government does not publicize this news. They want to create a very lively picture, showing that things are okay everywhere. But we cannot even see YouTube or Facebook or Twitter because they are blocked! I heard about a sister in Beijing who is in prison now. She made a video of another sister's testimony, and it became very popular. Because of this the government put her in prison, on the charge of attending an unregistered Christian church.

For me, married life is sometimes hard and sometimes good. Growing up, my mom never encouraged me to do any chores because she wanted my hands to be pretty. So before we got married, my husband's mom gave me two years of training. She would bang the pot with a spoon and shout, "Hey, watch!" Then I had to stand next to her while she taught me to cook.

I think a good wife should be honest and good at housework. She should have a willing heart for housework, instead of being lazy. I had also hoped my husband and I would share the chores, but that hasn't happened. Addison doesn't do anything to help at home. It is difficult to prepare all my lessons and do all the housework. I want to be a great teacher, but I feel so tired. I knew going into our marriage that I would have to work, but I wish I could just stay home.

My husband is really quite strict with me. He made me memorize every word of Proverbs 31 until I could recite it. The passage talks about the character of an excellent wife, so at first his idea felt like a threat. Later on, though, I felt that it wasn't bad to know these things. [Lightly did not recite Proverbs 31 on the spot, but I include it here for context.]

Proverbs 31: 10–31

[10]A wife of noble character who can find?
    She is worth far more than rubies.
[11]Her husband has full confidence in her
    and lacks nothing of value.
[12]She brings him good, not harm,
    all the days of her life.
[13]She selects wool and flax
    and works with eager hands.
[14]She is like the merchant ships,

bringing her food from afar.
¹⁵She gets up while it is still night;
   she provides food for her family
   and portions for her female servants.
¹⁶She considers a field and buys it;
   out of her earnings she plants a vineyard.
¹⁷She sets about her work vigorously;
   her arms are strong for her tasks.
¹⁸She sees that her trading is profitable,
   and her lamp does not go out at night.
¹⁹In her hand she holds the distaff
   and grasps the spindle with her fingers.
²⁰She opens her arms to the poor
   and extends her hands to the needy.
²¹When it snows, she has no fear for her household;
   for all of them are clothed in scarlet.
²²She makes coverings for her bed;
   she is clothed in fine linen and purple.
²³Her husband is respected at the city gate,
   where he takes his seat among the elders of the land.
²⁴She makes linen garments and sells them,
   and supplies the merchants with sashes.
²⁵She is clothed with strength and dignity;
   she can laugh at the days to come.
²⁶She speaks with wisdom,
   and faithful instruction is on her tongue.
²⁷She watches over the affairs of her household
   and does not eat the bread of idleness.
²⁸Her children arise and call her blessed;
   her husband also, and he praises her:
²⁹"Many women do noble things,
   but you surpass them all."
³⁰Charm is deceptive, and beauty is fleeting;
   but a woman who fears the LORD is to be praised.
³¹ Honor her for all that her hands have done,
   and let her works bring her praise at the city gate.

About a month into our marriage, my husband did something that made me feel very sad and angry. I prayed to God on my own and cried. "God, why is he not romantic or gentle? I don't like it!" I felt God reminded me of certain scriptures that helped my attitude, and he also helped me ask my husband to apologize. I found the strength to give Addison space and patience, and I felt that his attitude also changed. When we have a problem like this in our marriage, we try to pray individually or together for God to help. When I feel angry, though, I want to talk and pray together right away. I don't want to delay the problem. I want to solve the problem now! But my husband needs space to be alone and unwind before he can discuss a conflict. Afterward he'll come back and talk about his feelings. We can also seek advice from our pastors and talk with them for more help. I do feel that most of our problems get resolved.

We are facing a difficult dilemma right now, actually, so we are meeting with a couple who lead at our church this Thursday to discuss it. My husband was invited to start a youth group back in our hometown, but I don't want to go. I want to stay in Shenzhen until we move to our house in Xinjiang. But Addison is planning to move back into his parents' home so he can lead this group.

My life would be very difficult in that home, since his mother is very critical of every mistake I make and very angry with me. This has been an issue for one or two years, since before our wedding. Also, when we are at his parents' home it is very difficult to be alone or to have sex. His room is connected to the balcony where the family dries their clothes, and his mother walks through our bedroom anytime she wants to hang the wash. I think we need our own place, our own space, but my husband thinks it would cost too much to rent in our hometown. In truth, Addison never wanted to move out in the first place. He would have been happy living with his parents all along. He has a problem with letting his mom go, with leaving her. We call the kind of person who comes between a couple a dì sān zhě, or the "third party." It usually means a mistress, but I think his mom is our person.

Before our wedding, we never talked about a temporary move back to our hometown, and I never expected to live with his parents. I miss my own parents so much!

THE 1980S GENERATION

A Tale of Two Sisters
Arranged Marriages and Secret Boyfriends

LINGYU (B. 1986)

Lingyu is twenty-five and was raised in a small, poor village in Jiangxi province. The onward march of reform and modernization has barely ruffled this traditional pocket of China, where parents still arrange marriages and sons reign paramount. Lingyu's education terminated after she finished middle school, and she has worked various jobs for a decade since, ultimately moving to Shenzhen for better opportunities. She currently works in a shoe store and sends the bulk of her salary back to her parents each month.

Lingyu and I were introduced through a mutual acquaintance, and we met in a Western café near the fishermen's village in old Shekou. We sipped rose tea in mugs afloat with large flower buds while we talked. Lingyu is an attractive girl, and that day she was wreathed in a lovely smile and a silk scarf. She carried a designer bag, and somehow she paid for all of our drinks without my knowledge. When Linda signaled for our bill, the server looked confused and called back, "Already paid!"

In the beginning my English was quite poor, so talking with him was difficult. "Can you be my girlfriend?" he asked one day, at dinner. That much at least I understood. He had invited me to lunch nearly every day for the past three months, and I went, but I wasn't very interested in him. To begin with, he was almost twenty years older than me and divorced, and he also had children already. He was a foreigner from the United States.

"I need to think about it," I said.

One week later I gave him my answer. "Okay, we can try," I said, but I didn't have high hopes. This was two years ago, when I was twenty-three. My parents started pushing me to marry when I was twenty-two, but they did not arrange a husband for me. They will leave it to me, because they know I am stronger than my little sister. She has never had many of her own opinions or much power. It's my sister's personality that makes her this way, so my parents arranged her marriage to a boy from our hometown. That way they could be nearby to make sure everything was okay for her.

In our village, if your first child is a girl, you can try again for a boy. My parents tried again after me, and my little sister was supposed to be a boy, but she wasn't. My mom could have tried again in secret, but if the *fùnǚ zhǔrèn*, or "women's director," caught her pregnant, she would be taken to the hospital and forced into an abortion. Every village has this women's director, a cadre assigned by a big office in the cities. They are supposed to look for pregnant women and stop them after their second birth. Villagers aren't afraid of the hospitals, just the women's director. But the director can be avoided, since the village women usually warn each other about which day is a bad day to go to the hospital.

Some people from my hometown really wanted a son, so they hid in a nearby city to have babies until a son came out. Even today our national ID system is not very modern, so the government can't check your records right away. Back then families could easily exploit the confusion and escape notice in a crowded city. Once the desired son was born, they would move back to our village. The government couldn't do anything then, except fine them and require the wife to get her tubes tied. After all, they can't kill a baby.

In our village it was forbidden to date in school. It is a very poor place, so it was common to stop school after ninth grade and help your family. Even then, we were still supposed to wait until we were at least twenty years old to have any boyfriends. Very rarely a teenage boy might whisper "I like you" to a girl. But the couple would keep their feelings very hidden.

When the time comes, parents don't say something directly, like, "Okay, now it's time to get married." They just arrange a marriage for you. Among my peers, parents started to think about marriage when their children were seventeen or eighteen.

In my sister's case, nine families with sons came to visit my parents during the 2009 Chinese New Year. Each one offered a match for my sister. My parents cared first and foremost about the reputation of the parents, whether they were nice people. To find out more about these proffered families, my parents spoke with many people in the village. Next they considered whether the son was a nice boy who seemed controllable, for my sister's sake. They didn't really care much about the family's financial means or whether they owned a house, but they did look for a family with only one son. If there is more than one son, my sister would have to share the family's resources with another wife and her children too. My parents did not consider whether or not the boy was good-looking or educated.

My parents picked the best boy of the nine and then asked my sister what she thought. In the old days, a daughter always had to accept the match. Nowadays a girl can decline a particular boy if she doesn't like him. But my sister just said, "He's okay."

Very excited, my parents announced her engagement the next day. The boy's family came to our home to share a meal and to pay my parents the deposit money. This money was for my sister to prepare furniture, a TV, and other items that would be sent back to his home, where she and her husband would live after the wedding.

After this engagement party, my sister and the boy had one year to get to know each other better. Traditionally, the girl or her family can call off the wedding at any point during that year, as long as they return the deposit money. If the family is really powerful, though, then the girl really must marry the boy. The man's side can cancel the marriage too, but it's harder to get the money back in that instance, and they could lose ¥10,000 ($1,464), or even ¥100,000 ($14,641).

When they got engaged, my sister's fiancé was working in Xiamen and she was working in Shenzhen. They didn't visit each other during the first eight months of their engagement, since these cities are several hours apart. They just talked on the phone. His family wanted my sister to move in with him, but my parents said no. The man's family usually hopes that the couple will conceive during their engagement year, because a pregnant woman is very unlikely to cancel her wedding. I have a friend who realized she didn't want to marry her fiancé, but she got pregnant during their engagement and didn't have an abortion, so she had to go through with it. Eventually my sister did move in with her husband-to-be, but I told her about my friend's bad experience and discouraged her from having sex. She always listens to me, so she didn't do anything with him. [Lingyu smiled proudly.]

Since my sister had never been in a relationship before, she didn't know what to do when this boy did things she didn't like. She would call me, and then I would call him. "You should do some laundry," I would suggest. He would pause for a while and then say he was willing to try.

Frankly, my parents are upset with this boy because of something he did during that engagement year. My sister's wages from her job in Shenzhen were supposed to go to my parents, but he wanted the wages to go to his parents instead, and she obeyed. My parents didn't tell her they were upset. They just complained to me.

Even now, when I ask my sister if she is happy with her husband, if he is good to her, she doesn't know. She just says, "There are no problems. Life is okay."

My boyfriend and I are living together now, which is a secret from my parents. In the beginning, I met him through some mutual friends. One day soon after that he came into the shop I work in. He recognized me, and it turned out his office was nearby. He asked for my number.

This American boyfriend is very different from the only other boyfriend I've had. My first boyfriend was very bad. He hurt me a lot, and I gave up on men after him. But this man, he talks with me about things, and he really wants to know my opinion. He has also taught me a lot of things, like how to be a good girlfriend. He encourages me to tell him the things I don't like and the things I do like. He listens closely and comforts me, saying, "We can work things out."

In the beginning we had some problems. To begin with, we didn't know each other very well, but I also didn't know how to do anything. In China parents don't tell you anything about how to be in a relationship, they don't prepare you, so I didn't know. Now we talk out our problems and figure out how to solve them, and I feel happy about our love. [She fingered a silver ring on her middle finger.] My boyfriend gave me this. He called it a "promise ring." In China, if you wear a ring on this finger, it means that you love each other.

My boyfriend and I have talked about marrying each other, but he is already a father, and he is not sure if he wants more children. "I need a baby, and I won't marry without that," I told him.

I think a good husband is someone who loves me and is nice to me, who has a good job, and who takes his wife into account when he makes decisions. A good wife is competent at cooking and cleaning, and she does all the housework. I don't think a good wife needs to be beautiful, but she must understand her husband. She needs to understand that he is working very hard for the family. If he is not spending time with her or is getting drunk, she must not complain. If the son's parents want to move in, the wife should say okay. Maybe the wife will work, if the family needs money, but mostly the wife should be home, taking care of the children.

I think a married couple should own a home and share financial decisions. They should be good friends, but it is okay to keep some secrets too. In my hometown, people don't care about sex. Even if a couple is married, we think they shouldn't kiss or display affection in public. If they do, people will run a finger down their cheek and say, "They are not afraid of losing face!" It is a bad thing to get this attention.

Married couples often work in different places for the whole year anyway and maybe visit each other only once or twice. But I think it is important for a couple to be affectionate and to have sex, because those things help improve their relationship. Sometimes married couples have to live apart even when they work in the same city. Maybe one boards at a factory dorm, or maybe they must travel long distances from their apartment to work. I have some girlfriends who exploit these situations, claiming they are single so they can get a foreign boyfriend. They don't do this for love, but to get extra money.

Anyway, we will wait to get married until he can meet my parents. I might tell them this year. I might ask them to come to Shenzhen to meet him. They will object to his age and worry because he is a foreigner. But I can usually convince them of things. I think if I present the idea slowly, they will accept it. After all, they love me and want me to be happy.

She Cut Out My Chicken Eyes

LICAI (B. 1988)

Licai is twenty-four years old and grew up in Sichuan province. He is one of China's "modern migrants," part of a mass migration of millions of young people who have jumped from factory to shop to salon, and from province to province, coming from the village to the big city for work. Licai currently works at a barbershop in Shenzhen, the place where Linda gets her hair done, and he agreed to speak with us about his love life.

A tall, wiry young man with fashionably spiky hair, Licai has a serious demeanor and speaks in a low voice. We met him in a park near his shop, where he smoked a few cigarettes and told us about his first love, a woman who continues to haunt him through the shifting medium of modern life. Linda remarked that Licai had a poetic way of speaking, quite unusual for a boy who did not finish primary school.

When I was two years old, my mother, my grandparents, my baby brother, and one uncle were all killed on the same day. It made all the Sichuan newspapers. During family meals, we always dipped our food in some sauce. Well, I had another uncle, one with some kind of problem in his head, and he poisoned our dipping sauce that day. I didn't really eat the sauce yet, since I was so young. So I lived. My father also survived, since he had a construction job in a different city and wasn't home.

After everybody died, I went to live with my other grandparents and saw my dad during the Midautumn week and Chinese New Year. He remarried when I was seven and I got a younger sister. In my new family, we all tried to accept one another and be easy.

I never finished primary school. For three years I was a model student, always making the top-three student group. Then we started fourth grade, and an older boy got sent down to our classroom. He had been the bottom student in his class for an entire year and had to repeat the grade. I made friends with this boy and started going to his house after school, often sleeping over. He was very naughty. He was already drinking and gambling with cards and kissing girls.

After I met him, I didn't study at all. I just had fun every day with my new friend.

One time he put some sugar in a bottle of juice and gave it to me. I didn't know what it was, but it was sweet, so I drank it all. Then I went to bed and didn't wake up for three days and three nights. My friend was very scared. He thought maybe I was dead. Of course it wasn't juice; it was a fifth of Chinese liquor. When I finally pinched open my eyes, the room was spinning in circles. Somehow I had survived death a second time.

Sometimes my friend and I slept in a cave in the mountains instead of at his house. The cave bordered a footpath our classmates followed to school, and we would wake up very early to hide in the bushes on either side. When we saw a girl walking toward us, we would burst out and catch hold of her so we could kiss her. The boy students initially tried to protect the girls, but we stopped them. "It's not your business. If you try to stop us, we'll beat you," we warned. After that the boys stopped helping those girls.

Eventually I quit school and just stayed at home. Then, after a tedious year of doing nothing, I went out. I was very young, only fourteen years old, but I wanted to join my dad at his construction job, so I lied and said I was eighteen. They let me work as an assistant, carrying water and stones for the men. The site cook took pity on my bamboo-shoot limbs and snuck extra meat into my portions whenever he could. In those days my hands were a thick wax of calluses, plaster clumped in my hair, and puffs of dust punctuated any sudden movement I made. I looked like a ghost! But after three years of hard labor, cords of muscle covered every inch of my old bamboo-shoot self.

When I was seventeen, my cousin arranged a factory job for me and I left my father and the construction site. The new job was not nearly as taxing. I just had to add rubber handles to kitchen supplies. Every day I did the same thing. In the factory, people were mechanized, the children of the machines that huddled round, spoon-feeding us bits of other machines. After a while, even if I closed my eyes, I could do that work. I bore it for nine months before jumping to an electrical parts factory. After a while my cousin got a job in a mobile phone shop, so I quit factory life and moved to a new city to sell phones.

In the beginning, I felt like a fool, a bamboo reed with his bucket all over again. I didn't know anything about mobile phones or retail shops or communicating with rich people. My cousin and one manager helped me a lot. They taught me how to talk and how to sell. I grew up very fast and was soon promoted to "small leader," with two people under me. After one year, my manager took a new job in Dongguan, a city beyond the borders of Sichuan, and he invited me to join him.

We arrived on October first, the beginning of the Midautumn Festival and the first day of a big sale at the shop. We were supposed to push an old model that week, and I sold so many that my new boss promoted me to the small leader position in just a handful of days. This promotion upset many other workers, especially the older employees. "You've been here for one week and already you are a small leader," some muttered. "We've been here so many years, and still, we are only employees."

My promotion was a real problem. I needed to do something to show these employees that I was better than them, that I deserved my position. Luckily, the shop had a real problem too. There was a girl who worked there, a very naughty teenager. She never listened, but since she was the boss's relative, no one dared confront her. One day she wouldn't listen to me, so I spoke to her privately. I was very serious and very simple, and I made her cry. After that, she always listened very closely to me, and so did everyone else.

My first love started in that Dongguan shop. Initially I didn't have any feelings for the girl, and she had just broken up with a boyfriend. But I did have a problem with my feet. In Chinese we call this problem "chicken eyes," a kind of growth that must be removed with a knife. It is difficult to do on your own, so I endured them for weeks. One evening this girl stayed with me and patiently cut out all of my chicken eyes. It took many hours; we were awake until two thirty in the morning. After that night, I felt very warm and sweet toward this girl. I called my cousin, who still worked in the mobile phone shop in Sichuan, to ask her advice. "Ask her to dinner," she suggested. I did, and the girl accepted.

At that dinner, I was very straightforward. "I like you. How do you feel?" I said.

She surveyed me for a moment, her dark eyes a mystery. "I also like you, but I am one year older," she pointed out.

"That doesn't matter to me. I'll give you three days to think." She agreed.

On the second day, she ran up to me with a serious look. "Do you want to know the result?" Suddenly my head squeezed in around my eyes, like I was watching her down a long tube.

"If the result will be one I don't want to listen to, then you don't need to say anything." She paused for a moment but couldn't contain her sunlit grin. I hugged her very hard and then we were together. We went out with each other right then, and later that night we kissed. It was my first kiss.

Eventually my girlfriend and I moved in together, and we shared an apartment for the next two years. During that time she got pregnant, and we talked seriously about having the baby. But in the end, because my girlfriend had a very strong character and we were too young and didn't have much money, we took the baby off instead.

After some time, we heard about a new mobile phone shop opening in Shenzhen, a city close to Dongguan. We both applied and were hired for leadership positions, but my girlfriend's position was higher than mine. Technically speaking, she was in charge of me. We were nervous about telling this shop that we were boyfriend and girlfriend, so we told them we were sister and brother instead. At the shop next door, there was a boy who liked my girlfriend. She knew it, and I felt she was not being clear with the other boy. This made me very angry.

"Why don't you tell him I'm your boyfriend, not your brother?" I would insist. I also felt that she always tried to be better than me. We had many arguments about these problems, and finally I decided I needed to work in a different shop than her. So I quit and rode the bus back to Dongguan.

While we were apart, we called each other very often and argued nearly as often. One night, about a month after I left Shenzhen, I thought maybe there were no more shards of love left among all the anger. "If we are not happy together, we can separate!" I spat.

"Okay!" she shrieked, and we hung up on each other.

I immediately regretted those words. I tried to call her back, but she had already switched off her phone. Every day after that, I tried to call. Sometimes she picked up; sometimes she didn't. Sometimes she picked up only to poison me with indifference. I was twenty-one years old, and I had twice escaped death. But I was learning about a second kind of death, one it seemed I could not overcome.

After a while she called to say that she was homesick. She was going to leave the mobile phone business and return to her hometown in Sichuan. Someone later told me that she was in tears when she boarded the bus. She had been hoping I would come to say goodbye, or perhaps to say something more. Maybe that I still loved her, that she should wait for me. But I didn't go to say goodbye to her.

If you can believe it, two weeks later, this girl was married. And pregnant. We call this a shǎnhūn, or "lightening marriage," and it is very popular nowadays. After the baby came out, she divorced that new husband and gave him their child.

This was my first love experience, so it is lodged very deep inside my heart. For more than two years after our breakup, I avoided all other women. I moved back to Shenzhen and joined an uncle who worked as a hair washer in a small barbershop. I began as a hair washer too, but I learned many things and worked my way up to become a full barber.

This girl opened a clothing boutique in her hometown, and she still lives there. Almost three years have passed since we broke up, but I still hope that one day, when I have enough money and life slows down, I can go back to Sichuan and marry her. I have a new girlfriend now, but I still call this first girl at night sometimes to ask if she misses me. She always says yes. Then I say, "Okay, you wait for me, and one day I'll come back and marry you."

"You're drunk," she retorts. Then she sighs. "Ah, you are not suitable anyway. You are too young."

PART FIVE
The 1990s Generation
Unguided Love

I think love will be the most unforgettable experience . . .
Money and power are not important. True love
is the most important thing.

—Peony, b. 1999

The *jiǔlínghòu*, or 1990s generation, are the teenagers, university students, and youngest workers of current-day China. As they grow up, they are navigating a world flooded with foreign and domestic books, films, TV, and websites abuzz with possibilities for personal happiness and romantic love. While the Great Firewall was in place by 1998 and the government still does its best to censor the Internet, today's young people nonetheless enjoy unprecedented access to ideas, information, and communication. This single change has had immense effects on the 1990s generation's experience of love. They can ask questions about sex in anonymous chat rooms, browse articles about dating and marriage, flirt on QQ, or meet romantic partners on online dating sites. By contrast, their own parents knew nothing of sex and little of dating when they were teenagers.

Marriage is still a comfortable five to fifteen years away for most of this generation. Nonetheless, they are already experimenting with love, dating, and even sex, a clear indication that these things are no longer just the first step in the courtship process. Some even discuss such topics with friends, a remarkable break with tradition. Even the 1980s generation rarely brooked such "private" subjects with friends until they were much older. Perhaps most startling of all, members of this generation can comfortably say "I love you!" to a girlfriend or boyfriend, and many will hold hands in public.

Many of these young people are still in school. It is common for middle or high school students to board at public schools, staying away from their family five nights a week or perhaps most of the month. Those who do well in middle school advance to a college-prep high school, where they spend three intense years preparing for the college entrance exam. Their score on this single exam is the only criterion considered for admission to Chinese universities. There are no essays to write, no extracurricular activities to document, no recommendations to procure. Students with the highest scores get their top choice of university, and the leftovers filter down accordingly. In a few years this generation will be the most educated in China, as more than 25 percent are expected to go to college.

High school is not compulsory in China, and the children of the 1990s who do not make the cut usually attend a vocational school or stop their education altogether. For those who drop out after middle school, their teens and early twenties can be a confusing time. Many stay at home for a while but eventually "go out" to find work. Their life away from home is unsupervised and unstructured, and many find such freedom exhilarating but overwhelming and even dangerous.

Despite the popular media portrayal of the *jiǔlínghòu* as spoiled and selfish, many are very close to their families and do much both to honor their parents and to provide for them. Once members of this generation start work, they commonly send the bulk of their salary to their parents. This remittance is not quite a loss, as money is a joint affair in the Chinese family. Their parents will save the money, and they often assist their children in buying houses and cars when the time comes to marry.

Nonetheless, this generation's parent-child relationship is noticeably changing. Some young people have markedly different values and ideas than their forebears and may struggle to please their parents. Others report, however, that their parents are a bit open-minded. Some describe parents who tolerate dating in high school or even speak openly about love relationships, which is nothing short of revolutionary.

The members of the 1990s generation are the first to have grown up thinking of marriage and divorce as primarily a private matter of personal choice. In 2003 China again revised its marriage law, removing the requirements of work-unit approval for marriage and divorce. After forty-three years of centralized control, marriage and divorce suddenly became a simple process involving only the couple and the registration bureau. The marital amendments of 2003 also barred married persons from "cohabiting with a third party," a measure meant to curb the resurging popularity of kept mistresses in the big cities. While recognition of same-sex marriage has been repeatedly proposed, such an amendment has not yet passed.

More than any of the generations before them, the children of the 1990s grew up pondering the possibility of marrying for love. While their actual behavior still ranges widely, most believe that romantic feelings are natural and that individuals should be happy in love relationships. No generation before them has so clearly articulated such values. Some even told me they will not marry without love, an assertion I heard from none of the other storytellers. Make no mistake, though, this generation still cares a lot about financial stability, brand names, and material possessions. As one joked to me, "We used to dream about *báimǎ wángzǐ*, or "Prince Charming." Now we all want *bǎomǎ wángzǐ*, "Prince BMW!"

Some in this generation may well try to place romantic love in the center of marriage, but rough terrain lies ahead for those who do. Values and expectations have changed so quickly that they have grown up without any real-life examples of a such a marriage. Dating couples are still forming ideas about healthy romantic and sexual relationships, and nobody quite knows how to preserve such things inside the container of marriage. What will become of their parents? How can everything be balanced?

Most of these young people will engage in secret dating relationships, figuring things out alone along the way, until their parents push them to marry. Many question the traditional cult of silence about love and vow that when their turn comes, they will guide their children in matters of the heart.

Today the 1990s generation is 175 million people strong, making it the second smallest of the five generations in this book. Of course, that figure still outranks the populations of all but six nations on earth.

The Buddhist Oracle Said "No Boyfriends"

CARRIE (B. 1990)

Carrie is a bubbly, slender girl of twenty-two. She was born to Buddhist parents in the Year of the Horse and grew up in Fujian, a coastal province directly across from Taiwan. Carrie finished her undergraduate studies just last year and moved to Shenzhen for her first job.

We met on a Sunday afternoon, in the office of a mutual acquaintance who lent us a small conference room. Linda and I, Carrie, and Carrie's friend—an older, married man—gathered around a small round table. As we talked, we drank red tea from extremely fragile plastic cups. In her youth and sweet innocence, Carrie was very charming. She impulsively covered her mouth with her hand when she smiled and dropped her head into her folded arms when telling an embarrassing memory. Her baggy navy-blue dress was polka-dotted and trimmed with a high bib collar. A beige sweater hugged her small shoulders and square bangs skimmed the frames of her blocky red glasses. Her beauty was not striking, but her skin was creamy and her eyes friendly. When I asked Carrie if she remembered the first time she liked a boy, she giggled, covered her mouth, and said, "Yes, because it is happening right now!"

The first time a boy kissed me, I was fifteen. He was my classmate in English, but his scores were very poor, so I often whispered the translations to him. This bad student, well, he kissed me outside, at night! Behind my very own house! He tricked me into meeting him. He had been spending time with our friends nearby, he told me, and asked me to come outside because he had something to say. It was raining very heavily that night.

"I need to go outside," I said to my parents. They objected, but I said, "Well, I really need to go." Taking up an umbrella, I hurried out to meet him. We were just talking with each other, and then he kissed me! Actually, it was Valentine's Day, and he had asked the other students for my address. When I went outside, he told me he liked me but said he didn't want to disturb my studies. He pressed a rose into my hand, the one clutching the umbrella. I tried to push it away. "I don't want to receive this rose because I don't like you!"

When I turned to go, he kept my hand, pulled me in, and kissed me with rain-spattered lips. I wrested my arm away and ran back inside. *He is a bad boy!* I thought furiously. At that time I just wanted to cultivate friendship feelings and avoid loving anyone, so I never talked to him again. I really hated that boy after that.

Since he had forced me to receive his flower, I needed to take it into my home. I couldn't throw it away, because that would be cruel for the flower. Instead, I told my twelve-year-old brother my awful story and asked him to help me tend the flower. My parents didn't notice the rose for many days. "Who feeds this flower?" they finally asked.

"It is my rose. I feed it," my brother answered casually. So he helped me.

In my hometown, I never saw married people kiss or hug or say "I love you." Here in Shenzhen, though, I do sometimes notice a pair of affectionate lovers. When I do, it always seems they can make it only several feet before they must stop and kiss each other. I am always so surprised to see such people! I think they must love each other very much. But I could never do something like that in public. I think it's very strange! If I ran into my friends, well, I would be so ashamed. If a couple in my hometown ever kissed like that, everyone would gossip and say they were bad people. We think this way because of our traditional Chinese culture, and it is still the way of thinking in my hometown today.

My parents never hug or kiss or express their feelings openly, not even at home. They never say "I love you." They just take care of each other. If either one has a problem, the other will always help. But my parents would never do something like go out to dinner alone. And when our family sits down together, my parents only think to talk about my brother and me. For them, the purpose of marriage is to have children. But I don't agree. I think the purpose of marriage is to make your life colorful. You can depend on each other first and then have children together.

I want to experience all three kinds of love in my marriage— romance, friendship, and family love. But before I have romance, I want friendship. And after romance, I want family love. My parents never told me about love, but I think when I am a parent, I will tell my child about relationships. I will tell him or her something about love and about how to meet someone. [She laughed, ducking her head at the audacity of this plan.]

My parents had a *shǎnhūn*, or "lightning marriage." This means they married quickly, meeting only a few times before the wedding. A relative was their matchmaker. In my hometown, if a matchmaker introduces a couple and they have a good first impression, then they can date and get to know each other. If one doesn't like the other, she or he only has to say, "Not suitable." After that, they will both be introduced to other potential matches. We date only one person at a time.

My mother told me that in her day she was introduced to many guys but liked only two of them, my dad and one other guy. She couldn't decide who to choose, so because the family was Buddhist, my grandmother consulted a fortune-teller. The fortune-teller advised that her daughter should pick my dad. [Carrie broke into a wide smile, revealing uneven teeth for a brief second before her hand shot up to cover them.] Usually the fortune-teller considers your birthday and the alignment of astrological things, so this was how my dad got picked.

My family still follows the Buddhist way. We didn't read any special religious books growing up, but we did go to the temple when we had a problem. The last time I went was almost five years ago. I went with my mother, right before my college entrance exam. We needed to ask the Buddha about my studies and my health. We went to one side of the Buddha statues, where a woman waits who can explain everything. [Carrie wasn't sure of the word for this woman in Chinese or English, but based on her description, "oracle" seems appropriate.] This oracle is always a woman, never a man, and she is not a monk. If a visitor needs advice, Buddha will talk to this woman and she will convey what he says. There is no set fee for his guidance. You just need to make a donation.

After my exams, my parents again visited the temple to ask if I would "make a boyfriend" in university. The oracle warned them strongly, "She cannot make a boyfriend so early. The time is not suit-

THE 1990S GENERATION

able now." Throughout university, I did not forget these words. If a boy liked me, I thought, *Surely, I cannot do this!*

I remember the first time I witnessed a love relationship. One of my university classmates, a boy, was chasing my good girlfriend. On her birthday, he asked me and some of her other friends to help prepare a surprise for her. We decorated his dorm, arranging candles in a heart shape. We even had a rehearsal earlier that day, to practice our timing. That night he asked his girlfriend to come to his dorm. As she approached, we whispered, "One, two, three, turn out the lights!" She opened the door and found him smiling beside the glowing heart. It was very romantic.

That evening was the first time I had seen a romantic gesture like this in real life. *Oh, this feels very good!* I thought. The older generations just thought about the concerns of daily life, but I think romantic love is natural for young people nowadays. Since we can't look to our parents or older relatives to learn about love, we have to depend on other sources. For myself, I learn from friends and movies, and also from some love stories written by Chinese authors. I like these books very much. Love movies also touch my heart, but as much as they attract me, I can't help wondering whether someone like me can really do those romantic things? Many young people like me deeply desire to experience romantic feelings for ourselves, but sometimes we can't do what we what. Since we can't always find romance in reality, we need movies and books to help us taste those feelings.

Generally speaking, my generation doesn't know very much about love things or sex. I myself know very little. I don't know where people learn about sex, maybe from the movies? My friends don't talk about this subject. In fact, not one person I can remember has ever mentioned it with me. My friends back home don't kiss in public, and maybe they don't have sex until they are engaged. I think even in Shenzhen, maybe young people still wait to be intimate until they are in love and want to marry. As for me, it is hard to predict exactly what I will do! We will see. I think sex is important for a relationship, of course, very important. I think it will always be a private subject, though. I don't think I will ever talk about it with friends.

Since that oracle's prophecy, many boys have been interested in me, maybe because of my personality? I'm not sure. I smile all the time, and this is a strong point. Also, if I meet someone in trouble, I will help them immediately. I always make my friends happy. I am also good at communicating, and I like to chat. I never had any feelings for those boys who tried to chase me, though. I also wanted to follow the oracle's advice.

But now, for the first time, there is someone I like very much. Since I met him, I have wondered if maybe the oracle was wrong about not making a boyfriend after all. This boy I like is from Fujian province, like me, but he transferred to the Shenzhen office two months ago. We went out alone one time, to have dinner and drink some wine.

The first time I met this boy, he didn't make a deep impression on me. I just saw him sitting quietly in the office, not saying anything at all. The second time, one of my colleagues asked us both to go for a morning run through Hanshuling Park. We don't live in work-sponsored dormitories, but many of our colleagues live near the office, so we often meet each other for exercise and other activities. During the run this boy asked me to recommend an interesting place for him to see in Shenzhen. I suggested something, and then he asked me if I could take him to see it. I thought he was a good-looking boy, so I said, "If you behave properly, I will take you. But if you make me angry, then we won't go."

Several days later, I was moving into a new apartment and I needed help moving my heavy things. I didn't call him to help me, I called another colleague, but somehow he appeared too. He helped me to move and set up my things, and he even called a moving company to transfer my old sofa bed to my uncle's home. Since it was nighttime and I had to meet these moving men in my apartment, he stuck around. I began to wonder if he liked me or not. But he didn't tell me what he felt.

Sometime during the next week, he said, "I want to have dinner with you."

"Why?" I asked.

"Well," he began somberly, "last time, I helped you clean and decorate your new apartment, so I think you should treat me to dinner." Then he grinned at his joke. This was just an excuse, anyway. He paid for the dinner.

As I was getting ready for this dinner date, I knew he wanted to be alone with me, and I was very excited. My mood was a special feeling. But he hadn't told me he loved me or anything, so I didn't want to tell him how I felt.

We went to a Korean restaurant, and if he noticed that I liked any of the small side dishes, he gave me the whole bowl. We drank two glasses of Korean wine while we talked. Then he made this gesture with his hands. [She held up both hands, palms facing herself, then folded her left and right ring fingers down. Her fingernails were neat and unpolished and she wore no jewelry, only a watch.] This gesture has some symbolic significance: it means you are in a steady relationship. We think the fingers are associated with different relationships: the thumb with parents, the pointer finger with siblings, the middle finger with the self, the ring finger with a lover, and the pinky with friends. When he put his fingers that way, he could move them all, except his ring finger. He did not tell me anything directly; he just let me guess what he wanted me to know.

You know, we Chinese like to leave things implied. No matter how much we love each other, we seldom speak out clearly. We have a famous song about this, called "The Moon Represents My Heart." The lyrics say, "You ask me how much I love you. You think by yourself, you guess by yourself. The moon represents my heart."

I spent time with him again during a company outing to Zhaoqing, a place in Guandong province. We went there to climb a mountain, and he climbed behind me the whole way and helped with my bag. Later that night we all went to KTV [karaoke]. He can also sing very well. But he had too many drinks.

"You shouldn't drink so much," I suggested. He fixed me with a lopsided smile.

"Because you are here, it's okay for me." He meant that I would take care of him or take him home if he got too drunk.

Ever since that weekend, I have been thinking that maybe I like him! [Carrie covered her mouth and giggled helplessly.] But we are colleagues, so it's frowned upon to be boyfriend and girlfriend. It's a little embarrassing. We try not to be very obvious by showing up together all the time. [Carrie tucked her shoulders close together in front of her, clasped her hands, smiled, then covered her mouth and laughed uncontrollably again. Unable to stem her giggles, she dropped her head into her hands and then bent forward and sort of sprawled out on the table for a minute. As her mirth subsided, coming in just a few little eruptions, she collected herself, sat up again, and smiled at me.] I don't know why it's so embarrassing. I think it's difficult for us to say "boyfriend" or "girlfriend" out loud. If our colleagues know we love each other, they will tease us relentlessly. Also, everyone knows that if you have a love situation, you will be distracted at work.

Sometimes when we are both in the office this boy will do some, well, some very interesting things! [Dissolving into giggles again, Carrie put her head down on the table for a second time, seeking a moment of respite.] He teases me by hiding my water cup and then materializes beside me and laughs. When he walks by my desk, he makes funny faces, screwing up his tongue and crossing his eyes when no one is looking. One time, while he was pretending to methodically examine the items on my desk, he said, "Your water cup is dirty."

"Well, you can clean it for me," I joked. And he did. He went and cleaned it!

I don't really know the difference between liking and true love. But I don't plan to seek the opinion of an astrologer or fortune-teller or oracle to resolve my confusion. I don't like this idea. What if I love someone but the fortune-teller says not to marry him? If I listened to her advice, I would always wonder. Little things would make me think, *I should have married that guy.* I want to decide on my own who to love and marry. I do think the wedding date is important, so I would consult the astrologer for that, but mostly just because my parents would be upset if I didn't.

Things with this boy are also a little complicated because another girl loves him too, and she is both my colleague and my old roommate. *Titanic* 3D came out recently, and since *Titanic* was so wildly popular ten years ago, everybody is going to see the new version. This girl invited him to go see the movie with her, but he refused. [Carrie smiled triumphantly.] Next a different boy asked me to go to the movie with him, but I also said no. Then the boy that I like asked me to go with him. I didn't answer him yes or no. I just told him this move has too much love, too much emotion. Finally, my colleague, the one who also likes the boy, asked me to go with her. I said okay, and we saw Titanic 3D together.

I want to feel very natural with someone I love, and I feel so natural with this boy. An older male friend of mine told me that if you feel nervous when you see the person, then you know it's true love. But I don't agree. I think you should be able to talk naturally about many things. I don't like that nervous feeling! The boy I like told me he feels very nervous with that other girl but very relaxed with me. Every time when he has some problem, he will tell me his feelings about the situation.

This is the first time I have loved a boy from my heart, and I am very confused. He is really funny and good at music. He is clever, intelligent. He is an excellent boy. I really want to date him, but I don't think it is convenient for him to have another date with me. So I will just let everything go naturally.

Up to this very day, he has not spoken plainly to me, and we haven't made any arrangement to be boyfriend and girlfriend. I haven't held his hand, though I want to. I think Chinese people are too reserved! It is so hard for us to act or speak about love. Anyway, this relationship is not convenient for us right now. Every day when we leave the office, my girlfriends ask me to walk home with them. If I say no, claim to be busy, they will herd about me and squeal, "You have a date with a boy!" So for now I will just stay suspended in this difficult situation. Always something is limited, and I can't do what I like.

I Thought We Would Be Together Forever

ETHAN LI MINGWEN (B. 1994)

Seventeen-year-old Ethan was born in Sichuan, but his family moved to Shenzhen before he started the first grade. I met him at the end of his second year of high school and was surprised to learn of his plans to enjoy a "gap year" after graduation. After that he hopes to attend New York University and make his mark overseas. A sincere boy with eyes that crinkle when he asks questions, Ethan is both gangly and endearing.

We were introduced by a friend of mine who teaches ESL, and the three of us sat outdoors by Nanshan Book City, talking over sweating glasses of iced tea and lemonade. Like Carrie, Ethan expressed the opinion that it is "natural" for boys and girls to love each other. He was, however, the first person I spoke with whose parents thought he could handle a relationship in high school and whose teachers might give students a deterring pep talk rather than report their romance to their parents. This kind of tacit approval of romantic relationships from parents and teachers is nothing short of a seismic cultural shift, historically unprecedented in China.

I remember the first time one of my classmates got a girlfriend. I was maybe twelve, and boarding at primary school, when he announced to our dorm that he had asked a girl out and she had said yes. I was a little surprised, but I think it is normal for a boy to like a girl and to try to make a relationship.

Each classroom in our primarily school had a main teacher, and somehow ours always knew when a boy had some girl on his mind. She would quickly notice this boy and his girlfriend and have a little talk with him, maybe even with both of them. I don't think she would force them to separate. Teachers know these feelings are normal, so most will not demand you end your love, but some will try. Their little talks are intended to dissuade the couple by reminding them how important their studies are to their future. Oftentimes these teachers will only talk to the girl in question. Maybe they think she is more likely to be harmed by love. But some teachers will tell your parents about your love, and most parents will force the couple to separate for sure.

But not my parents. The first time I liked a girl, they told me, "We believe you can handle this. It's normal to love a girl, but you must handle yourself in the right way. Studies need to be the top priority." I don't know how they found out. They know everything, it seems! Once I left my QQ page open while I went to watch TV, and when I came back I found my mom studying it intently. I don't want my parents to talk about my love stuff, but maybe they understood me. I think they didn't try to stop my relationship because they fell in love with each other when they were my age.

Actually, my parents met each other when they were even younger than I am now. They were both studying accounting at zhōng zhuān, a kind of vocational high school. They were each other's first love. It's possible that they still have all three kinds of love—family love, friendship, maybe even romantic love—but I can't be sure because they never tell me anything about their relationship. This is common. I think most parents are too shy to speak with their children about themselves. I do know they were very young when they had me, because one time my mother told me so. She said they initially didn't want to keep me because they were so young, but destiny brought me out anyway. My dad was twenty-two at the time, and I don't know how old my mom was. Once I asked her how old she was, but she didn't want to tell me.

I also am not sure what kind of relationship they have because my father works in another province and my parents are not often together. When I was very small, my dad worked locally, but he stayed at the office until midnight most days. He works very hard. I remember once when I was young we traveled somewhere as a family. It's not a clear memory, but I remember being at a zoo, holding my mother's and father's hands. I felt happy. We haven't traveled much since then, as my dad prefers to rest at home instead.

When I was six we moved to Shenzhen because my father got a good job here. He brought my mother and me here so we could all live together. Then, two years ago, he got a job in Beijing, helping companies to join the stock market. Around that time I noticed that my parents were sleeping in separate beds. But nowadays I think they are sharing one bed again.

My own first love started in middle school, with one of my classmates. In the beginning she had some feelings about me, but I didn't have feelings for her. I just liked to tease her. Everyone thought I liked her because I always wanted to poke her ear, pull her hair, or tell her how the fat boy in our class liked her. The other boys teased me, singing, "You loooove her!"

"That won't happen," I always denied.

But after six months, it did happen. Somehow, I loved her. I could feel it inside, so I knew. I don't know why I loved her, I just did. She was a pretty girl, very quiet in a group, but in private maybe she could act a little crazy with friends. She was a good student, too. There was another boy in our class who liked her, and he tried to get her to be his girlfriend. Some of the girls helped him to get her. I felt frustrated and a little sad when she agreed, and that's when I realized I liked her. I tried to be close to her after she got this boyfriend, but she didn't want to talk to me, and I didn't know why. It made me feel very lonely.

In truth, I think she was a little reluctant to be this boy's girlfriend. One time in class he passed her a note, and it seemed like they were fighting. After one month, they broke up. A few days later, I was still feeling upset about this situation when I took my spot in class. Suddenly, another girl sat down next to me. She told me this girl I liked had some feelings about me. It was so exciting! "How do you know?" I asked, amazed.

"We were at lunch," she said. "And I asked her if she liked anyone else. She said yes: You."

That afternoon I passed a note to this girl: *Do you like me?*
A little bit.

I sent a second note: *Will you be my girlfriend?*
Maybe I can try. I will try, she replied.

We dated each other for the next two and a half years. For me, this relationship was very serious. She really turned me on, and I was crazy about her. We did separate one time, though, a few months into the relationship. It was the winter holiday break, and we didn't have cell phones or the Internet then. To call her, I would have had to call her

THE 1990S GENERATION

home number. And I was afraid that if I called, I wouldn't get her, but her mom or dad. So for the whole month, we didn't connect, and things were a little weird by the time we got back to school.

When we first got together, I wanted only to stay near her all the time. I didn't want to do other things. But after the new semester began, I felt awkward. I didn't dare to be as close, and she also stuck to her own friends a lot, so I had fewer chances to talk to her. Even when she was not with her friends, I felt a little afraid to approach her. I played soccer with my friends and didn't stay with her as much, so she thought I had lost interest.

Once, after school, I asked if I could walk her home, but she rejected me. She told me that one of the teachers in school knew her father, and she didn't want to risk being seen with me. But I doubted this was the real reason, because I had walked her home every day before the break. After a few weeks of this strangeness, I arranged through her friends to talk to her after class one day.

"Do you still like me?" I asked her. She said she didn't know. "What do you want?" I pressed. She was quiet for a few minutes.

"Maybe it's better to break up," she said. Later her friends told me that she ran home and cried that day. Maybe she thought I wasn't as serious as before.

We stayed apart for more than twenty days, and during that time I did a lot of things to try to win her back. She was crazy about this Chinese band called "Bang Bang Tang," so I bought her their CD. I gave it to her in class one day, and she accepted it and seemed happy about the gesture. I also chatted with her on QQ most days, and she wrote back to me. After twenty days, I emailed her: *Can we try again?*

Yes, she replied. When I read that email, it was like I went up to the heavens!" [He beamed in remembrance.]

The next month was her birthday. Lots of our classmates came, and we all went over to one friend's home to watch a movie. I knew another band she liked had a new CD, so I left the party to buy it here, at Book City, and I kept it out of sight when I returned. Finally catching her alone, I said, "I have something for you."

"What is it?" she asked, excited. I didn't answer but put it into her hands, and her face glowed.

ETHAN LI MINGWEN   229

Back then, if I said, "I love you; do you love me?" she always said yes. Then I would kiss her and give her a long hug. We never slept together, but now, in the last year of high school, many friends are having sex with their girlfriends.

The dreaded high school placement exams came at the end of ninth grade, and she and I were assigned to different high schools. This meant we couldn't see each other every day, maybe only once every two weeks, or even just once a month. Sometimes, when I asked her out for the next weekend, she would say her dad didn't want her to go. (Her father saw us once in middle school, walking together, and she was forced to introduce us.)

One day I really needed to see her, so I waited outside her apartment building. I called her to ask if she could come out for a quick chat, but she refused. This made me very confused and sad. I waited outside on a bench for a long time, but she didn't come. Later on she told me she hadn't wanted to come out because she wasn't dressed up. Did I believe her? I don't know, but I didn't know what else to do. We continued to see each other every few weeks after that.

By the second term of freshman year, I wondered if there was someone else. I had always wanted to know what she was up to and how she was feeling, but now I thought about this other possibility all the time. I became a little obsessed. I had her QQ password, and one day, while she was talking with me, I signed on to her page. An older boy student was also chatting with her, and my girlfriend seemed very happy to talk with him. After that day, I told her that I didn't want her to talk with this other guy, or anyone else for that matter, during our chats. "I don't talk with anyone else when I chat with you," I said. "I had to wait a long time for each reply, and that didn't make me feel very good." She said she wouldn't do it again, but it was a lie. Since I had her password, I logged on as her sometimes, and I saw these other chats. So maybe some of what happened was my own fault. Maybe she wanted more freedom and space.

I grew very unhappy in love. It got to the point where she could feel my heavy cloud every time we talked, and she didn't know how to cheer me up. My birthday came in June, on Children's Day, and I waited all day for her to send a celebration message. We couldn't meet up because of school, but I was expecting her message. After a while I called her and sent some text messages, but she didn't reply to anything. Finally, late in the afternoon, she called me. She said her phone had died and she had borrowed a cell phone from some guy. None of that made me feel very satisfied. As time went by, she always felt like I was unhappy, and I think this made her feel a little bit tired. [Ethan hooked a finger in the side of his mouth during this recollection and occasionally pulled his mouth to one side, overstretching it to cartoon-like proportions. Perhaps it was a nervous habit, but I felt it underscored his particular discomfort at that moment.]

One day I asked her if she still loved me. "I'm not sure," she said, not meeting my eye. I asked if I could walk her home from school that Friday, but she said no.

"Well, what about on Saturday or Sunday?" I pushed. I insisted until she agreed. But when we met up, everything was awkward. She didn't seem excited to see me. I didn't know it at the time, but it was the last time I would walk her home. The next week she texted me, *Bad news, maybe we break up.* I stared at her message for a long time. I felt very, very sad.

I saw her just once more, about a month later. I waited outside her apartment again, trying to catch her on her way to class. She was in a hurry, so we could talk for only a moment. I didn't tell her I missed her. I didn't say any of the things in my heart. Then, in a swirl of irritation, she was gone.

I felt miserable for the whole next year after that. I startled awake at night sometimes, thinking of her.

I learned a lot about love through this experience. I paid a lot of time and effort for love and got such an unexpected result. I thought we would be together forever, like my own parents. I thought we would marry each other. My parents knew our relationship ended, but they didn't say anything. I didn't want to talk with them anyway. I don't like for them to be involved in my love stuff. I did talk to my best friend, and he listened to me, but he didn't say very much either. Other friends asked about our relationship too, like my desk mate. She knew my ex-girlfriend, since they had been in an after-school program together. So I talked with her about the breakup.

It's been a year and a half since then, and I think maybe I don't love this girl anymore. I haven't met anyone else yet. Since I'm hoping to go to college in New York City, the timing is not so good right now. Next time around, though, I think I'll just go with nature, go with the wind, if I like someone. I will consider whether she is suitable. I want to marry for love, but I also want to marry a very considerate girl who really loves me back.

And I know I will marry a beautiful girl. We have a saying in China, *Qíngrén yǎn lǐ chū xīshī*, which means, "In a lover's eyes, there is always Xi Shi." Xi Shi, a favored concubine of the second-to-last Qing emperor, is celebrated as one of the four great beauties of traditional China. The expression means that if I really love a girl, I will think she is the most beautiful lady in the world.

You know, among my friends, I am definitely the most serious guy when it comes to love. Most of my friends fall in love, but it's not very deep. Others don't even experience love, they just date for fun. You know, some guys in high school will take advantage of the girls. They just want to have sex. This is a new problem in China, and one that parents and teachers aren't talking about. Maybe they feel too shy or don't know what to say, so they don't bring it up. But the Internet has some bad information, and when kids see it, they want to try it for themselves. I think if I get to be a dad, I will talk openly with my children. I will give them some guidance about love and sex and relationships, so they can choose the right path for their heart.

I Thought to Myself

YU LIHE (B. 1995)

At sixteen, Yu Lihe is a short and willowy girl with full pink cheeks and fashionably short hair. She grew up in Sichuan province with her mother, as her parents divorced when she was young. While many children mentioned growing up with only one full-time parent, Lihe was the first person I interviewed whose parents had actually split up.

After several halfhearted and turbulent attempts to finish middle school, she moved to Shenzhen last year and joined the staff of her uncle's barbershop. (Licai, from the 1980s section, is her colleague.) The day we met, Lihe was wearing a miniskirt, dark tights, high heels, and sparkly earrings. Her tawny skin was burnished with a hint of makeup, and her general demeanor bubbled with unexpected innocence.

I moved here because I wanted to change my life, and maybe I did. Now all I do is go to the barbershop, go to eat, and then go back to the dormitory to sleep. We call this the *sāndiǎn yī xiàn shēnghuó* kind of life. It means the "dorm-classroom-cafeteria kind of life," but it's an expression anyone can use to explain her boring and melancholy existence. It means I just sigh and follow the same daily route between three fixed points. But my life wasn't always like this.

I grew up in a small city in a good-status family. Maybe ours was the upper-middle status. My parents had only me before they divorced, and I spent most of my life with my mom, because my dad moved to a different city.

One of my uncles, who lived near our town, loved me very much. He ran a large and successful barbecue restaurant and was also the local Communist Party leader for his village. He was a powerful man. He needed to go out with many people and very often he took me with him. From a very young age, then, I understood how to drink and make a deal. I also saw many things that men did and I thought to myself, *Men are bad people.* Even so, I knew more about men than about girls, and when I was in school, I mostly played with the boys. I think I am much more mature than other girls my age.

When I was twelve years old, one of my friends, a boy named Guo Shi, liked a girl for the first time. It was the last year of primary school, and he needed help. He asked me to pass a message to this girl, asking if she would go out with him to the park that weekend. She agreed, and Guo Shi convinced me to join them too. We all met in the park, but Guo Shi and this girl disappeared almost immediately, leaving me with a cousin he had brought along. This cousin was a bit fat, and I didn't like him.

All of a sudden, this fat boy hugged me from behind. "I like you," he breathed in my ear. "Do you want to have a date with me?" I struggled out of his arms and sprinted a safe distance away. When Guo Shi and his girl reappeared, I confronted him, pointing at his cousin and recounting his bad behavior.

"My cousin has liked you for a long time," he explained with a shrug. "I invited you to come out today so you could see him again." This upset me greatly, because I secretly liked Guo Shi, not his cousin, and I was already jealous of his feelings for this other girl. How dare he purposely set me up with this fat cousin! I stalked off, fuming.

I didn't get very far before that fat cousin shouted, "If you don't agree to date with me, I will jump into this river!" I didn't care. I kept walking. But then he really *did* jump into the river! I had to go back, because otherwise maybe he would die or something. I thought to myself, *If I date him, Guo Shi will be jealous.* So I revised my strategy.

"Okay, let's have a date," I said.

My plan to bait Guo Shi didn't work out like I hoped, but this fat boy actually treated me very well. Every morning he came to wait for me at my apartment and we walked to school together. After school he always bought me a snack to eat, and we would ride our bicycles somewhere. We had lots of fun together. Sometimes we would sneak into the fields to steal watermelons and run away with them. During one of these melon escapes, my trousers caught on a thorn in the fields, tearing a gaping slash in the pant leg. This fat boy took his shirt and tied it to cover my pants so nobody would see my bare skin. He really cared about me.

After a while, though, I told him I didn't want to play anymore. It was the last year of primary school, and I needed to study very hard if I wanted to get into a good middle school. It was a little too late, though. My score on the primary school exam was only good enough to get me into a very average middle school.

The students in that seventh-grade class were bad kids. They got bad grades, they were very naughty, and they didn't study. Once I met them, I lost interest in studying too. Since our family had money and good relationships in the community, I told myself that I would find a good job even if I didn't do well academically.

When I was thirteen, I made friends with one very bad girl in my class. She smoked cigarettes, picked fights, and did other bad things. Of course, I studied her ways very closely. I became worse and worse and gave up my studies completely. Every day we skipped our evening classes to go out with older kids from the nearby high school. We called them our high school sisters and brothers.

Once, when I was waiting for my friends to come outside, a very tall boy came over and tried to chat with me. I was very proud of myself for ignoring him. I didn't care. He tried again. "What are you waiting for?"

"I'm waiting for Deng Wu," I informed him airily.

"Oh, I am her classmate. Do you have a boyfriend? Do you want me to introduce you to one?"

"No!" I said. "I don't need a boyfriend." Then that boy came very close, held my shoulders, and French-kissed me. Then he left, and I cried, because it was my first kiss and I had been forced.

Deng Wu came out a minute later and found me still sniffling. She asked what happened, and I told her, but I didn't know the boy's name, only that he was very bad. "You are so stupid," she sighed, blowing her bangs up with a sharp breathe. "Tomorrow I will arrange many people to help you beat this guy up."

Unfortunately, this plan did not pan out either. The next day, when we all met for the fight, it turned out that my high school sister knew that bad boy. In fact, they were friends. All the people she had arranged were his friends too, so of course they did not fight with him. Instead, this boy asked Deng Wu to help him chase me. He was also very handsome, so I relaxed a little. "Okay, I agree," I said.

After that my new boyfriend and I often skipped class to go out, just the two of us. One night I was supposed to meet him at the roller-skating rink. But when I arrived, I saw another girl hugging him, and I lost face. I confronted him directly about this girl. "Oh, we just hugged each other, it was not important," he shrugged.

"We are broken up," I said flatly.

"Okay," he said. He didn't care.

Then I cried again. One of my guy friends came to ask me what was wrong. "He kicked me out," I wailed quietly, wiping my wet, red face.

"Oh, all men are like this," my friend said, trying to comfort me. He gave me a tissue to clean my tears. I kept crying, but I also thought to myself, *For me, it's not difficult to find a man. Since one boy did this to me, I will do the same to another.* I looked at my friend, examining his eyes.

"Okay, now we will start dating," I announced.

"Why?" he asked. "You want to make your ex-boyfriend jealous?"

"No," I lied.

"Why, then?"

"Because you helped me clean my tears," I said. So we became boyfriend and girlfriend. But two hours later, I made another announcement.

"We had better just stay friends, rather than try out love," I said. That boy started, and for a moment he showed me only a blank face.

"Okay, if you are okay now, then I am okay to just be friends," he said, collecting himself. Then all of our friends teased him instead.

"Now you are kicked out!" they chorused.

I got worse and worse as I spent more time with all these bad students. We knew a lot of older students, and we also knew people from outside our school. Very often we banded together to fight people we didn't like. There were a lot of these people, so we had a lot of fights.

Toward the end of eighth grade, we went to another school to have dinner. A girl there leaned over with a whispered message. "That boy, Li Hu, likes you very much. Do you want to have a date with him?" This boy's father was in the local *hēishèhuì*, a kind of Mafia.

"Okay," I said, smoothing my hair.

THE 1990s GENERATION

Just like before, I started skipping school very often to meet this boy for a date. We would text message each other to do things. One time, in ninth grade, we went to climb a mountain with many friends. It had rained heavily the day before and the paths were slick. Since it was difficult for me to walk down safely, this Mafia boy carried me down the slippery slope. When we finally made it off the mountain, everyone was muddy and hot, and Li Hu invited all our friends to come to his house to clean up. He lived near the mountain, and his mother had her own business, so she was not at home during the day.

I was the last one into the shower, and by the time I came out, everyone else had already left. Only the Mafia boy was there, and we had sex that afternoon. We were both very shy.

"Why was there no blood?" he demanded when it was over. He narrowed his eyes. "Is this really your first time?"

"Yes, of course, it's the first time," I said indignantly. It was true.

His eyes turned cold and black. "You are lying to me."

I thought he had let it go, but I heard from someone else that he told his friends I had lied to him. Then another friend told me he was going out with another girl. I called him right then.

"Why did you do this? What happened?" He denied the rumor, but then a few weeks later, he broke up with me suddenly.

"We are finished." He admitted his lie and told me he had already been dating this other girl. I told him I didn't agree, and I didn't want to break up. "Even though you don't agree, I don't have any connection with you anymore," he said.

"But you were my first time," I managed, my voice very small.

"And you were mine!" he spat. "So now we are equal."

In China we think the first time is very important, so this boy really hurt me a lot. After that I felt very, very depressed, and my downhill spiral deepened all the more. I started to drink and smoke and use drugs. I didn't care about anything.

The school started to call my mom very often, and she was shocked because she didn't know anything about my world of bad things. "Why are you doing things like this?" she pressed me.

"Just for fun," I lied.

At the end of summer semester that year, three friends and I got into a big fight against just one other girl. We beat her so badly that she had head injuries and needed to be hospitalized. Someone called the police, and the four of us were arrested and sentenced to pay ¥2000 ($295) for this girl's hospital bills. My mom paid the fine.

One of the four girls in the fight got expelled, and my already bad reputation worsened with teachers and even with some other students. I wanted to switch schools. I was supposed to take my end-of-middle-school examinations to get placed for high school, but I didn't go. Instead, I switched schools and had to repeat the ninth grade. At least this new school didn't know I was a bad student, because my mom paid money to the first school to fix my record, taking out all the notes about my bad behavior. This kind of records tampering is very common. The three other girls' families paid to clean up their records too.

I was not any better at this new school, only worse and worse. Since my last boyfriend kicked me out, I thought to myself, *I hate boys. One day, when I am very powerful, I will punish all the girls that boy was with.* At that new school I got into more fights, had new boyfriends, and did everything the same way. Of course, that school kicked me out too, and then my mom really didn't know what to do. She sent me to live with my father so I could go to a private school. But still I could not make any changes, and finally I just stopped going to school completely.

After a while my bad news spread to the village where the uncle who used to love me lived. These reports made him lose face, and he was very angry with me. "You do bad things, you use drugs, and you have sex with men!" he yelled. He beat me very badly, so badly that I could not sit down for three days. My grandma cried and cried over this beating and my bad behavior. My uncle told me to change, but I could not change. I thought to myself, *I hate my uncle.*

Finally, a second uncle called my mother. He owned a barbershop in Shenzhen, a very big city in southern China, and he offered me a job. My mother talked to me for many hours that night, and she cried the whole evening. I realized that because of me, my whole family was very sad. My grandma was suffering so much because of my choices, and she is so old, and I love her very much. I thought to myself, *It is time to change.* I realized that I had been indefensibly bad and had wasted years of my life and my shot at an education. I wanted to change my life. I really *needed* to change it, so I came here to Shenzhen.

Now I work very hard and live very simply. I just live this "dorm-classroom-cafeteria" life at the barbershop, and every day is simple and melancholy. Every day is the same.

A Conventional Man

WILL GUO PINGYOU (B. 1996)

Sixteen-year-old Will Guo Pingyou was raised in central Jiangxi province by his parents and paternal grandparents. When he was six years old, his parents left their hometown and moved to Shenzhen in time for Will to start first grade. Their commitment to his education has panned out well, as Will tested into the best high school in Shenzhen.

When I met him, Will was a month away from finishing Senior Year 1 and from taking the dreaded Y1 exams. He sported a thin mustache and an NBA t-shirt, and his close-cropped hair had all the markings of a two-to-three fade (for those familiar with the taxonomy of standardized male haircuts). His English tutor introduced us and joined Linda and me for the interview. I thought he was rather brave to share his opinions about love, dating, marriage, and sex so frankly with three older women! As we sat down and greeted one another at the Coastal City Starbucks, a stooped little deaf woman poked at Will's shoulder, pointing to a card that asked for money. He reached into his pocket and gave her some.

I think a good girlfriend should love only her boyfriend. But if she falls in love with some other boy, then she should tell him. I am more conventional than other people my age. Others will break up. And if this happens because someone cheated or lied, as happens in maybe 40 percent of cases, then I think a breakup is best. But why are these people cheating? It is because they are not good at dealing with their lives. Their character is not admirable, so of course their dating life will not be wise.

An open-minded girl will act exactly this way: she will cheat, having two or three secret relationships. Because of this, I think a good girlfriend should not be very open-minded. She should have a lot of care and concern for me, and she should be conservative about kissing and hugging. She should maybe feel embarrassed about these things.

I am still together with my first girlfriend. We started one and a half years ago, the day before the final exams for middle school. She messaged me on my phone, sending a love poem. [I asked if he still had that message, and he admitted he had saved it.]

Before receiving this poem, I hadn't had much of an impression of her. I hadn't noticed her really, but she was concerned with me. I wondered why she liked me, what quality did she see? Her message really surprised me. I was so nervous and excited and embarrassed that I couldn't sleep that night. Thankfully, I still got a good score on the exam! *She is not so bad, maybe not bad-looking*, I thought. *Maybe I can try.* I felt excited because I had a secret, something my parents did not know about.

My parents' marriage is very traditional. They always warn me, "Don't love a girl." I think all parents instruct their kids like this. My parents seldom tell me anything else, but sometimes they caution me not to play around with girls. "Just find a girl to marry and give her all of your money, your concern, and your love," they advise. My parents still share some *yǒuqíng* and *qīnqíng*, the friendship and relatives kind of love, but I think *àiqíng*, romantic love, did not exist in their generation.

In some ways, I accept their advice. I think I can't put too much emotion into relationships at this age, since I am so busy with school. But in other ways, I think their advice is not so realistic. I've seen lots of situations on the Internet, and I cannot believe my parents' version of love. I learn about love online because TV and movies are not very realistic. Love is always too easy, too stupid, too happy in TV and movies. There is never any sadness, it seems.

I didn't reply to this girl's love-poem message, but I saw her the next day after our exams. I was embarrassed but excited! "Okay, I can try," I said. "I can try to be a boyfriend." I was very nervous. I am a boy, not a girl, so I should have been brave. But I wasn't. I would not have seen her again if she hadn't asked when she did.

We had our first date right then. We went to get Chinese food. We were both very shy, examining our plates and chopsticks as closely as possible. Maybe we stayed for one or two hours. I made myself stay, even though I had to work very hard to open my mouth and say anything.

For the next several months, we did not meet each other again. We only sent text messages. It was the summer holiday, and I had to prepare for the YI exams at the end of the next year. The teachers may not assign homework over the summer, but can they stop me from assigning homework to myself? Most days I studied for eight hours. After the vacation ended, I told one friend about my girlfriend. He was surprised that I could maintain my studies and a relationship. I think most people cannot do this, but I am willing to work very hard to succeed at both.

Actually, my high school has a special tradition of sending the older students to encourage the younger ones. They will talk with us about how to make life more colorful, more happy. Sometimes they talk about love. Many older students have told me how to balance the relationship between studies and dating. They think I can do everything if I am happy and my studies stay strong. This advice is away from our teachers' ears, of course. They will never know!

A month after high school started, bolstered with their encouragement, I sent my girlfriend a message: I miss you. It was the weekend, and I went to meet her in front of her dorm at school. It felt a little nice to see her, but I was afraid that if we went out somewhere alone, somebody would spot us and ruin the secret. So we just stood outside and talked. We didn't get into the same high school, so we can see each other only once or twice a month, against our parents' rules. We would both like to see each other more, but we are satisfied with how things are for the present. I seldom call my girlfriend because, for now, I think we talk often enough. If we can keep this relationship for many years, then we will know we are successful.

Nowadays some boyfriends will call their girlfriends lǎopó, or "wife." "Wife, I love you!" they'll say. It's like a pet name, a sweet nothing, but I think this word is wrong. It shouldn't be used before marriage. Some of my friends say this, for fun, but it's stupid. My girlfriend and I don't say "I love you" or "You're so beautiful" to each other. In America you say, "Talk is cheap," but for most Chinese, I think talk is expensive!

I couldn't honestly tell my girlfriend that I really loved her right now anyway, because I am confused about my feelings. I know that she loves me a little more than I love her. If I turn off my phone for one or two days, for example, I will have many messages from her. And she often sends gifts to me, via a friend, like sweets or cookies.

I think I am not a good boyfriend. In my heart, I should have more concern for my girlfriend. A good boyfriend should protect his girlfriend spiritually and physically and find ways to lessen her concerns and to comfort her when she is sad. He should tell her something funny or caring. I think helping each other like this is important because parents and teachers won't do such things. Teachers don't care about what you are thinking and feeling, just about your scores. This is okay, though; it is right. Parents do care about your spiritual self, but they are not sure what you really need. We don't tell them our deep things. They don't even know about our dating relationships! We don't view parents as friends, but we can talk freely with girlfriends and boyfriends, or schoolmates. A good boyfriend also cannot meet another girl without telling his girlfriend.

I think love is a natural experience. I think every Chinese person will have some brush with romantic love, since love with sadness is romantic too. It is easy to define romantic love: when you think your love is enough, then that is romantic love. I think my generation might marry only if they have this kind of love, and then, over many years, that love will change from romance to the family kind of caring. Maybe this will take thirty or fifty years, but every successful marriage will transition from romance to family love. Besides, I hear that romantic love can last in marriage for only three months. Passionate lovers must have sex every day, and they can only sustain that for about ninety days.

People my age learn about sex on the Internet mostly, but maybe also from their same-age friends or from older students. Nobody ever talks with their parents about sex. In middle school we had one forty-five-minute class about it, but our teachers only taught us all the illnesses and diseases you will get if you have sex. "So don't have sex, and then you won't die from all of these illnesses," they concluded.

I didn't need their motivation, though. I have my dreams. I study very hard like I do because I don't like Chinese universities. I want to go abroad, maybe to America or the UK. I want to study overseas and then become a crime investigator in the United States. To get there, I have to be the best. I have to do well on all my exams, but I am also focusing on my English. Three times a week, I ride the bus for one hour, from Luohu to Nanshan, just to take additional English classes. With these dreams, it is easy for me to make good choices. Other people don't have strong ambitions, so they care only about seeking happiness today. But that is not right.

I don't think any of my own friends have had sex yet, because they think like I do. My friends would never hug in public. Maybe some would kiss their girlfriends in private, but this is still rare. My girlfriend and I have held hands and hugged each other, but I have never kissed her. I think that even *thinking* about kissing her would be a little dirty. [He made a "yuck" face.]

More importantly, if I kiss her, then I create some responsibility. I am a conventional man! [He laughed at himself.] I think sex before marriage is stupid. You need to take more responsibility than that. If a kiss makes things serious, sex will really make them serious! I think the traditional Chinese way is better than the openness in the West.

Also, I would never divorce if my wife and I had a child. If we didn't have kids and our relationship went sour, then maybe I would divorce. But first I would communicate with her, ask her if I did something wrong. Could I do something more to make her happy? Regarding the man who cheats on his wife, I think he is so awful that he should not live. He should die right now! He should tell his wife that very same day, and she should divorce him on the second day. This man is a coward. He is not successful, because cheating would not happen in a successful marriage. I don't think my opinions are influenced by my parents or anything I heard. They just originated in my heart.

It doesn't matter if your wife is beautiful or not, as long as you love her. But I think every boy wants a beautiful wife! This is natural.

[I asked if he had heard the expression "The ugly wife is a treasure at home."] This is an old-fashioned saying, and I think it's not true. Physical appearance is important, but I think the spiritual self is more important. Still, I might break up with my current girlfriend. I don't know.

There Are Three Kinds of Chinese Parents

EMMA YANG XICHI AND PEONY LI DANDAN (B. 1999)

Emma and Peony were twelve years old and just beginning seventh grade, the first year of middle school, when we had our interview. They have known each other since preschool and were each other's first best friend. I anticipated this meeting with great curiosity, as I presumed that kids growing up in Shenzhen would have access to a wider variety of ideas than children growing up in villages or towns, or even other cities that are not special economic zones. I wondered if they might consequently think more progressively.

Peony has lived in Shenzhen all her life, with her parents and maternal grandparents. Her family comes from Hubei province—a place, she told me solemnly, that is famous for its noodles. Emma, on the other hand, was raised in Xinjiang until age four. She was our first interviewee to hail from that province, a huge stretch of desert and mountains in the northwestern corner of China. This fascinating province, the largest one in the country, borders Russia, Mongolia, Afghanistan, Kashmir, Kyrgyzstan, Tajikistan, and Kazakhstan and is the traditional home of China's Muslim population. Emma returns often to Xinjiang, as her father and other relatives still live there. She and her mother moved to Shenzhen for her education and live here during each school year.

Emma's mother accompanied the two girls to the interview. Initially I was concerned that they might not feel free to speak their minds with her there, although I certainly didn't want to cause them any trouble at home. Emma's mom set me quickly at ease, though. She had a very sweet energy about her, complete with eyes that crinkled up in the corners when she smiled. Plus, she didn't speak a word of English. The girls, on the other hand, were quite proficient and hardly needed any translation.

As it turned out, I needn't have worried about Emma's mother in the first place. She speaks openly with her daughter about love and boys and anything else Emma is wondering about. Peony, by contrast, lives in a more traditional home environment and cannot really speak with her parents or grandparents about love. Peony clearly longed for the kind of emotional support that Emma got from her mother, and her raw honesty made my heart go out to her.

We met at the Starbucks in Coastal City, where I ordered some drinks after the girls picked them out. When their iced teas arrived, I smiled to myself because they both declared the tea to be too cold and agreed they must wait one hour before drinking it. Adult women in China are always declining cold beverages, as ice is believed to cause stomachaches and harm the womb. Before that day, though, I hadn't realized twelve-year-olds would already be vigilant about womb warmth!

Emma: When I was very young, I thought *àiqíng* [romantic love] was too far away, too strange. When I was four years old, I thought this love was dangerous. I thought maybe it would hurt people very deeply, so I resolved never to have it. Then, when I was six, my older cousin began telling me about her love stories. She was always tangled up in love, so she often talked to me and to her mother. Then she would feel better and maybe go out on a date. Her mother is very open, so she accepted her boyfriend. *Maybe romantic love is nice,* I started to think. *Maybe it can have a good result.* Now that I am twelve, I think this love is good, if you can control your feelings.

Love is meant for boys and girls. They must spend a lot of time, money, and understanding on each other. Some people, when they first find this love, may also find their happily ever after. But for others, their love will end, and then they will feel very silly about their feelings. My cousin told me this. She is twenty-two and she told me everything about her broken heart. From her I learned that even though a couple loves each other, they need to be cautious. They need to share their feelings and understand each other well.

Peony: I agree with everything Emma said. I don't know how to define romantic love exactly. Chinese girls like us think this is a very strange question, because we have not fallen in love before. Our cousins will tell us their stories and we will feel very . . . I don't know. [She gestured toward her heart, indicating some emotional reaction.] I feel embarrassed and curious when I hear these stories. I think most girls will fall in love with hearing about these feelings.

Emma: Of course, we all have little love feelings about this boy or that boy. But if we need to talk with these boys or stand near them, we will feel very shy and won't know what to say.

THE 1990S GENERATION

Peony: I have a classmate, a boy, and he has a girl he wants to talk with every day now. If I go over to them, they want me to leave right away. This is the first time I have seen friends act openly this way.

Emma: Last year my best friend in sixth grade told me her secret: she had a boyfriend. She was happy but afraid too. She was a little bit afraid that her parents or teachers would have a different opinion. She was also not sure if the boy was suitable, so I suggested that she should just be friends first, so they could understand each other better. This year, in seventh grade, they are still in the same classroom, but she is beginning to think he might not be smart enough for her. Many times he cannot detect her subtlety. Also, when we get older, we will have to pay attention to our exam scores.

Peony: Chinese parents always think we need to focus all our attention on our studies! My parents tell me I should not fall in love now. If I do, they warn me, my scores will suffer for many years.

Emma: There are three kinds of Chinese parents, you know. The first kind are very traditional, and they are against your feelings. They are totally against students having these love feelings at all. The second kind are a little bit open. These parents are not against your feelings, but they want you to make good choices. My mother is this way; she is not against my heart, but she wants me to focus on my scores. The third kind are modern parents. They think you can continue love relationships as long as your scores are high, and they might even encourage your love. These parents are very rare. The best kind of parents are a little open but not modern. Modern parents will to be too irresponsible, and our teachers might think badly of them, because they are not making us focus on our studies.

Peony: Emma is right. My parents are the very traditional kind, so they won't let me have these love feelings. If I get older, my parents will still be against my love feelings. When I am twenty years old and in university, then they won't be against them anymore. But I think university is too late to learn these kinds of things!

I think most of us don't know how to talk with our parents about love and relationships. It is impossible to change their opinions, and they always hate my opinions by default! It feels like they can't say anything but "You can't do this anymore." Always my parents check my schoolbag, check my emails, and check every space in my room. I think they should trust me! They make me so sad. They are so worried about me, worried that I will love someone. They have threatened to take me out of school or something worse if I have a boyfriend. They are always very black and white. They don't try to understand me. When I am a mom, I will be open with my kids. I will let them share their ideas.

Emma: I think my mom is better. I can share my opinions with her and she will give me advice. She will help me make a choice. We actually started talking about love when I was only in primarily school. She told me these feelings are good and many people have them. She also said that she trusts me to be smart, to learn to control these feelings. When kids cannot talk to their parents, this is bad because it creates a secret. Instead, I think parents should treat their kids with respect. They should give advice when we need it, and they should care more about things outside of schoolwork, like our feelings.

Peony: Yes, I agree with the things Emma said. First, parents should listen carefully. They may hear something they don't like, but they should not interrupt me right away. They need to become good listeners. I don't even do anything! Why don't my parents trust me?

When our parents were our age, what did they feel and what did their parents say? Their parents would have been totally against their love feelings, as they could hardly accept love at any age. Most of their generation had to stop their love if they had it. My parents must have been so sad. Yet when their own children fall in love, they just parrot the same command to stop our hearts. Why can't they understand us? I wish they could accept and respect us.

Emma: When our parents were our same age, they didn't have these love feelings. They didn't think about romantic love. Maybe in high school, my mom said, they started to notice boys.

Q: Have you ever felt these love feelings?

Peony: I had this feeling in fourth grade and I wanted it to be a secret. I told Emma. She is my best friend, so I could tell her, because we can talk about anything.

Emma: I also had these feelings, in third grade, for the most popular boy in our class. But maybe the whole grade also admired him. He was smart, with good scores, but he also had a good temper and many other things. We thought that every good quality could be found in him. He knew all the girls thought this way, but he didn't say anything. He is still popular now, in seventh grade. When my cousin was my age, she said the popular boy *must* be the top student. But now, most of the popular boys in our grade don't have the highest marks. They are just friendly, humorous, good at sports and musical instruments, and all the teachers like them too. It is sometimes important that they are handsome, especially for first impressions. But when we understand them more, maybe then their appearance is not so important.

Peony: These boys must be kind and have good insides too. They must listen carefully when other people are talking and must have many things that others can see and like about them. This popular boy from third grade had a handsome face and many friends. Many people wanted to join his circle, but he would never reply. He always kept quiet about many things, so it made us feel that he was mysterious.

Emma: When we were younger, maybe you could tell your best friend about your feelings, but we never spoke about love in public. Then, in the first week of seventh grade, somehow love was a big topic. I don't know how. Our classmates were talking about love day and night, and we found out that other people had had our same feelings! Oh, it felt so good to learn that we weren't the only ones! I think one girl had an older cousin who started this topic.

Peony: This year I also read an article about love in an English magazine from our school. It said that if love is reciprocal, then it will bond you both together.

Emma: I have an article about this kind of love on my micro-blog. It is a little bit sad. It explains that if you love a boy and he doesn't love you back, then maybe you should let it go. Maybe you should put your love in the bottom of your heart, because even if your feelings are very strong, the result will not be good.

Peony: In *The Hunger Games* movie, Peeta loved Katniss, but she just wanted to stay alive. Maybe she had some feelings for him by the end, but she had a boyfriend already, so maybe it was a hard choice. But it was his love that saved their lives. I think, if I had a sweet lover like Katniss did, would I refuse him? That boy was willing to die for her! Oh, it makes me feel so many deep feelings. Nowadays most of our movies show us a love story. Even if it's just a subplot, there is always a little bit about love.

Emma: We have some books with love stories too, but you know, kids our age aren't so interested in reading about love. We really just like magic! Stories like *Harry Potter*. Magic stories have a lot of adventures, they are full of surprises, and there are lots of imaginary things to satisfy us.

Q: What do your teachers think of love?

Emma: At our age, our teachers always tell us just to study. I wish our teachers could treat us differently. Life doesn't always have to be about studies and exams. They should be more natural and should give us more chances for outdoor activities. The most important thing is they must assign less homework!

Peony: Yes, we just study all the time! We are very tired. We have three or four hours of homework every day, and it is like this: "Copy out the whole article three times in your notebook." Even if our teachers ask for our "opinion," everybody knows there is a right answer.

Emma: We think romantic love feelings would give us some relief. We could take a break and get our studies out of our minds. My mom thinks I should just pay attention to my studies before I am sixteen, though. When I an older, she says I can make this choice about love myself. It will be up to me. The most important thing is that she trusts me to make a good choice.

Peony: The point is that high school is the busiest time in a student's life, so we will want a boyfriend to distract us and help us relax. A boyfriend should also be very good at his studies, so he can help us with our homework. I might want to start with a friend first, a boy who has the same hobbies, who can talk easily with me, and we can grow into boyfriend and girlfriend. Sometimes we can't tell all of our secrets to certain girls, but if I could tell a boy my ideas and he could listen carefully, that would be good. I think love will be the most unforgettable experience.

Emma: At our age, girl friendships are complicated. Girls sometimes act like they want to make friends, but they really just want to learn something. Boys are simpler. It is easy to stay with them and get along. I also imagine love will be an unforgettable thing, but still I think we are too young now. Maybe when I am sixteen or seventeen it will be time.

Q: What is your opinion of a boy who puts his arm around a girl in public or a couple who hold hands on the street?

Peony: I haven't had that experience myself, so it's hard to have an opinion.

Emma: I think maybe they don't love each other, just like each other. If you really love each other, you don't need to say or do anything.

Peony: I am a little bit against these public displays. Money and power are not important. True love is the most important thing.

Emma: I think if the boy has his arm around the girl, or carries her bag, this is too showy and very false. But if they kiss or hug each other, maybe that's a genuine expression.

Q: Do you think your own parents have happy marriages?

Emma: My father is very busy but he always takes some time for family. My mom and dad still love each other and I am very proud. They care about each other. They care about all the details, even though they cannot visit during the school year. If my father is ill, my mother will tell him what he should eat and what he should do. Caring for each other is the most important thing.

Peony: I think my parents are happy. I've never seen an argument, but maybe I just didn't see it. I think they love me and take care of me, but they don't take the best way for love. They just take the way they want. This is a big problem between us. I don't know if my parents love each other, because they avoid these kinds of questions. But

I think our family is better than many others. I think a family must take care of each other and try their best to love each other.

Q: Do you girls want to get married? What do you see about marriage that is good? What is not good?

Emma: Marriage can make two strangers to be a family and create happiness. When I was six, I thought I hated marriage. I thought a wife's role was very annoying and boring. Women have to take care of many things! They must be very tired, I thought. But now I think having a family is more important than those problems. I think taking care of everyone's feelings is better than being alone. My cousin told me she won't marry. She is a little bit worried about making a new family with other people, because it is costly to support a family. But I think money in a family can be okay, because then every member is together, and you can deal with the problems together. So I think everything will be just fine if I marry, because our spirits will be together. Some families have arguments and many are not suitable. Maybe a couple made the wrong decision to stay together and their kids are hurt by their arguments. This is the bad side of marriage.

Peony: I think marriage is sometimes good and sometimes bad. There is a famous writer, Bing Xin, who said, "I don't know what family is, but when I arrive home, I forgot all my worries and unhappiness." She wrote this when she was ninety years old, and maybe she had grandkids. She meant that the happiest times in her life had been with family. [Xie Wanying (1900–99), a poet and writer known by her pen name, Bing Xin (Ice Core), has been called "the philosopher of love."]

But I do want to marry. I have a friend who told me she would never get married, and I was so surprised! She is so amazing to want to be single forever. I think she'll feel lonely.

Once I asked her why she wouldn't just wait until she was older and then get married. "I just don't have that feeling about boys," she told me. "I don't like the way the boys play. They have very different ways."

Emma: Many of my classmates think housework, babies, and taking care of parents will be too tiring. They think marriage is too far away, so they don't need to care about it now. But I asked them, "When you are older, what will you do?" They want to just continue working, they say. To have a family means less freedom, they think.

Peony: I think our generation has true love and modern love. Some couples just have this love relationship for money or for fun, like the teenagers in America. But my friends and I want true love. We would maybe not marry without it.

Q: What kind of man do you want to marry?

Emma: He must be responsible. Being responsible with his promises is the most important thing. He must also be hard-working and must care about himself and his family.

Peony: I haven't thought about this question before, so it is a little difficult to answer it. Just a handsome man, I suppose, and responsible, with a good heart. Someone who can take care of his family, who can sometimes help make the family harmonious.

Q: What kind of wife do you want to be? Do you want children? Will your parents live with you?

Emma: I want to do well in the kitchen. I want to be tender.

Peony: Taking care of my family will be the most important thing. I want to be a wife who can handle all of the small problems. Maybe I want to have children, if I am married. I think children give less freedom to the couple, but if the baby is cute and funny, that can give some happiness too. I think many people don't like children because they are too noisy and annoying. But if it's your own child, then you'll love that one, and will spend your time on him and think of him as a part of your own body and a member of your family.

Emma: I asked my mom if she had wanted to have a baby when she was young. She said she didn't always want one, she thought they were too loud, too noisy. When she had me, though, she said she felt her life was changed, that I was a part of her soul, her spirit. She was responsible for a whole new person, a new life. I think I'll want a baby when I'm married.

Peony: We both expect to live with our parents when we are older. In our tradition, we must take care of our parents. This is a big difference between China and other countries like America. Chinese parents might like to live with their kids, but they worry about being a burden. Maybe Chinese kids want their own life and think living with a parent is not convenient. In America children might see their parents only once or twice a week, but I think this is better. They still love each other. For me, though, I think I can't live apart from my parents because they would be so lonely if I did.

Emma: The trouble with parents living with us after marriage is that the daughter-in-law or son-in-law might not agree with your parents, and they might fight. But I think my parents would also get lonely if I moved out. Maybe parents don't get lonely in America.

Conclusion

Since the rise of China's Communist regime, marriage has somersaulted from a parentally arranged relationship that was never intended to include romantic love to a relationship chosen by spouses who now expect a little more from the institution. This transition unfolded over just sixty years, against a backdrop of political turmoil, social oppression, reform, and modernization. During the transition, romantic love catapulted from a nonentity in respectable social life to a significant player in matrimonial decisions. And yet marriage remains laden with practical purpose in China, and love is not yet the fundamental reason for tying the knot. Most young people still marry because it "is time," not because they are "in love." After the hardship of three decades of Maoism and the prosperity of three decades of economic explosion, the people of China are still negotiating the place of romantic love in their lives and marriages.

I originally plunged into this cross-cultural love and marriage adventure to understand the typical attitudes and experiences I encountered while living in Shenzhen, China. Beneath the veneer of custom and culture, I expected to find that most Chinese people wanted basically the same things out of love and marriage that I did. Unbeknownst to me, this book was really a search for universality. But after a year and a half spent engaged in dozens of formal interviews and countless conversations with friends, acquaintances, and strangers, I can't say that I've found it.

Nonetheless, I learned many things over the course of this remarkable journey of story collecting. The people I met introduced me to a cultural landscape that I knew next to nothing about, and their life experiences intrigued me. Along the way, my many unanswered questions pushed me to learn more about the changing forms of love, dating, and marriage in present-day China. While providing a neat conclusion to this complex mosaic is likely impossible, I will share what I have felt, pondered, and discovered over the past two years.

To begin, I am now convinced that our "personal" thoughts, attitudes, and expectations about love and marriage are not our own. These values are socially taught and are far more malleable than I previously imagined. I have witnessed how very hard it is for one person to pursue, or even *develop*, goals and desires that have been vilified, silenced, or dismissed by his or her dominant culture. I can only wonder what natural instincts have been inadvertently muted or gagged in my own homeland.

I was particularly struck by the power of language to shape people's attitudes and expectations about love and marriage. The changing connotation of *àiqíng* (romantic love) is a poignant example. This word existed in Old China but referred exclusively to illicit love with prostitutes and courtesans. As late as 1953, the anthropologist F. L. K. Hsu wrote that *àiqíng* had "no appeal" for China's young people, nearly all of whom would soon marry. By the 1960s and '70s, romantic love had inched inside the border of marriage, but only to describe cases in which a match provoked family conflict. Nowadays, romantic love has finally become a good word, a desirable experience, but its connotation is ephemeral and superficial. Romantic love can be enjoyed between dating couples, but most people expect it to evaporate within a few years of the wedding, leaving behind the solids of daily life and "family love." For the Chinese people, enduring romantic love is a myth, the sort of thing no realistic adult should expect.

These various definitions of love are powerful and surely shape Chinese people's interest in romantic love and their expectations of marriage. As Ziu Shouhe, a storyteller from the 1960s, described his introduction to his future wife in 1979, he said he "felt okay" about her. "We didn't really use complicated language for our feelings," he explained. "And we didn't have so many love words." Mr. Ziu had not expected or desired a deeper emotional experience, probably because he had never heard one described and his vocabulary barely even equipped him to think about one.

Even stronger than the influence of language is the power of China's social environment to shape people's attitudes and expectations about love and marriage. Not a single one of my storytellers grew up watching married adults who said "I love you," exchanged physical gestures of affection, or carved out "alone time" as a couple. Teachers taught that romantic love was harmful for young people and must be avoided. Friends rarely discussed boyfriends or love experiences. Very few people ever talked with anybody else about sex. With two exceptions, none of my storytellers' parents spoke directly to them about romantic love, sex, or the purpose of marriage. I got the sense that Chinese parents felt too shy to bring up these subjects, since nobody had ever discussed such things with them.

Consequently, people who did want something more than qīnqíng [family love] out of marriage were struggling to find it. With no real-life examples to draw from, those intrepid lovers had to invent their relationships as they went along, drawing inspiration from theory, the media, or their imagination.

I wondered what had caused this state of love and marriage in China. Where had this stunted vocabulary, these humdrum expectations, these unsentimental attitudes come from in the first place? As I read up on the history of marriage around the world, though, I realized that it was actually my own approach to marriage that was strange, not the worldview I saw in China. I contacted Stephanie Coontz, historian, author, and director of research and public education for the Council on Contemporary Families, to ask for some guidance. She pointed out that even after a society allows young people to choose their own mates, many different motives can underpin that selection. Broadly speaking, people usually seek either a "love-based marriage" or a "practical marriage," something Coontz has described as a "marriage of political and economic convenience" in her books. If you are looking for a love-based marriage, then you will care most about the fit between yourself and your partner, about the personal considerations that will allow the two of you to be a happy couple. On the other hand, if you are looking for a practical marriage, you will not focus primarily on the fit between yourself and your partner. Rather, you will base your decision on a wider range of considerations, such as economic stability, politics, and your parents' expectations.

Suddenly the whole picture in China made sense. All along I had wrongly assumed that once a society throws off the practice of arranged marriages, its young people will automatically pursue love-based matches as a sort of default. But that's not what I was seeing in China. I saw young people who were free to choose their partner (within a certain time frame), but those young people were primarily looking for practical rather than love-based marriages. They could marry quickly because they were not as focused on the fit between themselves and their partners. And their definition of a good marriage was not centered in their emotional, sexual, and social relationship with their spouse.

Marrying for love is still a newfangled and controversial issue in China, and in that light I finally understood my storytellers' skepticism and hesitation. The Chinese people are still grappling with how they *feel* about romantic love. They are still debating whether this love is desirable, unrealistic, or even harmful. People don't believe romantic love can survive in a marriage because they've never seen it done, and they aren't convinced such emotion ought to be there in the first place.

When I replace the words "romantic love" with my own society's hot-button issues—abortion, gay marriage—all of this hubbub becomes more familiar. The people of China are nervous about love-based marriages. They are not sure what will happen if romantic love is widely condoned as the fundamental reason for marriage. They are afraid of unleashing immorality and pandemonium if they allow young people to follow their hearts. Will society and tradition be ruined? Will parents be abandoned? Answers to these critical questions are being hammered and shaped as we speak, in the red-hot forge of a modernizing, globalizing China. The smoke is still puffing, the sparks are still flying, and nobody quite knows what love and marriage will look like when they cool.

Armed with some new perspectives, I went back to the ideas that had surprised me the most in the stories I collected. My storytellers believed that marriage was a must, with or without love, but that dating was distracting and harmful for anyone younger than twenty. Some thought that while love might be pure, sex was dirty or just for childbearing. While most couples got married expecting to live together forever, few expected their spouse to be their best friend or a source of emotional support. Monogamy was not assumed, and men in particular justified having girlfriends and "second wives" out of a belief that they could not confide in their wives. All of these perspectives make more sense in a world where people prefer practical marriages over love-based ones. As one traditional saying goes, "Marriage is mostly just firewood, rice, oil, salt, soy sauce, vinegar, and tea." It defines marriage as a primarily practical arrangement to supply daily needs, rather than a love-inspired relationship with emotional returns.

And yet crouching in the midst of this utilitarian portrait of marriage is the intriguing concept of *yuánfèn*. Mentioned by Mr. Yang, Ben Wang, and Riley, *yuánfèn* is the belief that destiny will bring a couple together at the right time, through a predestined encounter. It comes from the ancient Taoist vision of the cosmos as a tapestry being constantly woven. Time, place, and the trajectory of each life travel along the warp and the weft, or the horizontal and vertical strings of the weave. *Yuánfèn* is the intersection point, that pivotal spot where the path of one life meets another.

I was surprised to encounter this romantic idea in a culture of practical marriages, but like many other love-related concepts, *yuánfèn*'s meaning has morphed over time. The idea was traditionally used to force women to accept their spouses by emphasizing that the universe had predetermined their marriage. As Wen Ayi said, "Wives must bear their husband's lot and station in life as their own. They must not hope for change." Nowadays the term has had a facelift. People look for *yuánfèn* moments, pointing to serendipitous accidents as evidence that their romantic relationship is meant to be. Ben Wang's story of calling his wife during that critical three-minute window is one such example. "Many people I tell this story to think it is astonishing. A miracle."

I suspect the felt meaning of China's three-part concept of love will also eventually wiggle and morph to make room for love-based marriages. These three parts—family love, friendship, and romantic passion—came up often with my storytellers and helped me to appreciate that love had always been part of Chinese marriage in some form. In the old days people expected only family love. I believe they came to expect friendship in the Mao years. And nowadays people do hope to experience romantic love, they just don't yet expect it to be their main reason for marriage.

Rather, as Liu Wumin described, people now expect a marriage to transition through the three loves over time. Even Will Guo Pingyou, a young teenager, conceptualized a successful marriage in this way. "I think my generation might marry only if they have [romantic] love," he said. "And then, over many years, that love will change from romance to the family kind of caring." In other words, the ideal Chinese marriage relationship should pass gradually through passion to friendship and a deeper commitment to each other and the family. Perhaps one day Chinese people will be talking about how to balance all three loves simultaneously.

Ultimately, my storytellers taught me that however a culture defines and sets up marriage, it can be rewarding and loving or hellish and miserable. Marrying for love does not ensure a good marriage, and neither does marrying for practical convenience. Rather, the fit between people's expectations of marriage and what they actually get from the relationship seems to cause their happiness or dissatisfaction. My most contented older storytellers, like Jack Chou, Ma Yajing, and Liu Wumin, had not sustained a romantic connection with their spouses, but neither had they expected to. Each had found ways to infuse his or her marriage with the best of friendship and familial care, and I admired their relationships.

In the end, this experience of story collecting left me with many questions about the current state of love and marriage in China. I started this project to learn about people's personal experiences, but needed an objective overview to organize everything I had heard. I wasn't sure if my storytellers were typical people, and I wondered if other Chinese couples were more satisfied with their romantic and sexual relationships. I wanted to know how many husbands really sought emotional support from a mistress. What about the unfolding relationship between love and marriage? Do some young people marry because they fall in love, or do most still respond to parental pressure to marry at the right time?

I did a little digging and learned that present-day China is one massive nation of married people, the majority of whom are happy with their marriages and sexual relationships. People date a bit in their late teens and more in their early twenties. Before age twenty-five, most women respond to parental pressure to marry a financially suitable spouse, and the couple do their best to stay married and raise a family. Affairs, while disruptive, are sort of socially acceptable and may be on the rise. When a marriage ends in divorce, as one in five does these days, people marry again as soon as possible. Taking a closer look at these trends helped me to contextualize the stories in this book.

Dating

By the end of the 1990s, dating after high school had become socially acceptable in China. A 1997 study published in the *Journal of Sex Research* by Drs. Cheryl Renaud, Sandra Byers, and Suiming Pan found that 60 percent of married people in Shanghai and Beijing had had at least one serious romantic relationship before meeting their spouse. The study suggested that dating had become the norm, at least in urban China.

Dating was, and largely still is, thought of as the first step in the spouse-finding process. As such, it makes sense that society expects young people to delay romantic exploration until it is almost time to get married and start a family. This expectation explains why Chinese parents are struggling to stop China's latest romantic evolution: teen dating. Most parents and teachers do not approve of teenagers dating each other. When pressed for an explanation, they claim to disapprove because a student's studies and future career will inevitably suffer. While the workload of many Chinese teens is indeed enormous, I suspect parents have a deeper reason for their objections. When they were growing up, teen dating would have been completely immoral. Further, teen dating challenges the whole definition of dating. If the goal of dating is marriage, then surely no sixteen-year-old needs a boyfriend in a country that bars marriage before one's twenties. By dating anyway, teens are hinting that such relationships might be about love, friendship, getting to know themselves, or perhaps even sexual experimentation.

Despite strident prohibition by nearly all Chinese parents and teachers, teen dating is a popular and growing phenomenon. While having a relationship is still the exception rather than the rule, it is no longer the rarity it was in the 1980s. A 2010 study of Chinese high school students published in the *International Journal of Behavioral Development* found that 25 percent of boys and 10 percent of girls had had a boyfriend or girlfriend by age seventeen. While it is possible that Chinese girls are truly less likely to form relationships, one can't help wondering who those boys were dating if not their female classmates. Generally speaking, Chinese parents are much stricter with daughters than sons and expect girls to control their romantic feelings rather than act on them. Girls might therefore be more hesitant to report their romantic involvements to researchers for fear of shame or punishment.

Teenagers themselves are often ambivalent about these "early love" relationships too. The same study found that teenagers who are close to their parents are much less likely to date at all, in deference to their rules. Relatedly, Chinese teens reported feeling less trust and companionship with boyfriends and girlfriends than did a comparable sample of Canadian teens. Since young love is not yet socially acceptable, and many Chinese parents even consider it morally wrong, it might be difficult for conscientious teens to fully enjoy dating or falling in love.

Sex before the Wedding

As my storytellers' experiences suggest, sexual values and behaviors have changed dramatically in China since the early 1980s, particularly with regard to sex before marriage. Such behavior was historically taboo, and most 1970s couples did not even kiss or touch before marriage. By the end of the 1990s the tide had turned, and premarital sex was socially acceptable after engagement. Some groom-side parents even encouraged it, as storyteller Lingyu mentioned, hoping to ward off cold feet with a quick pregnancy.

A 2012 article in the *Shenzhen Daily* addressed the rapidity of this change, citing work by sexologist Li Yinhe, an expert from the Chinese Academy of Social Science. Li's studies pegged China's "premarital sex rate" at 15 percent in 1989, 40 percent in 1994, and 71 percent by 2012. Li pointed out that most societies take between one hundred and two hundred years to make the kind of behavioral shift China completed in just thirty.

The *Shenzhen Daily* article also cited a 2012 survey of sexual attitudes jointly conducted by the Qinghua School of Journalism and Communication and the magazine *Insight China*. The survey tapped twenty thousand people, most aged twenty to thirty-nine. Nearly half (43 percent) approved of premarital sex and believed it was an important step in selecting a life partner. On the other hand, one-quarter still considered such behavior "unacceptable and immoral."

A 2012 survey from Peking University's Institute of Population Research checked in with China's teenagers, 60 percent of whom were tolerant of sex before engagement. However, as only 22 percent had yet had sex, it is fair to say that most teens still wait until their twenties to personally apply those relatively tolerant beliefs.

While China's young people largely wait for their twenties to get sexual with a partner, most couples likely reach this stage before an engagement is announced. The 2007 *Face of Global Sex* report, produced by Durex, the British condom maker, tagged twenty-two as the median age of sexual debut in China. A 2012 study of 22,000 young people published in *International Perspectives on Sexual and Reproductive Health* confirmed this number, reporting that the average man now loses his virginity at the age of 22.5 and the average woman at 23.1. Engagements traditionally last one year in China, but as the median age of first marriage in 2011 was twenty-five for women and nearly twenty-seven for men, sex is clearly no longer reserved for only engaged or married couples.

Curiously, those who don't marry that first sexual partner don't wait long to get intimate in subsequent romantic relationships. According to the 2013 *Report on Chinese People's Love and Marriage Values*, most people younger than forty now expect to have sex within four weeks of a successful first date. This enormous survey, jointly produced by the dating website Jiayuan.com and the National Population and Family Planning Commission, reflects the expectations of 77,000 Chinese people.

Picking a Spouse and Getting Married

Thirty-five years ago, choosing a spouse in China was relatively straightforward. Nearly everybody was poor and undereducated, dating barely existed, and there were enough men and women to go around. With the exception of people's infamous political class status, known as their "family background," the playing field was pretty even. This equality simplified the search for the desired méndānghùduì, or "marriage between families of equal rank." Recently, China's economic explosion has stratified society into new classes divided by wealth, education, and power, complicating the modern criteria for a "good match."

In the midst of this volatile marriage market, what do today's young people consider when picking a spouse? Despite the growing interest in love, being "in love" is not yet a major precondition for marriage in China. Rather, income and property are the main requirements for China's young women and their parents. According to the 2011 *Chinese Marriage Situation Survey Report*, which boasted 50,000 participants, "92% of women think that a stable income is necessary for marriage." More than two-thirds of women surveyed also thought that men should get married only after buying a home, though 50 percent conceded that a down payment would suffice. A similar project, the 2012–13 *Survey Report on Chinese People's Love and Marriage Values*, found that only half of Chinese women believed a man had to own a home before his wedding day. Amusingly, the report added that 66 percent of Chinese men did not agree.

Four-fifths of single women surveyed in 2011 took things even further, saying a man should not even think about *dating* until his monthly salary hit ¥4,000 ($635). This figure might not sound high, but it is nearly three times higher than Shenzhen's minimum monthly wage, which is the highest in all of China. Furthermore, ¥4,000 is 81 percent of what the average Chinese person made all year in 2011 (though it is just under Beijing's average monthly salary). Whether or not their expectations are realistic, the demands of today's brides simply demonstrate that marriage is still primarily about financial security in China.

These requirements are not exactly traditional, though it is true that marriage has always been sealed with a financial transaction in China. Historically, the wedding of a son was often the most expensive thing his family ever financed. In addition to providing the celebration itself, the groom's family paid a hefty "bride price" to their daughter-in-law's family. Her family was entirely not off the hook, though, since daughters were often sent into their new life with a dowry of furniture, cash, or other goods. As marriage was never intended to be about passion or emotional connection, these financial transactions made sense. The son's family was getting the lifetime labor of a daughter-in-law, who would provide both grandsons and old-age care. She was a valuable prize. The daughter's family no longer needed to provide for another person, but they lost the labor and company of their offspring, so their smaller expression of financial gratitude is also fitting.

Despite these historical roots, I think the stipulation that a groom have a home and an unusually high income has a distinctly modern flavor. In a very short time, some people in China have gotten very rich. Across the country, the average wage quadrupled between 2000 and 2010. The expectations of young brides are growing at pace with the wealth they see rising around them, and sometimes faster. For example, the minimum requirement from the 2011 survey, of a boyfriend with ¥4,000 a month, represented a full 10 percent increase over the figure named by women in the same survey in 2010! Demonstrating the mind-set of her peers, one twenty-two-year-old dating show contestant famously rejected her suitor in 2010 with these words: "I'd rather cry in a BMW car than laugh on the backseat of a bicycle."

Moreover, both the 2011 and 2012 surveys mentioned that financial hopes are increasing rather than decreasing with the post-1980 generations. Women born in the 1970s are less likely to insist on the financial outlays desired by younger women. Arguably, they grew up in a poorer China, watching the simpler engagements of twenty and thirty years ago. On the other hand, as women are considered "leftovers" if they are unmarried by their twenty-eighth birthday, their parents will push them to marry before all chance of finding a husband evaporates. Some may consequently be willing to accept a husband without any real estate to offer.

Almost tragically, the Supreme People's Court of China recently upset the financial calculations of millions of wives who married with security and house keys in mind. In 2011 the court declared that any real estate purchased entirely by one party would remain fully his or hers in the event of a divorce. Ostensibly intended to slow the divorce rate, protect men and their parents from prospective gold diggers, and perhaps change the purpose of marriage, the new interpretation deprived a disproportionate number of wives of property they had always believed was jointly owned. Dubbed "the law that makes men laugh and women cry," this controversial maneuver sparked outcry among mainland wives.

While the majority of marriage deals may well include money and property, not every bride has bought into the fiscal frenzy. If 50–70 percent of women believe a man must own a home before marriage, then 30–50 percent also don't believe it. These days, some of these women are opting for a luǒhūn, or "naked marriage." In this version of matrimony, the couple does not seal their union with an apartment, car, diamond ring, or elaborate party. Instead, they pay a scant ¥9 ($1.45) for a marriage certificate at the Office of Civil Affairs, and they may have a small party with family and friends afterward. Many storytellers mentioned their uncomplicated nuptials, such as Ma Yajing, whose worldly possessions fit on the bicycle her groom rode to the train, or Xu Kiwi, who married on a day she had off from work. Naked marriages are not always sweet or altruistic, though. Ming-Ming went into marriage concerned that her boyfriend was not bringing his savings into their married life, and the couple divorced just a few years later.

Remaining Single

In a marriage market that orbits money and property, there are predictable winners and losers. Poor men, the identified losers, have always struggled to marry in such conditions. In Old China, people resolved this problem with at-birth betrothals and child brides, as described by storyteller Liu Wumin. Today such solutions are no longer legal, and the marriage prospects of poor men are further complicated by China's substantial gender imbalance.

The One Child Policy collided disastrously with Chinese culture, where sons had always equaled a secure retirement. Millions of parents, unwilling to raise a daughter instead of a son, resorted to infanticide and sex-selected abortion to make room for a boy. With sad irony, this abominable situation now haunts those coveted sons, punishing them with a serious shortage of potential brides and dooming them to fail their parents. The marriageable generations now have twenty-three million more men than women, resulting in a "marriage squeeze" felt most sharply in the countryside. The men at the bottom are simply more likely to lose the financial competition for China's available women. Unfortunately for them, the 2013 policy amendment, which allows couples to try for a second child if either spouse is an only child, will come far too late for these men.

The difficult truth is that many of them will never find a wife. In 2010 single men made up 75 percent of all unmarried people between ages thirty and forty-four in China. This figure isn't expected to improve anytime soon, even though China's unnatural sex ratio (the number of girls per one hundred boys) is slowly and thankfully reversing. By 2030, 25 percent of Chinese men in their late thirties will remain unmarried, according to a 2010 analysis in *Foreign Affairs* magazine. What will happen to this country, so traditionally obsessed with marriage and grandchildren, when one in four men cannot marry?

Interminable singleness is not just a male problem. China's highly educated urban women, the infamous *shèngnǚ*, or "leftover women," are also coming up short. According to the latest Chinese census, these accomplished women are the most likely to remain unmarried past age twenty-seven. The danger of becoming a *shèngnǚ* is one of the most talked-about issues in China, and single women are constantly reminded of their looming expiration date. In 2013 *Business Insider* shared this cheery hint, offered by the All-China Women's Federation: "The tragedy is, they don't realize that as women age, they are worth less and less, so by the time they get their M.A. or Ph.D., they are already old, like yellowed pearls."

Given all the fuss, I was surprised to learn how few "yellow pearls" dot the cities of modern China. According to 2010 UN World Marriage Data, 22 percent of Chinese women age 25–29 are unmarried, along with a mere 5 percent of women age 30–34. Go older, and all but 2 percent are hitched. In Singapore and the United States, by contrast, 25 percent of women in their early thirties are still single; in Japan, 35 percent are unwed, and in the UK it's nearly half. Compared to women in the developed world, Chinese women are much more likely to get married. Perhaps the real reason for the media onslaught lies in the government's desire to get these "A-Quality" women married so they can make smart babies. Ultimately, China's leftover women may face a challenge in finding a good husband, but it is the millions of leftover men who truly deserve our sympathy. At least a financially independent woman can buy her own apartment and support her parents. By contrast, a poor man will always struggle to meet his parents' expectations.

Married Life

Most Chinese people are married before their twenty-fifth birthday and spend much of their life as a spouse, even if they change partners. On the mainland, the sheer ranks of the coupled are staggering. More than two times as many people are married right now in China than are alive in the United States and Great Britain combined. Ninety-nine percent of women and 93 percent of men born before 1975 have married at some point, and in 2010, nine out of ten people between thirty and sixty years old were married. These numbers contrast sharply with the West, where only 50–75 percent of British and American adults of similar age were married.

Marriage is such a habit, such a normal part of life, that most of my storytellers had never considered any philosophical explanation of its purpose. As Stephanie Coontz, the marital historian, described it in one of her books, getting married in China is more like going to high school in the West. It's something everybody "should" do, something you have to do to get to the next stage of your life. While everybody agrees on its necessity, few people expect high school to meet their deep emotional needs, nor do many expend much energy finding the "perfect fit" high school. Instead, many people in the West just go to a convenient high school, the one nearest their home or perhaps the one their parents or friends suggest. While it is not a perfect analogy, there are many parallels between the approach to high school in the West and the approach to marriage in China.

As such a comparison suggests, many people in China do not expect marriage to be a highly emotional experience. In a 2001 paper, Ge Gao, a communications professor at San Jose State University, wrote that in Chinese society, emotional experiences like love are spread out and shared more broadly across the family and "in-groups." As such, people don't expect love, or other emotional experiences, to be highly intensified within just one relationship. Gao noted: "A committed relationship in the US culture, in contrast, is formed on the basis of strong emotional experiences. Love is everything to US Americans and it is the major precondition to marriage."

In the context of all I had learned about Chinese people's practical approach to marriage, it made sense that the spousal relationship was not supposed to leap up from the emotional landscape like Mount Everest. I understood Gao's depiction of a society where people enjoy a moderate emotional connection with many people, including their spouse. I agreed that most Chinese people did not seem to judge the quality of their marriage based on the intensity of their emotional connection to their husband or wife. Furthermore, when I thought back over how my storytellers typically described the process of meeting and marrying their spouse, I could see with fresh eyes that emotional intensity had not often been part of the story. Not one person had framed this experience as his or her season of falling in love.

And yet I suspect this neat depiction of China's "mild marriages" is not the whole story. Many people I talked with did want, or had enjoyed, a strong emotional experience with a lover. Consider Lucy's desire to have "that spark" with someone, Fangfei's deep sexual connection with Sam, Sally's early feeling that her ex-husband was her soul mate, Lightly's passion for and impatience with her boyfriend, Licai's emotional despair as things unraveled with his girlfriend, and poor Ethan and his broken heart. Some of the people I spoke with struck me as being just as hungry for that emotional Mount Everest as we are in the West. Perhaps China's age of practical marriages is coming to a close.

There is reason beyond my storytellers' accounts to suspect that the definition of a good marriage is shifting in China. Another annual survey, this one called the Chinese People's Love and Marriage Happiness Survey, asks one thousand married people to rank the top ten factors affecting marital happiness. The survey, which is conducted by the Communist Party–affiliated *Xiaokang* magazine and the Tsing-hua University Media Research Laboratory, reports that a majority of 2011 participants ranked "income" as the most important matter affecting happiness, followed by "mutual affection." By 2012, however, income had nosedived to fifth place, trumped by mutual affection, ability and willingness to communicate, mutual fidelity, and children. People believed a good income mattered more for happiness than a good sex life, but interestingly, sex life now outranks the quality of the notorious mother-in-law relationship.

Values may be in flux, but most married people are nonetheless pretty happy with their relationships. This same *Chinese People's Love and Marriage Happiness Survey* reports that 60 percent of married folk were relatively happy in 2012, while 18 percent were very happy, landing 78 percent somewhere in the happy zone. A much larger nationwide survey of ten thousand married couples, conducted by the All-China Women's Federation from 2009 to 2010, returned similar findings. Sixty-two percent of participants were happy with their marriages and loved and respected their spouses. Notably, happiness was easier to find on the east coast, where those with higher levels of wealth and education tend to congregate. Among eastern couples, 65 percent were happy, compared to 63 percent in central China and only 58 percent in the less developed western provinces.

These surveys are encouraging, as they suggest that China's marital satisfaction lags only slightly behind that of the United States, the UK, and Australia. Recent, large-scale studies from these three nations report that 65–85 percent of married couples are satisfied or very satisfied with both their relationship and their sex life. Considering that China is less developed and has had far less time to sort out a strategy for establishing a satisfying connection between married couples, this picture of marital satisfaction is pretty good.

More encouraging still, the nation's "naked marriages," the ones that skip the exchange of cash and apartments, appear to fare just as well as other, more wealth-focused unions. The aforementioned 2011 *Chinese Marriage Situation Survey Report*, coproduced by the China Association of Social Workers and the matchmaking website Baihe.com, found that 70 percent of "naked" couples were satisfied with their relationships. Given the new law separating women from their husbands' apartments and the satisfaction rate among couples who marry simply, the naked marriage could be a harbinger of things to come.

Sexual satisfaction trends are less consistent for married people in China. The same 2010 All-China Women's Federation survey reported that 64 percent of married couples were "satisfied" or "very much satisfied" with their sex life. Another survey from the same year echoed this average, though it split the results by gender. Twenty-five percent of husbands, but half of wives, said their physical relationship was "unsatisfactory," which leaves a total of two-thirds rating things in the bedroom as "satisfactory." The survey, conducted online by the Shanghai Academy of Social Sciences and the China Population Communication Center, added that nearly one-third of couples felt their marriage was "in a crisis." The report did not specify whether the people in crisis were also the ones who were sexually dissatisfied.

An older article from the *International Journal of Comparative Sociology* sheds some light on this seeming abundance of sexual problems. In 2002 the authors forecast that as the sexual relationship grew increasingly important to China's couples, better education and awareness about sex, sexual problems, and sexual pleasure would be sorely needed. More than a decade later, talking about sex is still largely taboo, and some couples with intimate concerns might truly have nowhere to turn.

Extramarital Affairs

A growing number of Chinese people are tolerant of extramarital affairs. In some ways this tolerance is an updated version of China's traditional culture, in which men had broad license to pursue sexual pleasure. Such permissiveness was stamped out by the conservative wing of the Communist Party, which wanted to change this aspect of social life for the better. (Though, ironically, Mao himself was quite friendly with the ladies.) As such, the party targeted adultery, multiple wives, prostitution, and all manner of sexual sins between 1949 and the 1980s. Adultery was officially considered a "crime against the family" and offenders could be imprisoned. Under Mao, prostitution was nearly eradicated and did not come back in force until the period of "reform and opening up." People like Mr. Yang, a storyteller from the 1950s, grew up in a world seemingly devoice of affairs, and one in which sex itself was almost invisible. In his opinion, "Having an affair . . . is a new thing, borrowed from Western ideas."

Nowadays, many Chinese men and women believe a lover could be an important emotional supplement to adult life. Some consider affairs acceptable as long as a spouse does not find out and the side relationship does not cause any family trouble. In 2011 the *New York Times* reported the distress of Chinese wives, many of whom complain their husbands think of a mistress as a marital prerequisite. Zeroing in on these attitudes, the 2010 *Chinese People's Love and Marriage Happiness Survey* found that only 58 percent of married respondents were "fully committed to avoiding an affair."

Being tolerant of cheating and actually cheating are different things, though. Since infidelity came up regularly in my storytellers' experiences, I wondered how common affairs were in the average marriage in China. Surprisingly, solid current-day statistics were difficult to find, especially for husbands. One survey of thirty thousand college-educated wives living in big cities, sponsored by Sina.com in 2004, found that 33 percent had had at least one affair, while 8 percent admitted frequent affairs. An older survey, the 1999–2000 Chinese Health and Family Life Survey, is also worth noting. This project, which collected a rare, nationally representative sample of China's adult population age twenty to sixty-four, found that 21 percent of men and 5 percent of women had had at least one extramarital affair. It also reported that men and women from higher socioeconomic backgrounds were the most likely to stray. While these figures are now outdated, such a high-quality survey is a helpful benchmark to compare with modern trends.

Common sense suggests that infidelity is on the rise in present-day China. Richard Burger, author of *Behind the Red Door: Sex in China*, says Chinese men have entered a "new golden age of sexual infidelity," conjured from the combination of their newfound wealth and their age-old sense of sexual entitlement. In fact, Shenzhen is home to one area so chock-full of rich men's girlfriends that people call it "Second Wife City." The "second wife" concept refers to a classic sort of mistress, one who expects full financial support in exchange for exclusive sexual access. While subway advertisements, online sites, and politician's scandals involving such women are easy to find, people say this kind of formal arrangement is declining in popularity. Chinese men have discovered cheaper alternatives like casual girlfriends or friends with benefits.

While wives traditionally had little choice but to turn a blind eye, many are not putting up with affairs quite so readily these days. Cheating is now the "top marriage killer," according to the 2012 *Chinese People's Love and Marriage Happiness Survey*. A report aired on the *Beijing Evening News* in 2011 said that 70 percent of divorces are now initiated by wives, and these women most commonly cite a cheating husband. In his book, Richard Burger also wrote of one Beijing court that found 60 percent of divorce plaintiffs had initiated proceedings after discovering a spouse's lover. In this particular court, husbands were only twice as likely as wives to be the guilty party, suggesting that wives are becoming more "open-minded." One study by the All-China Women's Federation, widely cited in 2001, found that 30 percent of divorcing wives had been unfaithful.

Ultimately, I think some of these extramarital relationships are a symptom of what is missing, as expectations for romantic love and intimacy are increasing faster in China than marriage can change. The number of affairs will likely not decline until the need for an "emotional supplement" to marriage is addressed. Many Chinese husbands believe they cannot confide in their wives or share their troubles, especially if their problems are financial or family-related. They justify a lover because they need to get support and emotional intimacy somewhere. Indeed, one Chinese word for "confidante" is *hóngyán zhījǐ*, which means "beautiful female soul mate." When a man says he wants to find a *hóngyán zhījǐ*, he is never thinking of a wife. If husbands and wives could find a way to bring that kind of intimacy and emotional fulfillment into their marital relationship, they might put a lot of second wives out of business.

Divorce and Remarriage

Divorce has been increasing in China since the late 1970s and is now a generally acceptable alternative to an unhappy marriage. Early in the new millennium, China cancelled the requirement for couples to seek permission from their work unit or neighborhood committee before getting a divorce. Overnight, divorce became a private matter that could be finalized within three days, and people rushed to sever soured ties. At least one in five marriages now ends in divorce in China, according to a 2009 report by China's Ministry of Civil Affairs.

Not surprisingly, the post-Mao generation (born after 1976) have a higher divorce rate than their elders. But the trend in Beijing, where 39 percent of marriages now break up, trumps even the record of the younger generations, suggesting that urban culture is a more powerful influence on divorce habits than sheer age. This figure brings China's capital nose to nose with the United States and the UK, where just over 40 percent of first marriages ultimately end.

Curiously, very few Chinese people who get divorced actually stay divorced. According to UN world marriage statistics, only 2 percent of Chinese women and 3 percent of Chinese men under age sixty were currently divorced in 2010. In America and Great Britain, by contrast, 6–19 percent of adults under sixty were divorced at that time. So, while just twice as many couples divorce in the West as in China, the actual number of divorced people available at any given time is exponentially higher in the West. People in China may simply remarry more quickly.

From political leaders to parents, everybody is understandably concerned about this substantial uptick in divorce, but cries of alarm might be premature. Lamenting the state of divorce, the All-China Women's Federation asked in 2013, "What is affecting Chinese people's marital happiness? Is it money, relationship matters, or children?" One cannot automatically interpret rising divorce rates as proof of souring relationships, though. Especially in China, where marriages are not necessarily formed with marital satisfaction in mind, those marriages might never have been happy to begin with.

Historically speaking, a spike in divorce rates in developing countries usually indicates that desires for mutual affection, compatibility,

and even sexual satisfaction are challenging old notions of marriᵉ
as an altruistic duty and obligation. Infidelity, unkindness, and phys
ical abuse will always crop up in some marriages, and China is no
exception. Other couples will struggle endlessly to get along, finding
it difficult to live with each other or the relatives that come with the
marital package. In China's recent past, only morally degenerate or
crazy people got divorced, so couples soldiered through their unhappiness to save face and preserve a symbolically integrated family. Few
people expected romance or fairness anyway, and the back-up plan
for divorced women—hometown shame, maybe prostitution—was
hardly a better alternative.

China's rising divorce rate may well be an indicator that people now
have the freedom to end the bad marriages they would have endured
in the past. People are starting to value their own happiness and are
hoping for mutual affection, communication, and sexual faithful-
ness in their marriage. As these ideas take hold, the nation should
expect to pass through an unstable couple of decades as divorce loses
its stigma and a backlog of unhappy couples break up. America went
through such a stage in the late 1960s and '70s. But such instability
will likely not last forever. Future generations will learn from their
parents' mistakes and divorce rates will drop as couples increasingly
marry with compatibility and happiness in mind. The very same thing
has been happening in the United States, where divorce rates have
been dropping since 1980 among the younger generations.

Divorce never feels good, not to the couple or family involved and
not to the society that must handle the mess. But on a much broader
scale, think of divorce as a public health measure, like air bags. Anyone who has ever been hit in the face with a car air bag knows that
innocuous little cushion is really a controlled explosion that will
hurt, bruise, cut, or even burn you. But it will also save your life. The
option to divorce without suffering enormous social consequences
is just like that controlled explosion. While it hurts society, it also
has the power to change the nature of marriage and to give people
a second chance. Husbands might think twice before heading to a
KTV bar and wives might pause before secretly spending their husband's money to finance their younger brother's expensive educa-

ım Liu's story). Both spouses might choose a partner who
ıd wants to stay with them. Ultimately, if China's peo-
'orporate romantic love and sexual satisfaction more
ırriage relationship, then rising divorce is the para-
must be paid.

Homosexuality

Homosexuality is a current social issue in China, but not for religious reasons. Rather, homosexuality is a problem partly because gay people get married and partly because they don't. The second problem is easier to explain. Simply put, homosexuality presents a major challenge to parents' hardwired traditional belief that everyone should marry and have a child. Living life with a gay partner would subject a man's family to shame and bar him from fulfilling what most parents consider his highest filial duty: bearing a son. His options are to live a lie with a straight wife and please his parents or be himself but become a bad, unfilial child. Choosing the latter is a big deal in China, which is why this weighty moral dilemma hangs so heavily over China's gay population.

As Riley's story demonstrates all too clearly, the idea that a child might not want to marry someone of the opposite sex and might instead want to live with a same-sex partner is cause for full-fledged parental desperation. Parents want gay children to "change their mind," marry, and produce a child, which brings us back to the first problem: gay people getting married.

Same-sex marriage is not yet legal in China, but gay and lesbian people marry in droves. According to a 2013 article in the *Wall Street Journal*, four-fifths of gay men in China probably take a wife. Reporters Olive Geng and Josh Chin spoke to Zhang Beichuan, an HIV/AIDS researcher and sexologist at Qingdao University. As Mr. Zhang explained, "They feel they have the responsibility to pass on their family names—to be so-called filial sons."

Lesbian women face similar pressure but sometimes have a little more freedom just by being female. As Li Yinhe, a sociologist at the Chinese Academy of Social Sciences, told the *New York Times* in 2011, "Traditional society basically overlooks women in some ways, and there is a certain freedom in that. . . . But that free space isn't necessarily power." Women do not traditionally continue the family line in China, but many younger lesbian women are still the only child of parents who expect an heir. Either way, parents lose face in a big way if their daughter doesn't marry.

The plight of women who marry gay men has come to light recently as well. Known as *tóngqī*, which means "wives of comrades," these women often endure loveless, nearly sexless marriages with their husbands. A 2011 article in the *Shenzhen Daily* attested that many women are unaware of their husband's sexual preference until after the wedding but continue the marriage because of parental pressure to have children and avoid divorce.

Unfortunately, the expectation that gay and lesbian individuals should marry an opposite-sex partner makes sense if marriage truly is a practical, baby-making arrangement between two families. But the young men and women such marriages would affect are clearly less and less likely to agree with such a definition of marriage. As China's concept of marriage widens to balance the quality of the spousal relationship and the couple's obligations to their parents, such unions will become increasingly nonsensical.

Overall, this examination of current-day trends in China suggests that my storytellers' love and marriage experiences were fairly typical, albeit a bit more intense than their fellow countrymen's. Nearly 30 percent of them had been through a divorce, landing them in the crosshairs of statistics for the nation, young people, and Beijing. Of the sixteen who were married when we spoke, just over half were satisfied with their relationship, a figure slightly below average. Only one person was currently divorced, which is typical, but two people born before 1975 had never married, which is more unusual. Thirty-five percent of the married storytellers had experienced an affair, but the dearth of good statistics makes this figure had to contextualize. Of the seven who were yet unmarried, most weighed a blend of financial security and mutual affection when thinking about a future spouse, which is normal. But some intended to marry for love, and that is a more progressive aspiration.

As this book comes to a close, the people of China are still chewing over the ideal relationship between love and marriage. In many ways the "ugly wife" of ancient lore is still a treasure at home. This ugly wife has become a metaphor for the Chinese notion of the "good choice" wife, the kind of stable, selfless, unassuming woman many men and mothers-in-law still prize. When marriage is practical instead of love-based, it follows that husband and wife must each focus on carrying out their role in the bargain. An ugly wife is expected to labor tirelessly for her children, parents, and spouse, asking her husband for little but financial support in return. She should never leave her husband, even if he barely acknowledges her on his way out to see friends or his mistress. She may be a treasure at home, and she may be holding the family together, but I question whether she is happy and personally fulfilled. I think the Chinese people are starting to ask the same question.

The best way for today's young people to rescue the ugly wife is to allow marriage to continue along its evolution from a practical bond to a love-based union. As marriage becomes a relationship dominated by the couple's personal fit and emotional connection, more of the nation's traditional spousal roles and obligations will grow flexible. As couples begin to care more about relationship satisfaction, they will want to find ways to adjust their lives to fit their needs. Perhaps the next generation will find a way to sustain all three kinds of married love, the coveted triumvirate of family care, friendship, and romantic love, throughout the years of their marriage.

Love and marriage in China may well be headed in this direction, but with values in flux, anything could happen. A majority of married people now believe that mutual affection affects marital happiness more than income, which is one indicator that love is infiltrating marriage in historically unprecedented ways. The rising divorce rate reflects people's rejection of traditional roles in favor of personal satisfaction and fulfillment. And an encouraging number of people are even happy in naked marriages, unions entered into without the traditional exchange of wealth and property. However, with premarital financial demands on the rise among younger generations, China's future marriages could come to revolve around security and economic stability even more than they do today.

CONCLUSION

I have come to appreciate the quiet strength of the Chinese concept of family love and I know it brings happiness to many people. And yet part of me hopes today's younger generations will find a way to preserve some of the lasting sweetness of romantic love. Marriage need not be a constantly passionate, heart-fluttering daily experience, but many way stations dot the path between ardor and asexual cohabitation. I hope future couples can find ways to preserve their sexual relationship and special connection while also meeting the needs of their parents and children.

As Louis de Bernières wrote in *Captain Corelli's Mandolin*, "Love itself is what is left over when being in love has burned away, and this is both an art and a fortunate accident." Perhaps China's youngest generations will be those lucky artists. Perhaps they will finally free the ugly wife.

Timeline of Recent Chinese History (Emphasis on the Mao Years)

1911: Fall of the Qing dynasty, ending thousands of years of emperor rule and "feudal society." Rise of the Nationalist Party (Guómíndǎng), headed by Sun Yat-sen.

1915–30: Various leaders vie for head of state position.

1921: Foundation of the Communist Party of China.

1927: Civil war breaks out between the Nationalist Party and the Communist Party; Nationalist government purges Communist members in Shanghai.

1930: Chiang Kai-shek leads Nationalist Party.

1931: Japanese army invades the northern Chinese territory of Manchuria; occupation persists until the end of World War II. In the modern day, this region is generally referred to as Northeast China (Dongbei) and consists of Heilongjiang, Jilin, and Liaoning provinces, though some extend its borders to include parts of Inner Mongolia, Russian territories, and Sakhalin Island.

1932–43: Lin Sen leads Nationalist Party.

1934: The Long March, the infamous Communist retreat to escape massacre by the Nationalists, is survived by only 10 percent of the starting forces. Mao Zedong's leadership in this movement marks the beginning of his ascent to power.

1937–45: Second Sino-Japanese War (known in China as the War of Resistance against Japanese Aggression), which ends with the atomic bombing of Hiroshima and Nagasaki.

1945: Chiang Kai-shek returns to power. The Nationalist Party is a founding member of the United Nations.

1949: After protracted civil war, the Communist Party establishes the People's Republic of China under the "Great Helmsman" Mao Zedong. Nationalist Party retreats to Taiwan.

1950: The Agrarian Reform Law, aka the Land Reform Movement, redistributes the land of landlords and wealthy farmers to millions of peasants. "Class enemies" (e.g., former landowners or wealthy citizens) are denounced, or even killed, in violent public "struggle sessions." China joins ally North Korea against the United States in the Korean War.

1951: The fourteenth Dalai Lama signs the Seventeen-Point Agreement for the Peaceful Liberation of Tibet, establishing Chinese sovereignty over Tibet.

1956: The Hundred Flowers Movement. The Communist Party calls for debate and criticism of its methods from China's intellectual and artistic set, to let "one hundred flowers bloom, and one hundred schools of thought contend." The original intention is unclear, but popular criticism quickly spirals beyond Mao's intentions, and the movement triggers the Anti-Rightist Campaign.

1957: The Anti-Rightist Campaign, a massive purge leading to the imprisonment, reeducation, or internal exiles of thousands of "Rightist" intellectuals, artists, religious adherents, and others.

1958: Great Leap Forward begins, a nationwide endeavor to catapult Chinese agricultural and economic development forward. As Henry Kissinger explains in *On China*, Mao intended to surpass Great Britain in steel production within a handful of years and to quickly ratchet up agricultural production during the same interval. Any remaining private businesses were largely dismantled, and rural communities were reorganized into people's communes, pooling food and labor. Peasants were conscripted in semimilitary brigades to accomplish massive public works projects. The production goals of the Great Leap Forward were far out of the realm of possibility, but to avoid frankly acknowledging these failures, local cadres took to falsifying output numbers to fulfill their quotas, which were promptly exported.

1959–62: Famine claims the lives of an estimated thirty million people.

1959: Sino-Soviet relations deteriorate dramatically and Soviets begin restricting transfer of science and technology to China.

1960: Sino-Soviet split. Khrushchev recalls Soviet advisors and technical experts in China, resulting in open conflict between China and the USSR.

1962: The Himalayan border dispute and the Sino-Indian border crisis. China reasserts its perceived historical authority over Xinjiang and Tibet, western portions of the countryside over which India also had a historic claim. Clashes ensue along the disputed borders.

1963: "Sending Down" begins. Some urban residents are sent to the countryside to redistribute the population after the famine years and to fulfill Mao's ideological call for a return to agrarian life.

1964: Test of first atomic bomb in China.

1966–76: The Cultural Revolution. Nationwide political purges bring on social chaos bent on destruction of "The Four Olds": old ideas, old culture, old customs, old habits.

1967: Test of first hydrogen bomb in China.

1969: Sino-Soviet border conflicts.

1970: First satellite launch in China.

1971: Henry Kissinger, U.S. defense secretary, makes a secret visit to China. Lin Biao, Mao's handpicked successor, is killed in an airplane crash while fleeing after an attempted military coup.

1972: U.S. president Richard Nixon visits China. Normalization of relations between the United States and China begins. Signing of Shanghai Communiqué (first Sino-U.S. Joint Communiqué), in which the United States acknowledges the "One China Policy" regarding Taiwan but does not endorse China's version. Mao's health fails and Zhou Enlai and the Gang of Four struggle over internal leadership of China.

1976: Chairman Mao Zedong dies at the age of eighty-two. The Gang of Four (including Mao's widow) tries to seize control but fails.

1977: Hua Guofeng starts the Open Door Policy, which is later incorporated in Deng Xiaoping's Four Modernizations Program. Deng Xiaoping outmaneuvers the Gang of Four and rises to power.

1978–79: Deng Xiaoping introduces stepwise economic reforms, the Four Modernizations, prodding China toward open business and diplomatic relations with the West.

1979: Twenty-nine-day border war with Vietnam. Introduction of China's Family Planning Policy, often called the "One Child Policy," at the provincial level.

1980: The first special economic zone, which allows private, joint public-private, and foreign enterprises to operate, is established in Shenzhen. The One Child Policy is implemented nationwide.

1984: Margaret Thatcher visits China, signs the Sino-British Joint Declaration. Fourteen test-bed coastal cities are opened to foreign investment.

1989: Crackdown on Tiananmen Square demonstrations with military power, known in China as the "June 4" tragedy (official death toll: two hundred). Martial law is declared in Tibet. EU-wide arms embargo declared against China. Stock markets are opened in Shanghai and Shenzhen.

1991: First McDonald's restaurant opens in Beijing.

1992: Jiang Zemin takes over as head of state. Deng Xiaoping accelerates market reforms to establish a "socialist market economy" after visiting the special economic zones in the southern province of Guangdong.

1995: Educational legislation stipulates a nine-year compulsory education.

1997: Britain's ninety-nine-year lease of Hong Kong expires. Hong Kong becomes a "special administrative region" of China under the One China, Two Systems Policy. Death of Deng Xiaoping.

1998: Great Firewall of China established to censor Internet content.

1999: Portugal turns Macau back over to China. Falun Gong is banned.

2001: After years of negotiations, China becomes a member of the World Trade Organization.

2003: SARS outbreak. China's first manned space mission goes into orbit carrying astronaut Yang Liwei.

2004: Hu Jintao succeeds Jiang Zemin as head of state.

2008: The most violent ethnic protest in years erupts in Lhasa, Tibet's main city. An earthquake strikes Sichuan province, killing 69,000 people. Summer Olympics come to Beijing. Premier Wen Jiabao accepts responsibility for a milk-powder scandal that might have affected more than 50,000 children.

2009: Sixtieth anniversary of the People's Republic of China.

The following is a list of books and scholarly articles that were especially helpful in researching this book. Newspaper articles, interviews,
and web sources are referenced directly in the text. English translations of articles concerning the love and marriage surveys mentioned
in the conclusion can be found on the All-China Women's Federation's
official website, http://www.womenofchina.cn.

Burger, R. *Behind the Red Door: Sex in China*. Hong Kong: Earnshaw, 2012.

Cai, Y. "China's Below-Replacement Fertility: Government Policy or Socioeconomic
Development?" *Population and Development Review* 36.3 (2013): 419–40.

Chang, J. *Wild Swans: Three Daughters of China*. London: Simon and Schuster, 1991.

Chang, L. *Factory Girls*. New York: Spiegel and Grau, 2009.

Coontz, S. *Marriage, a History: How Love Conquered Marriage*. London: Lindauin, 2006.

Diamant, N. *Revolutionizing the Family: Politics, Love, and Divorce in Urban and Rural
China, 1949–1968*. Berkeley: University of California Press, 2000.

Gao, G. "Intimacy, Passion, and Commitment in Chinese and U.S. American Romantic Relationships." *International Journal of Intercultural Relations* 25.3 (2001): 329-42.

Gil, V. E. "The Cut Sleeve Revisited: A Brief Ethnographic Interview with a Male
Homosexual in Mainland China." Clinical notes. *Journal of Sex Research* 29 (1992):
569–77.

Guo, W., Z. Wu, X. Qiu, G. Chen, and X. Zheng. "The Timing of Sexual Debut among
Chinese Youth." *International Perspectives on Sexual and Reproductive Health* 38.4
(2012).

Hsu, F. L. K. *Americans and Chinese: Passage to Difference*. 3rd ed. Honolulu: University Press of Hawaii, 1953.

Kissinger, H. *On China*. New York: Lindauin, 2011.

Lee, H. *Revolution of the Heart: A Genealogy of Love in China, 1900–1950*. Stanford CA:
Stanford University Press, 2006.

Li, Z. H., J. Connolly, D. Jiang, D. Pepler, and W. Craig. "Adolescent Romantic Relationships in China and Canada: A Cross-National Comparison." *International
Journal of Behavioral Development* 34.2 (2010): 113–20.

Money, J. "Peking: The Sexual Revolution." In *Handbook of Sexology*, ed. J. Money and
H. Musaph, 543–50. Amsterdam: Excerpta Medica, 1977.

Parish, W., and M. Whyte. *Village and Family in Contemporary China*. Chicago: University of Chicago Press, 1978.

Renaud, C. E., S. Byers, and S. Pan. "Sexual and Relationship Satisfaction in Mainland China." *Journal of Sex Research* 34.4 (1997): 399–410.

United Nations Statistics Division (UNSD). World Marriage Data. 2010. http://data.un.org/.

Xinran, X. *China Witness: Voices from a Silent Generation.* New York: Anchor, 2010.

———. *What the Chinese Don't Eat.* Great Britain: Vintage, 2006.

Yan, Y. *Private Life under Socialism: Love, Intimacy, and Family Change in a Chinese Village, 1949–1999.* Stanford CA: Stanford University Press, 2003.